Growing in Newness of Life

Christian Initiation in Anglicanism Today

Papers from the Fourth International
Anglican Liturgical Consultation
Toronto 1991

David R. Holeton, *editor*

The Anglican Book Centre
Toronto, Ontario

00 709011 07

1993
Anglican Book Centre
600 Jarvis Street
Toronto, Ontario
Canada M4Y 2J6

© 1993 by the Anglican Consultative Council for the International Anglican Liturgical Consultation

Typesetting by Jay Tee Graphics Ltd.

Canadian Cataloguing in Publication Data

International Anglican Liturgical Consultation (4th : 1991 : Toronto, Ont.)
   Growing in newness of life

ISBN 1-55126-045-X

1. Initiation rites – Religious aspects – Anglican Communion – Congresses. 2. Initiation rites – Religious aspects – Christianity – Congresses. 3. Anglican Communion – Liturgy – Congresses. 4. Liturgies – Congresses. I. Holeton, David, 1948– . II. Title.

BX5021.I67 1993   264'.03   C93-093238-2

Growing in Newness of Life

TABLE OF CONTENTS

Introduction

When it was decided that Christian Initiation would be the primary topic for the Fourth International Anglican Liturgical Consultation, the Steering Committee knew that the Consultation would be addressing one of the major ongoing issues facing Anglicans today. Given the vastness of the topic and the constraints of time we would face at the Consultation itself, we followed a pattern set at IALC-1 in Boston: a number of participants were asked to prepare resource papers so that members of the Consultation could reflect on the issues facing us. As our work was to be divided among four working groups, it was important that the breadth of issues to be discussed, as well as the variety of contexts in which the issues are lived out within Anglicanism, be presented before the Consultation actually began.

The papers fall naturally within those four working areas: the renewal of initiation theology; baptism, mission and ministry; confirmation and the renewal of baptismal faith; rites of initiation. A general context for our work was created by a number of papers describing experiences in various parts of the Anglican Communion.

It is almost twenty-five years since Lambeth 1968 set the renewal of patterns of Christian initiation as a common task for the entire Anglican Communion. As chair of the Consultation, I posed the introductory question: How are we doing? What, if anything, has taken place across the Communion? In light of the mixed response to that question, I attempted to delineate some of the issues that I believed the Consultation would need to address as Anglicans seek to renew this aspect of their common life.

The renewal of initiation theology

The renewal of initiation theology was the subject of the first working group. In his preparatory paper, Professor William Crockett addresses the importance of theological integrity in the reform of Anglican initiation practice. He generates five theological principles which are fundamental for the renewal of Christian initiation in Anglicanism.

For a long while, Anglicans have not been asked to make apology for their traditional practice of infant baptism. Today, however, the practice of indiscriminate baptism of infants is under attack from many quarters. Gordon Kuhrt examines the theologies on which the practice of pædobaptism has been based, and calls for a renewal of the theology of covenant as a biblical and pastoral way forward.

The relationship between baptismal practice and theology is dialogical. Gregory Kerr-Wilson and Timothy Perkins look at the effect some of our renewed practices will have on our ecclesiology and eucharistic theology.

Baptism, mission, and ministry

When Lambeth 1968 put Christian initiation on the agenda for the Anglican Communion, it did so in the context of the working group on Mission and Ministry. It was a concern of the Consultation that the issue remain solidly rooted in that context. In the first paper in this group, Louis Weil articulates the principle that our models for baptism inevitably flow from our understanding of the nature of the church as it pursues its mission in the world.

As Anglicanism seeks to renew its understanding of mission, it is looking for new ways in which to integrate its life of worship and mission. In an increasing number of provinces, the catechumenate has become one of those integrating factors. Robert Brooks examines the restoration of the catechumenate as a challenge to the church to re-order its life so that it might be prepared to enter the twenty-first century.

In this Decade of Evangelism, John Hill and Paul Bowie suggest that it is only through the rebuilding of an ordered ministry of pastoral and liturgical catechesis that we can surmount our inherited patterns of a privatized, infantalized, and marginalized baptismal practice, and restore to our ministry of evangelization this critical element of effective initiation and response.

In an age in which attention has focused increasingly on adult candidates for baptism or on the infants of committed families, Ronald Dowling draws our attention to the important ministry of the preparation of parents (many of whom may have had only a casual relationship with the Christian community) for the celebration of baptism.

Confirmation and the renewal of baptismal faith

The question of confirmation and the renewal of baptismal faith is where Lambeth 1968 began the present process of renewal, and, it often seems, it is on this issue that patterns for renewal often falter. Addressing the issue head-on was imperative for any significant reform in this aspect of Anglican life. In his essay on the subject, Bishop Colin Buchanan gives an overview of Anglican theological positions on confirmation, and concludes that, while confirmation might remain an ongoing pastoral ceremony for those ratifying baptismal faith at an age of discretion, it must be excluded from playing any initiatory role or from remaining a requisite component of initiation or completion of baptism.

Rites of initiation

As liturgical texts are a primary expression of the present belief of the churches in matters of initiation, it was important that the Consultation have an overview of both historical and present practices. Professor Thomas Talley draws on his vast knowledge of the Christian liturgical tradition to look at recent Anglican texts in the context of the larger liturgical tradition, pointing out anomalies (such as the Anglican restriction of confirmation to bishops) and areas which have yet to be explored more fully (the restored catechumenate both for adults coming to faith as well as for infants who will be baptized later, after a period of instruction).

Kenneth Stevenson, like Jeremy Taylor before him, sees the evolving shape of Christian initiation as related to the needs of the church in particular ages. The present church, he suggests, can draw on its past but may need pastoral remodelling in order to meet the needs of the future.

Leonel Mitchell looks at one particular dimension of the celebration of Christian initiation that increasingly is becoming a concern within Anglicanism. He discusses baptismal anointing both as an ecumenical question and as a response to the Lima Document's call for vivid signs to enrich the baptismal liturgy.

In this same context of vivid signs, Philip May explores the power of baptismal symbols not just to describe reality but also to create it. Baptismal symbol helps create the grammar of Christian language and dialogue. As such, the symbols must be robust enough to crowd out all that is mere speculation, and submerge people in what is happening.

Kevin Flynn undertook the massive work of surveying the plethora of initiation texts which have appeared in the Anglican Communion over the past few decades. In presenting his findings, he challenges the extent to which many of the texts reflect a renewed theology of initiation.

Patterns of initiation: An Anglican mosaic

The Anglican Communion, like all churches who see their mission in global terms, is a mosaic. IALC-3 at York took that cultural diversity seriously as it addressed the question of liturgical inculturation in the Anglican Communion. IALC-4 could not address the question of renewal of initiation practice without a similar attention to the contextualization of its practice.

In telling the story of the New Zealand experience, Archbishop Brian Davis and Bishop Tom Brown show how one province implemented new patterns of nurture, overcoming both pastoral hurdles and legal challenges.

In the Canadian context, Bishop Joachim Fricker reflects on his experience of new pastoral practices in the celebration of Christian initiation. As his role has evolved from that of ''confirmer'' to ''baptizer,'' he has come to see a new episcopal role in encouraging parishes in their vocation as baptizing communities.

The Anglican Communion contains older, established churches as well as younger, struggling churches. Two markedly contrasting views of this reality are seen in the papers of Donald Gray and Juan Quevedo-Bosch. Canon Gray looks at the complex questions faced by an established church living with religious pluralism, and asks how the church can best serve the nation. Professor Quevedo-Bosch writes from the perspective of a church which is a small minority within a minority, where Christian practice itself has been strictly regulated by a communist regime. As the government shows signs of relaxing the restrictions on religion, the church is faced with developing new models for initiation.

Three very different experiences are described in the short papers of Winston Halapua, Themba Vundla, and Francis Wickremesinghe. The Fijian experience is described as one in flux, in which older, clerically dominated models no longer adequately serve a church discovering that the joy of welcoming newcomers is the celebration of the whole church.

Themba Vundla looks at traditional initiation practices (birth, puberty, marriage, childbirth) among various peoples of Southern Africa, and raises questions about the implications of these traditions for Christian initiation, which, as practised, is generally not seen as initiatory in the African sense.

Francis Wickremesinghe describes a new ecumenical baptismal rite prepared by the churches of Sri Lanka which makes a serious attempt to address the question of liturgical inculturation.

Elizabeth Smith volunteered a paper which deals with initiation in a context which will be novel to many readers. As the Anglican Communion renews its practice of initiation in a wider context, her words should be read with care.

Part of the strength of the IALC is the rich variety of experience included within its membership. Its meetings include bishops, parish pastors, scholars, church administrators, and lay persons. It is to be expected that some of our diversity finds itself reflected in the variety of writing styles in this collection. While the papers served as resources for the whole Consultation, each paper is the opinion of its author. How this wide variety of opinion found itself reflected in the work of the Consultation itself can be seen in a careful reading of the Toronto Statement: "Walk in Newness of Life."

In the process of editing this volume the authors were given the opportunity to revise their papers. This accounts for the references to the Toronto Statement in some of the papers themselves. Without the assistance of my tutor, the Rev. Dr. Thomas Harding, this collection would never have found itself onto disc in final edited form.

"Walk in Newness of Life" marks a high degree of consensus achieved in consultation among a representative body which includes most of the liturgical scholars active in the Anglican Communion. As a text, it should be taken with particular seriousness as provinces continue in the ongoing process of renewing their theology and practice of initiation. This collection of papers is published in the hope that it will service as a useful resource in facilitating that important dimension of our common life.

David R. Holeton,
Chair, IALC.

Shrove Tuesday, 1992.

The Contributors

David R. Holeton is Professor of Liturgics at Trinity College, Toronto and Chair of the International Anglican Liturgical Consultation.

William R. Crockett is Professor of Systematic Theology at the Vancouver School of Theology.

Gordon Kuhrt is Archdeacon of Lewisham in the diocese of Southwark.

Gregory Kerr-Wilson is Rector of the Church of the Holy Family, Heart Lake in the diocese of Toronto.

Timothy Perkins is Associate Priest in the parish of St. Luke, Baton Rouge in the diocese of Louisiana.

Louis Weil is Professor of Liturgics at the Church Divinity School of the Pacific in Berkeley, California.

Robert Brooks is Political Officer of the Episcopal Church and a member of its Standing Liturgical Commission.

John W. Hill is Rector of the Church of St. Augustine of Canterbury in the diocese of Toronto.

Paul Bowie is Assistant Curate of St. George's Memorial Church, Oshawa in the diocese of Toronto.

Ronald Dowling is Rector of the Church of St. Mary the Virgin, South Perth, Australia.

Colin O. Buchanan is Vicar of St. Mark's, Gillingham and an Assistant Bishop of Rochester in the Church of England.

Thomas J. Talley is Professor Emeritus at The General Theological Seminary, New York.

Kenneth W. Stevenson is Rector of Holy Trinity and St. Mary's, Guildford and a member of the Church of England Liturgical Commission.

Leonel L. Mitchell is Professor of Liturgics at Seabury-Western Seminary in Evanston, Illinois.

Philip May is Priest-in-Charge of the parish of St. Richard of Chichester, Islington in the diocese of Toronto.

Kevin W. Flynn is Rector of the Church of St. Stephen-in-the-Fields, Toronto and Tutor in Liturgics at Trinity College, Toronto.

Brian Davis is Bishop of Wellington and Primate of New Zealand.

Tom Brown is Assistant Bishop of Wellington, New Zealand.

Joachim C. Fricker is Area Bishop of the Credit Valley in the diocese of Toronto and Chair of the National Doctrine and Worship Committee of the Anglican Church of Canada (1989–1992).

Donald Gray is Rector of St.Margaret's Church, Westminster and a former Chair of the International Anglican Liturgical Consultation.

Juan Quevedo-Bosch is Professor of Liturgics at the Seminario Evangelico de Theologia, Matanzas, Cuba.

Winston Halapua is Dean of Fiji, diocese of Polynesia.

Themba Jerome Vundla is Archdeacon of Durban South in the diocese of Natal and a former member of the IALC Steering Committee.

Francis Wickremesinghe is a layman in the diocese of Seychelles and has served as secretary of the (Anglican) Church of Ceylon Liturgical Commission.

Elizabeth Smith is a deacon in the Anglican Church of Australia, presently engaged in graduate studies in California.

Christian Initiation:
An Ongoing Agenda For Anglicanism
David R. Holeton

It is almost twenty-five years since Lambeth 1968 set the renewal of patterns of Christian initiation as a common task for the entire Anglican Communion. A quarter of a century later it is not inappropriate to ask: How are we doing? What, if anything, has taken place across the Communion? As with most issues that face us as Anglicans, provincial reaction has encompassed everything from total disregard for the question, to a reform of initiation practices which is probably far beyond the most visionary imaginings of any bishop present at Lambeth in 1968. A restored catechumenate, communion of all the baptized, repeatable affirmations of baptismal faith with episcopal imposition of hands probably were not in the minds of many of the bishops who voted for Resolution 25.[1] Yet each of these reforms is a natural consequence of a serious examination of our baptismal theology and practice.[2]

---

[1]Resolution 25 states: "The Conference recommends that each province or regional Church be asked to explore the theology of baptism and confirmation in relation to the need to commission the laity for their task in the world, and to experiment in this regard" (*The Lambeth Conference 1968: Resolutions and Reports* [London and New York: SPCK and Seabury, 1968], 37).

The resolution must be read in the context of the Report of the Working Section on The Renewal of the Church in Ministry which recommended the following alternatives as "possible lines of experiment":

(a) Admission to Holy Communion and confirmation would be separated. When a baptized child is of appropriate age, he or she would be admitted to Holy Communion after an adequate course of instruction. Confirmation would be deferred to an age when a young man or woman shows adult responsibility and wishes to be commissioned and confirmed for his or her task of being a Christian in society.

(b) Infant baptism and confirmation would be administered together, followed by admission to Holy Communion at an early age after appropriate instruction. In due course, the bishop would commission the person for service when he or she is capable of making a responsible commitment (*Lambeth 1968*, 99).

[2]Some of this development I have pointed out previously in "From Lambeth to Boston" in *Nurturing Children in Communion*, Grove Liturgical Study 44, Colin Buchanan, ed. (Bramcote, Notts: Grove, 1985), 39ff.

The renewal of both our theology and practice of initiation is clearly bearing fruit in those dioceses and parishes where there has been serious pastoral implementation. Even in parishes where the reforms have been introduced as little more than a veneer, attitudes towards the nature of church and Christian community have changed. Who is included and who is excluded from the sacraments—particularly the eucharist—has changed basic understandings of the nature of the church, even among those who frequent her altars only at Christmas and Easter, when they are confronted by communicants who may be only infants in arms. Church is not like it once was; age and knowledge are no longer the primary and definitive criteria by which we are invited to sup at the Lord's table. For many, a whole world of theological constructs has been turned on its head. As one of my older students remarked some years ago: ''Before I could go to communion I had to go to classes for months. Now I look around me at the altar rail and see all those little sandbaggers who haven't done anything at all receiving communion too!''

In a number of provinces the sequence: baptism-confirmation-first communion, so carefully observed within Anglicanism since the last century (and taught as if it had scriptural warrant), has been irreparably broken. Baptism admits to the eucharist regardless of age. Confirmation, or affirmation of baptismal faith, may take place on repeated occasions as the individual becomes aware of having entered a new and significant stage on his or her journey of faith. Some, baptized as infants, who have grown up within the life of the faith community, sharing regularly in the parish eucharist and taking on their responsibilities in the life and mission of the church, have never come to a point where they felt the need to be confirmed. Several provinces now have significant numbers of those in their late teens or early adulthood who do not remember a time when they were not welcome at the Lord's table, who have always been actively involved in the life of the Christian community, and who have not been confirmed.

I would suggest that no bishop at Lambeth 1968 imagined this situation as a possible consequence of Resolution 25. Yet, on reflection, we should not be surprised to see it as an outcome of that resolution. In retrospect, and in the context of the initiation practices of other churches (notably the Orthodox and oriental churches) where the practice of confirmation has never been known, the emergence of this pattern is quite natural. At the same time, our own pastoral experience should tell us that there is more than one occasion when individuals want to make a public profession of faith before the gathered assembly, and particularly in the presence of their chief pastor, the bishop.[3]

Pastoral experience over the past several years (and here it is difficult to ascertain whether or not this is merely a phenomenon related to our own uncertain age) has shown that our traditional practice of a routine and unique confirmation in early adolescence, without the possibility of a similar event later in life, has left many dissatisfied. In many situations this has led to individuals turning to other churches where they can experience a dramatic renewal of faith commitment and, not infrequently, actually be re-baptized. In provinces where there is provision made for repeatable *confirmations* or *affirmations of baptismal faith* (neither of which is understood as the "seal of the Spirit"[4]), this felt need is met, and individuals are finding that Anglicanism can satisfy their need for the ritual expression of important moments on their faith journey.

If these are signs of Anglicanism in renewal, there are at least as many signs of Anglicanism in stagnation, if not actual retrenchment, as far as the reforms of initiation practice are concerned. Only a minority of provinces appear to have responded to Lambeth 1968's call "to explore the theology of baptism and confirmation in relation to the need to commission the laity for their task in the world...." Of those provinces which have acted positively in response to this mandate to "explore," only a fraction have gone on to "act."

Often the reports of theological and liturgical commissions have fallen on deaf ears. In some provinces, the advice of theological and liturgical commissions, as well as that of Christian educators, has been dismissed cavalierly by bishops who are determined that "their sacrament" will not be touched by reform. Not infrequently, significant synodical majorities in favour of the renewal of Christian initiation in the Houses of Laity and Clergy have been vetoed or blocked by an Episcopal House which appears to work on a mythology of liturgical history and pastoral practice that is, at best, somewhat naïve.

---

[3]It is interesting that at the Faith and Order Consultation on Children and the Eucharist held at Bad Segeberg, the Orthodox theologian Cyrille Argenti pointed to this "felt need" among some Orthodox for whom there is no possibility of a western style profession of faith.

[4]I would suggest that, from an examination of the theological content of their prayers and the rubrical directions for their celebration in the context of the Prayer Book theology of confirmation, these two rites are theologically and liturgically indistinguishable.

If one were to judge progress in the renewal of initiation practices in Anglicanism in the light of the eight recommendations of the Boston Statement from the first International Anglican Liturgical Consultation, the assessment would be rather gloomy.[5] While it is perhaps unrealistic to expect many tangible results in just six years, most provinces still do not admit all the baptized to the eucharist, the normal celebration of baptism is liturgically minimalist, canonical changes have been few, some provinces have acted to affirm confirmation as the normative rite of admission to communion,[6] and there does not appear to be any ecumenical dialogue, in which Anglicans are engaged, that has given the general communion of all the baptized a significant place on its agenda.

Is the renewal of Christian initiation faltering within Anglicanism? An honest answer would appear to be the very Anglican "Yes and No." Having been mandated to produce a statement on the question, the Fourth International Anglican Liturgical Consultation can hope to give fresh

---

[5]The Boston Consultation recommended:
(i) that since baptism is the sacramental sign of full incorporation into the church, all baptized persons be admitted to communion;
(ii) that provincial baptismal rites be reviewed to the end that such texts explicitly affirm the communion of the newly baptized and that only one rite be authorized for the baptism whether of adults or infants so that no essential distinction be made between persons on basis of age;
(iii) that in the celebration of baptism the vivid use of liturgical signs, e.g., the practice of immersion and the copious use of water be encouraged;
(iv) that the celebration of baptism constitute a normal part of an episcopal visit;
(v) that anyone admitted to communion in any part of the Anglican Communion be acknowledged as a communicant in every part of the Anglican Communion and not be denied communion on the basis of age or lack of confirmation;
(vi) that the Constitution and Canons of each Province be revised in accordance with the above recommendations; and that the Constitution and Canons be amended wherever they imply the necessity of confirmation for full church membership;
(vii) that each Province clearly affirm that confirmation is not a rite of admission to communion, a principle affirmed by the bishops at Lambeth in 1968;
(viii) that the general communion of all the baptized assume a significant place in all ecumenical dialogues in which Anglicans are engaged (*Children and Communion*, IV).

[6]*Christian Initiation Matters*, GS983 (London: General Synod, 1991), the Report of the House of Bishops to the English General Synod of July 1991, is perhaps the most astounding example of this. Not only did the bishops affirm a traditional order of baptism-confirmation-first communion, but they called for the ending of experiments of admission to communion before confirmation, albeit "at a pace which...gives due regard to the pastoral difficulties in individual dioceses and parishes" (p.3)!

courage to those provinces which have been bold enough to act for reform, and a push to those for whom the issues have yet to figure on the agenda for the renewal of their provincial life in mission and ministry.

Renewal of baptismal theology

It is not by accident that more has been written about the theology and practice of Christian initiation over the past three decades than has been written during all the preceding centuries of Christian history. As the inherited structures of established Christianity broke down, it became evident that the Anglican patterns of Christian initiation associated with them—general baptism in early infancy, confirmation in early adolescence followed by first communion—no longer met the pastoral needs of the church. Or, at least, the model no longer appeared to be working. Confirmation was in crisis. The disparity between those who were presented for baptism as infants and who later returned for confirmation was enormous. Even more marked was the disparity between those who made a "mature" profession of faith and commitment at confirmation and those who continued to practice their faith in the context of the Christian community a year after their "mature" acceptance of their own baptismal vows. When confirmation and first communion were not held at the same time (as was often the case in many urban dioceses), many young confirmands did not bother to return for first communion.

Models that had been left unexamined became the subject of serious examination. What did baptism have to do with infancy or confirmation with adolescence? Who ought to be baptized? What are the effects of baptism? It would appear that many of these questions have yet to be resolved within Anglicanism.

In creating the Lima Statement, *Baptism, Eucharist and Ministry*,[7] the section on baptism was the easiest to write, largely because those who were delegated to produce the text believed that there was general agreement among the churches on the theology of baptism.[8] Only after the

---

[7]Faith and Order Paper No.111 (Geneva: WCC, 1982).

[8]This was particularly true after the major advances made between pædobaptist and believers' baptist churches in the *Louisville consultation on Baptism*, Faith and Order Paper No.97, published in the *Review and Expositor* 77.1 (1980).

text was approved at Lima and sent to the churches for further discussion did we come to realize how much disagreement there was on the subject, not just between pædobaptist and believers' baptist churches, but also between Roman Catholic and Orthodox churches[9] as well as churches issuing from the Reformation of the sixteenth century.[10] We should not be surprised to find these questions being debated within the Anglican communion.

The social and theological assumptions implicit in *The Book of Common Prayer* were both legitimate and comprehensible in a church reforming its life and liturgy in the middle of the sixteenth century. It is evident that those assumptions are no longer universally applicable within Anglicanism. Whether or not they are applicable anywhere is a moot question.

Who may be baptized and who ought to be baptized are questions which must be addressed. We see within our communion those who would defend a policy of "open" baptism in which all who present their children for baptism (whether or not either parent or any of the sponsors practice the Christian faith in the context of a gathered Christian community) would be received with few or no conditions.[11] In some provinces the new baptismal rite would make such an eventuality impossible.[12] There are those who would restrict baptism to believing adults and the children of practicing parents. There are also those who would restrict baptism to those who can answer for themselves alone. The advocates of each of these positions see themselves as defenders of a "catholic" (rather than

---

[9]During the Roman Catholic-Orthodox dialogue in Bari, it was suggested by an Orthodox bishop that Roman Catholic baptism was no baptism because it was not immediately followed by chrismation and communion.

[10]The question of whether or not those who have been baptized in water but have not received the eucharist have, in fact, received the fullness of baptism is becoming a growing division among some churches.

[11]Mark Dalby in *Open Baptism* (London: SPCK, 1989) is probably the most recent and articulate advocate of this position. See also R.R. Osborne, *Forbid Them Not* (London: SPCK, 1972).

[12]The question in *The Book of Alternative Services* (Toronto: Anglican Book Centre, 1985), "Will you be responsible for seeing that the child you present is nurtured in the faith and life of the Christian Community?" (p.153) was introduced at the request of the Primate, Ted Scott, to assure that there could be no baptism without commitment to active participation in an actual Christian community.

"sectarian") understanding of the church. Without some clear articulation of an Anglican theology of baptism, there is no way forward through these disparate liturgical and pastoral demands.[13]

It is in this context that dialogue is important between provinces. The pastoral practices of some provinces can easily give scandal to others. Older established or pseudo-established provinces are confronted with requests for baptism, to which they assent, which would be refused in many provinces in which Anglicanism is a minority church. Some of the principles of liturgical inculturation, which were presented in *Down to Earth Worship* by the York Consultation (1989),[14] need to be put to the test in any attempt to provide some common ground to the question: Who *may* be baptized and who *ought* to be baptized?

What are the effects of baptism? Does baptism convey grace or is it a sign of grace already given? What is the relationship between baptism and the remission of sin? Is that sin inherited or is it only actual sin that is forgiven? Can we speak of sin at all in relationship to baptism, or should we be speaking of baptism only in terms of welcoming into God's family.[15]

To some, these questions may seem contrived. It is my experience that they are not. They are being asked widely throughout the communion and the answers given become the theological foundation for new baptismal rites. The disparity of answers given risks seeing rites produced which are mutually exclusive theologically and erode the primary basis for our unity as a communion. That is not to say there cannot be a plurality of understanding of baptism within our common life, but that, unless there is some definition of the theological continuum, there may be no common life.

---

[13]Last Advent IV I attended the eucharist in a South London parish. Within the context of the liturgy, there were three baptisms. Neither the newly baptized, their parents or sponsors (nor any of their friends) received communion. While the parish may have discovered there is a relationship between baptism and its weekly renewal in the parish eucharist, that discovery was considerably undermined by those seeking new life for three infants apparently being uninterested in the source of nurture for that life for themselves.

[14]*Findings of the Third International Anglican Liturgical Consultation*, David Holeton, ed. (Bramcote, Notts.: Grove, 1989), 3-10, and *Liturgical Inculturation in the Anglican Communion*, David R. Holeton, ed. (Bramcote, Notts.: Grove, 1990), 8-13.

[15]A proposed baptismal rite was defeated at a recent synod with the argument that "in our age it is no longer appropriate to speak of baptism in relationship to sin but, rather, as welcoming into the family of the Church."

What are the consequences of baptism? Is it admission to full membership in the church with full title to all that the church has to offer (particularly the eucharist), as was articulated in the Boston Statement?[16] Or does baptism admit to some sort of junior membership which only achieves its fullness when other requirements have been fulfilled (learning, age, confirmation, etc.), as most confirmation manuals would have us believe? Having thought that Boston was quite clear on this matter, further deliberations make it seem as if a theological principle needs to be articulated once again.[17]

This question is of importance not only for young Anglican communicants who find themselves refused communion as they visit or move to other provinces, but also for those from other ecclesial traditions who ask for eucharistic hospitality at Anglican eucharists or who wish to move into Anglicanism from some other Communion.

The Lima document acknowledges the uniqueness of baptism and cautions against any practice which might be interpreted as re-baptism.[18] This outlook challenges two Anglicans customs. The most widespread is the practice, common since the nineteenth century, of not confirming the Orthodox and confirmed Roman Catholics who wish to become members of an Anglican church, but insisting that all others must be confirmed, including those who had been confirmed by a bishop who was not within the "historic" episcopate. While this practice does not suggest re-baptism, it does suggest quite clearly that there is something wanting in the baptism of many churches which we would in no sense doubt as Christian. How can we enter into dialogue with another church made up of what our confirmation manuals would call "junior members"? Less widespread, but not uncommon in some provinces, is the routine re-

---

[16]*Children and Communion: An International Anglican Consultation Held in Boston U.S.A. 29-31 July 1985* (Bramcote, Notts.: Grove, 1985), also published in *Nurturing Children in Communion*, 42-49.

[17]It is surprising that in Martin Reardon's discussion paper, *Christian Initiation — A Policy for the Church of England* (London: Church House, 1991), only six lines in its sixty-six pages is given to the experience of the Anglican Communion (p.40), and neither the Boston Statement nor any other non-English Anglican document is cited in the bibliography.

[18]Baptism, 13: "Baptism is an unrepeatable act. Any practice which might be interpreted as 're-baptism' must be avoided."

baptism of those who come into Anglicanism from other ecclesial traditions, notably from the Roman Catholic Church.

The theological consequences of baptism must be addressed if we are to maintain a sacramental integrity within the life of our own Communion (a communicant anywhere in the Anglican Communion is a communicant everywhere), and if we are to maintain more than a passing fidelity to the ecumenical agreements to which we are a party.

A more recent challenge that has been presented to a number of provinces concerns the formula with which we baptize. While the formula "I baptize you in the Name of the Father and of the Son and of the Holy Spirit" is not the only baptismal formula known in the western church, it has been universal within Anglicanism.[19] Today that formula is being challenged on at least two fronts. In some provinces where gender inclusive language is a major pastoral concern, there have been local initiatives at modifying the formula to meet particular theological and pastoral demands. In other provinces, the intention to be faithful to one particular reading of the Book of Acts has led to the practice of baptizing in "the name of Jesus" alone. While I believe there are ways in which at least the first concern can be resolved satisfactorily,[20] both questions must be addressed before the validity of baptism within some provinces begins to be challenged both by other provinces and other churches.

The context of baptism

When Lambeth 1968 set the Anglican Communion to work on the renewal of its theology and practice of Christian initiation, the first generation of reports from theological commissions and the liturgical texts which, in turn, found their way into new prayer books did not look into the wider context of baptismal preparation and its concomitant liturgical rites. As some provinces began to experience the consequences of a renewed theology of baptism as celebrated in their new baptismal rites—particularly in parishes where candidates for baptism were adults rather than infants—

---

[19]In some recent texts the Orthodox formula "N. is baptized in the Name of the Father and of the Son and of the Holy Spirit" has been introduced.

[20]See, for instance, my "The Liturgical Implications of Feminist Proposals to Change the Trinitarian Baptismal Formula" in *Ecumenical Trends* 17.5 (1988), 69-72.

questions were raised about the possible restoration of the catechumenate.[21] In many communities, it became anomalous not to mark candidates' journeys towards baptism with liturgical rites which celebrated the growing faith of the catechumen as well as the community's commitment to that person.

While there is considerable evidence that a restored catechumenate is playing an important role in many parishes' recovery of a sense of mission,[22] the matter is not without controversy. In one province, the restored catechumenate has been made an integral part of the Decade of Evangelism. At the same time, there are those who question the theological appropriateness of interposing a lengthy period of preparation between a request for baptism and the baptism itself. Others wonder whether a restored catechumenate is not simply another device for the further clericalization of the church. Both the successes and the anxieties need to be taken seriously if a way forward is to be found. This question will become more pressing over the coming years, particularly as some provinces, where infants were once the normative candidates for baptism, find an increasing number of adults coming to faith and seeking baptism. As provinces work towards the second generation of baptismal rites, the IALC can make a significant contribution to this work if its members can engage in a frank discussion of the theological, liturgical, and pastoral implications of a restored catechumenate.

The renewal of baptismal faith

It was with confirmation that the present initiatives in renewing Anglican initiation practices began, and often it seems that it is with confirmation that they will come to an end. It was with confirmation that the first generation of reports from theological commissions and rites from

---

[21]While some provinces (notably Southern Africa) have admitted to the catechumenate for many years, little had been done to provide a liturgical matrix for the community celebration of the journey towards baptism.

[22]Robert Brooks was the first to report to the IALC on this matter at Brixen in 1987. See his "The Catechumenate: A Case Study" in *A Kingdom of Priests: Liturgical Formation of the People of God* [Papers prepared for IALC-2 at Brixen, 1987], Alcuin/GROW Liturgical Study 5, Thomas J. Talley, ed. (Bramcote, Notts.: Grove, 1988), 15-19.

liturgical commissions broke down.[23] There seem to be several factors operative: biblical, historical, theological, and what can perhaps best be called the *pompa episcoporum*.

While it is often said that confirmation is "a rite in search of a theology," the problem within Anglicanism is that confirmation has too many theologies. Rather than limiting themselves to theologies consonant with the liturgical rites, the proponents of confirmation often create theologies of confirmation which are impossible to justify, either in scripture or in any of the liturgical rites known to the church. This fertile inventiveness leads to the conclusion that there is no substantive theology of confirmation, and that most of what we are presented with is merely bogus. The Prayer Book tradition is being asked to bear a theological weight for which it does not have the undergirding.

While there may never be a precise and incontestable answer to the question "What did Cranmer think he was doing?" when it comes to matters of baptism and confirmation, I would suggest that there is incontrovertible evidence that the development of the baptismal and confirmation rites in the first two Prayer Books were not merely a continuation of the medieval rites in which confirmation was the completion of baptism. I would suggest (as have others in the past) that Cranmer intended to take the entire theological content of medieval baptism and confirmation and place it in his reformed baptismal rite.[24] Prayer Book baptism is complete initiation. Prayer Book confirmation is not the same as medieval confirmation (i.e. it is not a completion of baptism), and it is inappropriate to ask it to bear the theological weight of the medieval rites.

In producing a rite for confirmation Cranmer clearly accepted the late

---

[23]I have tried to trace this process in "Christian Initiation in Some Anglican Provinces," *Studia Liturgica* 12.2/3 (1977), 129-150.

[24]It is not infrequently suggested that this is a North American (perhaps revisionist) theory of Cranmer's intentions. The accusation is somewhat unfair. While Marion Hatchett was the first to revive the theory in our time (*Thomas Cranmer and the Rites of Christian Initiation*, unpublished S.T.M. thesis, General Theological Seminary, New York 1967, p.123), the question was raised in 1690 by Hamon L'Estrange (*The Alliance of the Divine Offices*, Library of Anglo-Catholic Theology [Oxford, 1846], 370, 406-7) and in 1710 by Charles Wheatly (*A Rational Illustration of the Book of Common Prayer of the Church of England* [London, 1864], 354-6). Both L'Estrange and Wheatly considered the baptismal unction in the 1549 Prayer Book to be the anointing from medieval confirmation.

medieval/renaissance idea that there was a "pure" confirmation that can be found in scripture, whose theological focus is the mature affirmation of baptismal faith after the completion of catechesis. As this idea would have it, this purified rite was apostolic, though it had nothing to do with confirmation as the medieval church celebrated it.[25] While there is no historical substance to the idea (which was based on the acceptance of Pseudo-Dionysius as an apostolic witness), Anglicans have the misfortune of inheriting a rite which is a radical break from its medieval homograph and yet, because it bears the same name, begs confusion. Apart from some basic understanding of the liturgical/historical context in which Cranmer was working, and on which he founded his new creation, there is little wonder that two distinct rites with the same name quite naturally lead to confusion—particularly when, in the nineteenth century, some Anglicans began reading the Roman theology of confirmation into the reformed rite.[26]

Any progress that is to be made in renewing confirmation within Anglicanism must make a serious assessment of what took place under Cranmer. If Cranmer's own reforms were reviewed, and not read in the light of either a medieval or Tridentine theology of confirmation, Anglicanism would have a far greater freedom for the renewal of its life in this area than is often imagined.

The pastoral dynamic which led to the "invention" of reformed confirmation in the sixteenth century[27] was the need to provide adolescents with an occasion to publicly "own" their faith.[28] Some tell us this need

---

[25]See my forthcoming book, *The Beginnings of Reformed Confirmation.*

[26]As the two (or now, many more) theologies have become so hopelessly confused, and as we now know that there is no historical basis for "primitive" confirmation, it is probably time that Anglicans grasped the nettle and dropped the word from their theological vocabulary, except when discussing a Roman rite which does not exist in Anglicanism.

[27]See n.25 above.

[28]While the candidates for this newly invented rite would be counted as adolescents by some contemporary standards, they were in fact young adults, of an age to marry, to establish independent households, to fight in time of war (and to be expelled from the community should they be unwilling to be confirmed!)

continues to exist today; and that perception must be honoured.[29] What has happened, however, is that we have taken the initiative away from the candidates and made confirmation so routine and programmed that there is little correlation between confirmation and a mature profession of faith.[30] It is only in acting decisively in this matter that we can begin to respond to the task set by Lambeth 1968.

Initiation and episcopal ministry

From a number of the papers presented to the Consultation, it is clear that the renewal of Christian initiation in Anglicanism depends on the active support and goodwill of the bishops.[31] In the space of a very few years, a diocese can move from one model of initiation to another if the reform has the clear and active support of the bishop. A lukewarm or negative response to the synodical actions of a province can assure that little or nothing takes place in a diocese. Too many bishops act as if the sacraments and liturgical life of their dioceses are their personal property rather than the possession of the whole church. Serious questions need to be posed as to whether it is true *episcope* to dismiss the express will of synods as well as the findings of theological, liturgical, and educational commissions.

What needs to take place to win the support of the majority of bishops in renewing the pastoral celebration of baptism and the affirmation of baptismal faith? There are at least three dimensions. The first is the matter of eduction; the second, a renewed place for bishops in baptism; the third,

---

[29]I noted Cyrille Argenti's comments on the need for such an occasion in Orthodoxy in n.3 above. It is perhaps ironic that the same need finds itself worked out in various parts of the Roman Catholic Church where there is a public *profession de foi* completely unrelated in time to confirmation (which often has taken place years before) and for which there are no sacramental claims made.

[30]One of the early scenes in the film *If...* is a fair satire of much of our pastoral practice. As the boys return to school for a new term, they pass before the matron and prefects. As the matron examines each one, a prefect keeps record and asks the questions: "Ringworm? Eye disease? VD? Confirmation class?"

[31]This is strikingly evident in the paper by Archbishop Davis and Bishop Brown, "Child Communion: How It Happened in New Zealand," and Bishop Joachim Fricker's paper, "A Bishop in Initiation," both in this volume.

a matter of ego: what Colin Buchanan means when he warns us ''never to underestimate the bishop's need to be needed.''

1. Baptism, confirmation and education:

The matter of education is not unimportant. When addressing questions of baptism and confirmation, bishops are given to making some of the most astounding statements.[32] Recently one bishop told me that, ''as the church has always taught, in baptism you become a member of the local church and of the local church alone. It is only through my apostolic ministry of confirmation that you become a member of the whole church.'' Surely no theological college would allow a student to pass ''Introduction to Systematics'' holding such an opinion; it is not only erroneous but also formally heretical.

Bishop Hugh Montifiore tells us that:

> Confirmation was administered to Samaritans who had been baptized but who could not yet enjoy the Christian experience (Acts 8:17); and also some Ephesians who had only known John's baptism. The New Testament shows the origins of confirmation; but its function has changed with differing circumstances. Its use cannot be proved necessary, but it is a vital, symbolic, useful and meaningful part of the discipline of the Church of England. We ''need something outward to mark full membership of our church.''[33]

Here the bishop can only be writing *qua* bishop and not as the reputable biblical scholar he is. The theological theme, however, is common: ''Confirmation marks the end of 'junior' membership in the church.''[34] To suggest that baptism does not admit to full membership in the church, or that there are categories of ''junior'' and ''senior'' membership within

---

[32]It is in encountering some of these episcopal dicta that one is reminded of Martin Luther's observation: ''I allow that confirmation be administered provided that it is known that God has said nothing about it [in scripture], and knows nothing of it, and what the bishops say about it is false'' (''Von ehelichen Leben,'' *Dr. Martin Luthers Werke* [Weimar: 1907] X.ii, p.282).

[33]''Scriptural Basis of Confirmation'' in *Confirmation Notebook: The Content of Christian Belief* (London: SPCK, 1984/5), 10. By 1989 the book was in its 14th printing. This ''biblical'' apology for confirmation is clearly being widely disseminated.

[34]John B. Taylor, *Going On: Guidelines for the Newly Confirmed* (London: Daybreak-Darton, Longman and Todd, 1989), 3.

the body of Christ are assertions unsupported by any liturgical text Anglicanism has ever owned. To continue to propagate these concepts as "episcopal truths" does significant damage to the renewal of Anglican life.

Similarly, there are liturgical/historical canards which are continually repeated and, because they are made by bishops, go unchallenged. A commission on which I sat was told by a senior bishop that, "he was very glad that in the primitive church, with its classic shape of the seven sacraments, the two sacraments which involved human touch were reserved to bishops alone: confirmation and ordination." To someone who has a formation in liturgical history, the assertion is clearly without substance, even risible. But lay people hear and repeat the statement and, when asked for their source, quote this senior bishop. The resulting quandary is both difficult and embarrassing. Should one let it pass unchallenged, thereby perpetuating a clearly erroneous belief which frustrates the recommendations of a national commission but leaves the bishop's authority unchallenged? Or should one point out that it is impossible to baptize and anoint without touching (let alone to anoint the sick), and that it is extremely difficult to give communion without touching the communicant, or that the classic sign for the reconciliation of a penitent was the imposition of hands—all actions regularly performed by presbyters? In taking the latter course one feels disloyal, and is aware that the effect is to erode the authority of the episcopal office generally, which certainly would not be my intended purpose.

The plea to bishops is not only to read the documents that have been produced on baptism and affirmation of baptismal vows by their theological and liturgical commissions but also, perhaps far more important, to set their own reflections alongside those documents and ask themselves if some of the assertions they have been making in confirmation sermons are true. No credit is done to the episcopal office if it is allowed to become the perpetuator of an episcopal "folk theology" whose aim is to undergird confirmation while undermining the work of the biblical, theological, and liturgical scholars of the church.

2. The liturgical role of bishops:

I have pointed out elsewhere that the liturgical texts we have inherited gave a very restricted role to bishops in the ongoing liturgical life of Anglicanism.[35] While this can be explained historically in terms of the

---

[35] "The Bishop Leading His Diocese" in *The Bishop in Liturgy*, Alcuin/GROW Liturgical Study No.6, Colin Buchanan, ed. (Bramcote, Notts.: Grove, 1988), 25ff.

era in which our texts were born (the immense size of many dioceses, no suffragan bishops, and no possibility of retirement), the effect has been to form a mold in which many bishops have seen their primary liturgical functions as confirming and ordaining. To preside at either baptism or the eucharist was an exception. How many bishops even thirty years ago regularly presided at the baptism of those other than their children, grandchildren, or godchildren? How many bishops of that era would "preside from the throne" while the parish priest celebrated the eucharist? The sacramental ministry of bishops was defined in terms of two "nondominical" sacraments; the regular celebration of the "dominical" sacraments had become a presbyterial, not episcopal, office. (The Prayer Book Ordinal itself re-enforced this.) There is little wonder that, when the question of admitting unconfirmed children to the eucharist was first raised in the Canadian House of Bishops, a former Bishop of Toronto warned the House: "Take away confirmation and I will have no right to enter a parish church."

While we can understand the genesis of this situation, we can no longer allow it to go unchallenged. To allow bishops to remain "confirmation machines," and to define their own episcopal roles in terms of confirmation, does infinite damage to the life of the church by imposing such a limited understanding of *episcope*. In provinces where the reformed rites of baptism and affirmation of baptismal faith assume a bishop as the usual presider at baptism, affirmation, and the eucharist, many bishops have come to have a quite different understanding of their own liturgical ministry, and have discovered new possibilities for the exercise of *episcope*—possibilities which do not begin and end with confirmation.

In my own province, bishops were recently surveyed about their practice of baptism and confirmation. The shift in practice from what was normative twenty years ago is remarkable. Only two bishops reported using the *BCP* confirmation rite exclusively (and in both cases it was in an indigenous language into which the new rite has yet to be translated). Most bishops prefer to use the rite in which baptism and confirmation/affirmation are celebrated together. Only sixteen percent of the bishops preferred confirmation without baptism; eighty-two percent of the bishops always celebrate the eucharist when they confirm.[36]

---

[36] Twenty-five years ago most confirmations in urban Canadian dioceses took place apart from the eucharist. The baptism of infants during a confirmation was virtually unheard of. Unbaptized adults were usually baptized privately by the parish priest a week or so before they were to be confirmed. Not infrequently, this private baptism took place minutes before the confirmation service began.

The shift in liturgical practice has had a significant effect on the way bishops have come to understand their episcopal ministry. By becoming ministers of baptism, and by celebrating the affirmation of baptismal faith in the context of baptism, many bishops are finding new ways to preach the mission of the church and the common ministry of the whole people of God. Their vision of their own *episcope* has grown as their sense of being the chief pastor and minister of both word and sacrament has grown. The central role once played by confirmation in the general understanding of *episcope* has diminished. Now half the Canadian bishops are prepared to say that, should confirmation be discontinued, their understanding of their role in the life of the church would not be affected significantly. An increasing number of Canadian bishops feel that the disappearance of confirmation would enhance their pastoral opportunities during a parish visit.

The narrowness within which many Anglican bishops have come to define their *episcope*, and the experience of those bishops who have set out to explore new models of episcopal ministry, would seem to point to the necessity of a fresh look at the role of the episcopate in the sacramental life of the church. All the signs indicate that bishops would find their pastoral role enhanced, and that they would find themselves at the heart, rather than on the periphery, of the ongoing liturgical life of the diocese. I do not doubt the need of bishops to be needed; I only hope they will find this new way in which they are needed more fulfilling than being the "confirmation machine" of which so many complain.

3. The pompa episcoporum:

The third dimension which needs serious examination in the renewal of the episcopal role in baptism and confirmation/affirmation of baptismal faith is the disparity between what bishops claim to want to see happen and what is actually happening.

When interviewed, as well as when producing recommendations from the episcopal bench, bishops repeatedly claim that they see confirmation as a time when they can establish a pastoral relationship with the confirmands.[37] At the same time, bishops stress the importance of

---

[37]Some bishops refine this and suggest that confirmation is a time to maintain a pastoral relationship with the parish.

confirmation as a mature affirmation of faith. Both of these desires are laudable and beyond reproach.

The actual pastoral practice, however, falls short of coming close to these often articulated ideals. In the survey of the Canadian episcopate, forty-nine percent of the bishops reported spending time with confirmation candidates before their confirmation only occasionally or seldom. Seventy-seven percent of the bishops reported spending up to three hours with the candidates while thirty-eight percent reported spending no more than an hour with the candidates. Sixty-one percent of the bishops reported that their time with the candidates was devoted to the meaning of confirmation and for nineteen percent that time included dinner. At the same time, every bishop reported that there was some sort of reception and gathering held after the confirmation at which they met parents and family, wardens, synod delegates, and parishioners, in addition to the confirmands. This was time included in the calculation of hours spent with the candidates. While there are some bishops who regularly spend time with the candidates, either individually or in small groups, and enter into genuine conversation with them (rather than talking *at* them), is it not time that most bishops asked themselves if their present confirmation practices are the most effective way of building genuine pastoral relationships with confirmands? Are there not other models which would better achieve this end, so that time could be devoted to the confirmands themselves rather than being diverted to the vast retinue of well-wishers who show up for the *pompa episcoporum*?

I have suggested repeatedly that there is a need for an occasion for the affirmation of baptismal faith, a need which should be honoured. In Canada most bishops express the desire that this should be a "mature" profession of faith. Yet three-quarters of the Canadian bishops say that the average age of confirmands is between thirteen and fifteen years, an age which is well below their own stated "ideal" age and one which most Christian educators deem inappropriate for such a profession of faith. Yet in Canada, there is only one bishop who will not confirm adolescents under the age of sixteen years and only one diocesan synod has called for a five-year moratorium on the "routine" confirmation of young adolescents.

Changes in who are confirmed and when they are confirmed are probably more at the discretion of individual bishops than any other pastoral activity. As the Anglican Communion is the only church which restricts confirmation to bishops alone, there seems little reason why bishops cannot take strong initiatives to see that the candidates for confirmation come closer to those the bishops consider to be ideal. If there is good news, it is that children who have received communion from an early age feel no pressure to be confirmed at an early age, and, when they are confirmed, the maturity of commitment comes much closer to what bishops are hoping for when they lay on hands at the affirmation of baptismal faith.

The final question is the seductive quality of the actual practice of confirmation to which Colin Buchanan alludes in his paper entitled "Confirmation" in this present volume. The dynamic of this seduction is easy to understand. It poses, however, the question of whose needs are really being met in the celebration of confirmation: the confirmands' or the bishop's? Bishop John B. Taylor writes:

> bishops love to hear people say: "Hello, Bishop, you confirmed me." With any luck you might even be able to tell the bishop what he preached about or what the text was, and that will make his day.[38]

As a teenager, I said something similar to the bishop who confirmed me, several weeks after the event. He replied (jokingly?): "I hope I didn't do you any harm." I was speechless and embarrassed. There was no attempt to continue the conversation on his part. I guess he didn't need to be affirmed; but I guess we hadn't managed to establish much of a pastoral relationship either.

The question is obviously a sensitive one but it needs to be posed. Is confirmation, as presently practiced, meeting the ends its practitioners profess? Whose needs are being met? This question is particularly acute in those parts of the communion where confirmation is truly the *pompa episcopi* who, when acting as tribal chief, receives all the honours of a local prince and returns home, car or jeep stuffed with the offerings of the faithful.

Liturgical texts

One of the concerns which lay behind the creation of the International Anglican Liturgical Consultations ten years ago was the foundation of a forum in which those responsible for the reform of liturgical texts in

[38]*Going On — Guidelines for the Newly Confirmed*, 4.

their respective provinces could discuss the development of new liturgical texts. While there has never been any intention to dictate the content of new liturgical texts (the apparent intention to do so was one of the reasons underlying the resistance of the IALC to the establishment of a Pan-Anglican Liturgical Commission), there is more need than ever to think collegially about the developing shape and content of rites for baptism and the affirmation of baptismal vows.

The rites which have been produced by a wide variety of churches in the light of the Lima statement[39] have clearly brought new life to those churches. Indeed, that document has had a significant influence on the development of baptismal rites in a number of Anglican provinces. Those provinces have often adapted the Lima shape to meet particular Anglican sensibilities, however. It is perhaps time to see if some consensus can be achieved on the general shape Anglican texts might take as we embark on the next generation of baptismal texts.

In surveying the renewed rites, it becomes apparent that there are areas where a collegial reflection on common problems could bear much fruit. Some directions will probably emerge quite naturally as a result of the Consultation. The eucharist, rather than the office, as the context in which baptism takes place could be a position achieved with little difficulty. Provinces seem to be slower, however, in responding to the second recommendation in the Boston Statement: that there should be a single baptismal rite regardless of the age of the candidate. It would be highly desirable, also, if some consensus on the role of the signation, a ceremony long defended by Anglicans, could be achieved. At present the signation is being used for a wide variety of (sometimes incompatible) purposes, ranging from the Christic and interpretive at baptism to the pneumatic. In some renewed rites the signation has been dropped from baptism and reserved for confirmation, a practice which only serves to exacerbate the confirmation question.

Consensus on the shape and intention of rites for confirmation/affirmation of baptismal vows may be difficult to achieve, but this matter is of great importance to many provinces. Currently, a number of provinces are living with rites which had a unity and theological integrity when they left the hands of the liturgical commissions which produced them, but were altered on the floor of synod and are now left eviscerated or

---

[39]See "The Celebration of Baptism" in *BEM*, Baptism, 17-23.

else claim to do what their drafters never intended them to do!

An overview of the existing rites also leads to questions about the variety of ceremonies that are possible and helpful in a single rite and, in light of the York Statement (*Down to Earth Worship*), how the rites themselves can respond to the diverse cultural contexts in which Anglicanism has flourished.

Anglican baptismal rites range from the relative simplicity of the historic Prayer Books, in which the ceremonies were often reduced to the use of water and the sign of the cross, to a dense richness (chrism, candles, white garment, other traditional indigenous signs of belonging) found in some of the renewed rites. This rapid development in baptismal rites raises questions about the seriousness with which we take the fundamental sign-acts (death, new birth) as well as the role to be played by the interpretive acts which often, in their actual celebration, risk overshadowing the acts they are said to interpret. Here the third Boston recommendation needs to be taken with particular seriousness.

As provinces take the inculturation of their liturgies more seriously, they not infrequently encounter questions of whether a rite associated with initiation in their own culture carries connotations which may impair the purpose for which its use is intended in another culture. Here a discussion among sister churches may help clarify questions being raised in local churches.

The Toronto Statement can only hope to be the beginning of an ongoing conversation, one more part of the ongoing agenda given to the provinces by Lambeth 1968. It is imperative that it give clear answers to the questions raised by Lambeth 1988 and by ACC-7 and 8. We hope it will be read with more attention than have been some of its predecessors.

I The Renewal of Initiation Theology

Theological Foundations
for the Practice of Christian Initiation
in the Anglican Communion
William R. Crockett

Background

During the last twenty-five years, fundamental changes have been taking place in the theology and practice of Christian initiation, both within the Anglican Communion and ecumenically. The fundamental issues which have surfaced in this re-examination are: the unity of Christian initiation, infant and adult baptism, the relationship between baptism and admission to communion, the relationship between baptism and confirmation, and the role of the bishop in relation to Christian initiation. These theological and pastoral shifts also reflect widespread cultural changes.

In the light of developments taking place in the various provinces of the Anglican Communion in the practice of Christian initiation, the Lambeth Conference in 1968 commended two alternatives as ''possible lines of experiment'':

(a) Admission to Holy Communion and confirmation would be separated. When a baptized child is of appropriate age, he or she would be admitted to Holy Communion after an adequate course of instruction. Confirmation would be deferred to an age when a young man or woman shows adult responsibility and wishes to be commissioned and confirmed for his or her task of being a Christian in society.

(b) Infant baptism and confirmation would be administered together, followed by admission to Holy Communion at an early age after appropriate instruction. In due course, the bishop would commission the person for service when he or she is capable of making a responsible commitment.[1]

Lurking behind these two alternatives are two quite different understandings of confirmation. In the first alternative, confirmation is

---

[1] *The Lambeth Conference 1968: Resolutions and Reports* (London: SPCK, 1968), 99.

separated altogether from Christian initiation and admission to communion, and understood as the renewal of baptismal vows and commissioning for service in adulthood. In the second alternative, confirmation is understood as an element in Christian initiation which ought to be re-integrated into a unified rite of Christian initiation followed by early admission to communion. The later renewal of baptismal vows and commissioning for service by the bishop is no longer called confirmation.

Lambeth 1978, in turn, "recommended that each province of the Anglican Communion should re-examine the theology and practice of initiation with particular reference to the bishop's role."[2] In 1982 the World Council of Churches Faith and Order document *Baptism, Eucharist and Ministry* appeared, which posed an ecumenical challenge to all the churches to re-examine their theology and practice of Christian initiation.[3] This was followed, in 1985, by the Boston Statement of the International Anglican Liturgical Consultation which recommended that baptism in principle lead to admission to communion, and asked the provinces of the Anglican Communion to cease to require confirmation or any other postbaptismal educational requirement or attainment as a prerequisite for admission to communion.[4]

In 1987 the Anglican Consultative Council encouraged the provinces to study both the *BEM* document and the Boston Statement and posed a number of questions concerning the latter.[5] The report "Mission and Ministry" of the Lambeth Conference in 1988 acknowledges the importance of both *BEM* and the Boston Statement and recommends, "that the text of the Boston Statement and the ACC questions put to it should be widely circulated throughout our Communion and a careful study made by Provinces which have not so far considered it."[6] Resolution 69 "requests all Provinces to consider the theological and pastoral issues involved in

---

[2]*The Report of the Lambeth Conference 1978* (London: CIO, 1978), 86.

[3]Faith and Order Paper No.111 (Geneva: WCC, 1982).

[4]Text and accompanying essays found in *Nurturing Children in Communion: Essays from the Boston Consultation*, Grove Liturgical Study 44, Colin Buchanan, ed. (Bramcote, Notts.: Grove, 1985).

[5]*Many Gifts, One Spirit: Report of ACC-7: Singapore 1987* (London: Church House, 1987), 68-72.

[6]*The Truth Shall Make You Free: The Lambeth Conference 1988* (London: Church House, 1988), 71.

the admission of those baptised but unconfirmed to communion (as set out in the Report of ACC-7), and to report their findings to the ACC."[7]

The aim of the present paper is to further this process of study within the Anglican Communion by attempting both to outline the theological issues presently facing the Communion in the area of Christian initiation and by attempting to indicate solid theological foundations for developing Anglican practice.

The unity and theological richness of Christian initiation

The primary theological affirmation that must be made is the unity of Christian initiation. Christian initiation is the action of the triune God whereby we are united with Christ in his death and resurrection, sealed with the Holy Spirit, and incorporated into the church. This unity, however, is unfolded in the New Testament and in the liturgy of the church "in various images which express the riches of Christ and the gifts of salvation."[8] This theological unity and richness is admirably summarized in the *BEM* document:

> Baptism is participation in Christ's death and resurrection (Rom.6:3-5; Col.2:12); a washing away of sin (I Cor.6:11); a reclothing in Christ (Gal.3:27); a renewal by the Spirit (Titus 3:5); the experience of salvation from the flood (I Peter 3:20-21); an exodus from bondage (I Cor.10:1-2) and a liberation into a new humanity in which barriers of division whether of sex or race or social status are transcended (Gal.3:27-28; I Cor.12:13). The images are many, but the reality is one.[9]

BEM goes on to state:

> In God's work of salvation, the paschal mystery of Christ's death and resurrection is inseparably linked with the pentecostal gift of the Holy Spirit. Similarly, participation in Christ's death and resurrection is inseparably linked with the receiving of the Spirit. Baptism in its full meaning signifies and effects both.[10]

---

[7]*Lambeth 1988*, 239.

[8]Baptism, 2.

[9]Baptism, 2.

[10]Baptism, 14.

In the early church this wealth of theological imagery was unfolded in a rich liturgical sequence without obscuring the unity of the act of initiation. As a recent Canadian report stated:

> Because the images of baptism are so rich, the liturgies quickly began to use a variety of symbols and sign/acts to interpret the richness of God's act of grace in baptism. Thus we find the baptismal action including not just the use of water, but also the use of oil or chrism, the imposition of hands, and the giving of both light and a new baptismal garment. It would be unfair to these ancient ceremonies to invest any one of them with a particular meaning or efficacy independent of the meaning of baptism as a whole. Their purpose was to make clear particular dimensions of the richness of God's gift of new life in baptism. Thus, for example, the willingness of some contemporary commentators to say that chrism or the imposition of hands is the "moment" when the Holy Spirit is bestowed would have been incomprehensible to a Christian who lived at the time this liturgical action first took place. God's Spirit was seen as operative throughout the baptismal action, just as the Spirit had been operative in calling the baptized to Christ. Any assertion that there was just one moment in the liturgy when the Spirit was active would have been greeted with incomprehension because it would have undermined the Spirit-filled quality of the entire baptismal celebration.[11]

Sacramental efficacy: The relationship between grace and faith in Christian initiation

In the patristic period the unity between the sacraments as signs of faith and means of grace was clearly attested. Augustine makes this abundantly clear in relation to baptism:

> "Now you are clean through the word which I have spoken to you." Why does he not say, you are clean through the baptism with which you have been washed, but "through the word which I have spoken to you," save only that in the water also it is the word that cleanses? Take away the word, and the water is neither more nor less than water. The word is added to the element, and there results the sacrament, as if itself also a kind of visible word.... And whence has water so great an efficacy...save by the operation of the word;

---

[11]*Report of the Confirmation Task Force of the Anglican Church of Canada* (Toronto: Anglican Church of Canada, 1989), 15-16.

and that not because it is uttered, but because it is believed? For even in the word itself the passing sound is one thing, the abiding efficacy another. "This is the word of faith which we preach," says the apostle, "that if you shall confess with your mouth that Jesus is the Lord, and shall believe in your heart that God has raised him from the dead, you shall be saved. For with the heart we believe unto righteousness, and with the mouth confession is made unto salvation." ...The cleansing, therefore, would on no account be attributed to the fleeting and perishable element, were it not for that which is added, "by the word."[12]

It is clear in this text, moreover, that Augustine is not speaking of faith in a purely individualistic and subjectivist manner; he is speaking of the faith of the church into which the candidate is baptized as a believing member. This has important implications for the way in which we view both the baptism and the communion of children. Since the Middle Ages, sacramental theology has tended to oscillate between a purely objectivistic understanding of sacramental efficacy on the one hand (*ex opere operato*) and a purely subjectivistic understanding of the sacraments as signs of the faith of the believer on the other. This polarization has obscured the grace-faith relationship and the nature of sacramental efficacy.

The Anglican tradition rejected both extreme objectivism in relation to the sacraments and an extreme subjectivism. Article 25 speaks of the sacraments as "effectual signs of grace," and in the *Laws of Ecclesiastical Polity* Richard Hooker speaks of the sacraments as "moral instruments":

Sacraments serve as the instruments of God...moral instruments, the use whereof is in our hands, the effect in his... [They] really give what they promise, and are what they signify. For we take not baptism or the eucharist for bare *resemblances* or memorials of things absent, neither for *naked signs* and testimonies assuring us of grace received before, but...means effectual whereby God when we take the sacraments delivereth into our hands that grace available unto eternal life, which grace the sacraments represent or signify.[13]

As I have written elsewhere:

---

[12]*Homilies on John* 26.18.

[13]*Laws* 5.57.5.

Hooker attempts to steer a middle course between ''Zwinglianism'' on the one side and the doctrine of the medieval Church on the other. To explain the relationship between divine grace and the sacraments, Hooker, like Aquinas, employs the language of instrumental causality. The sacraments are not causes of grace in an absolute sense. God alone is the author of grace. The sacraments are causes only in a secondary or instrumental sense. God uses them as a means of imparting grace. As means of grace, however, the sacraments do not produce their effect automatically, but only conditionally. The sacraments are *moral instruments*, not mechanical or physical instruments. Hooker is employing here what we would call a ''personalist'' rather than a naturalistic or mechanical model of sacramental causality. The operation of the sacraments is analogous to the offering and acceptance of a gift between free moral agents. It is conditional both on God's free offer of grace and upon the faithful response of the recipient. The offer of grace is unconditional in the sense that the sacraments depend upon the divine promise.... The acceptance of the gift, however, is conditional upon the free and faithful response of the recipient.[14]

The baptism of infants and adults

The primary candidates for baptism in the early church were adults. Nevertheless, the children of Christian parents were baptized from a very early period. Since in the early church proclamation and faith, the water bath, and sealing with the Spirit (whether expressed in the water bath itself or in accompanying sign-acts such as anointing or the imposition of hands) constituted a unity, when infants were baptized they were baptized with the full rite of initiation culminating in the eucharist. We are presently moving into a period when it is increasingly the case that persons of various ages are presenting themselves for baptism. This means that the appropriate age for baptism (and communion) has again become a matter of debate within the Anglican Communion.

The case for infant baptism needs to be placed in the context of an adequate theological understanding of the nature of sacramental efficacy and the relationship between grace and faith. If the primacy of grace in the act of baptism is emphasized to the exclusion of faith, this can lead to the indiscriminate baptism of infants. On the other hand, if the role

---

[14]*Eucharist: Symbol of Transformation* (New York: Pueblo, 1989), 179-180.

of the personal response of the believer becomes paramount, the children of Christian believers are excluded from the community of faith. Infant baptism is only arguable on the assumption that those being baptized are the children of Christian believers.[15] It must not be turned into an argument for indiscriminate baptism.

So far I have spoken of the grace-faith relationship from the perspective of a *personalist* rather than a *mechanical* model of sacramental efficacy. This needs to be broadened, however, to make it clear that, from a biblical perspective, when we speak about sacramental activity we are speaking about those sign-acts which initiate and renew the covenant relationship between God and the community of faith. Such an understanding makes it clear that when we speak about baptism, we are speaking not only about the individual's personal relationship to God but also about the incorporation of the baptized person into the believing community. The primary theological basis for baptizing the children of Christian believers is the divine invitation to participate in the covenant community. A covenant model undercuts the tendency towards an individualistic and subjectivistic understanding of faith, which has more to do with the heritage of western culture than with the bible or the early church.

The relationship between baptism and confirmation

In the early church baptism was a single rite within which a variety of sign-acts interpreted the theological richness of the sacramental action. Historical research has shown the emergence of two basic patterns of Christian initiation in the early patristic period, each in the context of a single rite. These were the East Syrian and the western (Justin, Tertullian, and Hippolytus). The sequence of baptism in the East Syrian tradition was: 1. an anointing with olive oil on the head, 2. the water bath, 3. the eucharist. The striking feature of this pattern is that the anointing precedes the water bath. The western pattern was: 1. catechesis, 2. oil of exorcism, 3. water bath, 4. anointing with chrism (Tertullian) or oil of thanksgiving (Hippolytus), 5. imposition of hands by the bishop (in Hippolytus this is accompanied by a final anointing on the forehead with

---

[15]See Colin Buchanan, *A Case for Infant Baptism*, Grove Booklet on Ministry and Worship No.20 (Bramcote, Notts.: Grove, 1973).

consecrated oil as a "signing" or "sealing"), 6. the eucharist.[16]

This early unitary sequence (with its regional variety) eventually dissolved in the west and "finally collapsed into three separate and isolated moments of water-baptism, confirmation, and eucharist."[17] This dissolution was unique to the Roman rite and its spread in the west. The Roman rite (the rite used in the city of Rome itself and the surrounding area) was further unique in having two anointings after the water bath, following the pattern in Hippolytus. The various local rites which were used throughout the rest of Europe had only a single anointing following the water bath. In the course of time, the imposition of hands and the final consignation with oil on the forehead in the Roman rite became separated from the rest of the rite and acquired a separate identity as the sacrament of confirmation. Moreover, while the normal practice in both the eastern and western churches outside Rome was to delegate the presidency of the entire baptismal celebration to presbyters when the bishop could not be present, the church in Rome was unique in reserving the laying on of hands and the final anointing to the bishop.

With the evangelization of western Europe by Roman missionaries, and the subsequent attempt by Charlemagne in the ninth century to impose political and liturgical unity on western Europe, the Roman rite came to replace the former local rites. The dioceses which were thus created by missionary and political expansion were vast areas where it was not possible for the bishop to be present for every baptism. The final part of the initiatory sequence, therefore, was delayed until the bishop could be present.

Once separated from baptism, however, the imposition of hands and final anointing became a rite in search of a theology. Faustus of Rietz, a fifth-century Gallican bishop, speculated that, "in baptism we are born anew for life, after baptism we are confirmed to fight; in baptism we are washed, after baptism we are strengthened."[18] This passage

---

[16]See Aidan Kavanagh, *The Shape of Baptism: The Rite of Christian Initiation* (New York: Pueblo, 1978), 40-54.

[17]Nathan D.Mitchell, "Dissolution of the Rite of Christian Initiation" in *Made, Not Born: New Perspectives on Christian Initiation and the Catechumenate* (Notre Dame: University Press, 1976), 50.

[18]Pseudo-Eusebius, *Homily for Pentecost* 4, cited in the *Report of the Confirmation Task Force*, 10. For the text in its context see Bernard Leeming, *Principles of Sacramental Theology* (London: Longmans, Green, 1956), 624-626.

subsequently found its way into the False Decretals, from which it was quoted by Peter Lombard, and became the foundation of standard medieval theologies of confirmation including that of Thomas Aquinas. Confirmation, therefore, in the medieval tradition, became commonly understood as a further strengthening by the Holy Spirit after baptism.

A second and quite different meaning of confirmation derives from the period of the Reformation:

> By the fifteenth century, beginning in Bohemia, a liturgical novelty had appeared. Humanism, with its religious expression in the devotio moderna, brought its new-found concern for religious knowledge into a liturgical setting. Adolescents, after a period of intensive religious instruction, made a profession of their own faith in the context of the liturgical assembly. Never before in the history of the church had such a practice been required of those who were already baptized.

> Erasmus, through his correspondence with the Bohemians, learned of the practice and proposed that a similar procedure be introduced in the church in the Low Countries. Adolescent boys, Erasmus suggested, should be instructed by the most learned priest in their city or town and should mark the conclusion of this religious catechesis in a solemn liturgical assembly presided over by the bishop. Erasmus' idea spread and became the model for what was to be called confirmation in the churches issuing out of the sixteenth century Reformation.[19]

According to this second (Reformation) meaning, confirmation is not a part of initiation but the renewal of baptismal vows by adolescents. These two quite different meanings of confirmation were inherited by the English reformers. The source of the present confusion in Anglican thinking about confirmation has its roots in the fact that the term carries two quite different meanings stemming from the two quite distinct historical backgrounds which we have described. The first (medieval) meaning refers to the laying on of hands and final consignation which had become separated from the early unitary initiation rite in the Roman tradition and became known as the separate sacrament of confirmation. The second (Reformation) meaning of confirmation was the renewal of baptismal vows by adolescents.

---

[19]*Report of the Confirmation Task Force*, 11.

What did Cranmer think he was doing when he came to revise the inherited initiation rites? Recent liturgical scholarship has cast new light on Cranmer's intention in revising the rites of initiation in the first two editions of *The Book of Common Prayer*. There is a growing consensus among liturgical scholars that Cranmer had a twofold aim in revising the initiation rites. In the first place, it now seems clear that Cranmer's aim in revising the baptismal rite was to restore the unity of Christian initiation. Secondly, while he retained a rite for confirmation in the Prayer Book, he followed the Reformation rather than the medieval model and interpreted confirmation as the renewal of baptismal vows rather than as the completion of baptism.

The evidence for this is that in the medieval baptismal rite, the first anointing following the water rite took place on the crown of the head, while the final anointing by the bishop (confirmation) was on the forehead.

The Prayer Book baptismal rite, however, specified that the chrismation (1549) or the signation/signing with the cross (1552) take place on the forehead (the place of confirmation) and not the crown. In addition, the language accompanying the chrismation in 1549 ("unction of his Holy Spirit") and signation in 1552 ("we receive this child into the congregation of Christ's flock...and manfully to fight under his banner") was the language of medieval confirmation, not of medieval baptism.

[Moreover, the] authors of the Prayer Book drew on a variety of sources. Among these was the Hispanic *Missale Mixtum*, which represents the liturgical use in Spain before the arrival of the Roman Rite. Thus it contained a single, unified, baptismal rite presided over in its entirety by either bishop or presbyter. In either case the presider performed the final baptismal sealing.

This background makes it more than plausible that the baptismal rite of the English reformers was not created by mere chance but was explicitly intended to achieve everything previously effected by the two former rites of baptism and confirmation. Modelled on the unitary initiation rites of Spain, Gaul, or Milan, rather than the two-stage Roman rite, the baptismal rite of the Prayer Books affords full initiation requiring nothing more to complete it. Confirmation, in the Roman sense of the final baptismal anointing, had been deliberately incorporated into the baptismal rite itself.[20]

---

[20]*Report of the Confirmation Task Force*, 11.

Cranmer's confirmation rite was now modelled on the Reformation rather than the medieval pattern; it was no longer the completion of baptism but the renewal of baptismal vows. Moreover, it was separated from the baptismal rite in the Prayer Book and preceded by the Catechism. This fits exactly with the pattern found in the Bohemian Reformation and in Erasmus, where the laying on of hands comes as the conclusion of a period of catechetical instruction.

The relationship between baptism and eucharist

It is clear from our discussion thus far that the eucharist was the culmination of the initiatory sequence in the early church. The separation of baptism and confirmation in the west has obscured this original unity of baptism and eucharist. In the early church, baptism was incorporation into the eucharistic community. The Boston Statement employed a *koinonia* ecclesiology in its attempt to provide a theological basis for the intimate link between baptism and the eucharist, and drew from this conclusion that all the baptized, whatever their age, ought to be admitted to the eucharist:

> The church is the whole body of the faithful. It is created through baptism into the death and resurrection of Jesus Christ, which is the sign of faith and of participation in God's act of redemption. The faithful sustain and proclaim their unity with their Lord and each other as they meet each Lord's Day and as they regularly participate in the eucharistic assembly by sharing the Word of God, the prayers, the kiss of peace and the eucharistic gifts. In this way a sharing community, a *koinonia*, is formed and nurtured. The people of God together form a communion. The shared identity first established in baptism is exhibited and reinforced in communion.... The baptized life in Christ is a eucharistic life. The *koinonia* of God's people is a *koinonia* of the baptized.

> ...Consideration of the arguments for the baptism of infants, insofar as they are ecclesiological arguments, suggests that the communion of such infants should take place from the time of, and on the basis of, their baptism. Baptism is one (Eph.4:4); if infants are baptized, they are baptized into Jesus Christ just as adults are, and their baptism is in principle initiation into the eucharistic life just as is the baptism of an adult. To postpone their participatory inclusion into the eucharistic community obscures the meaning of their baptism, and even creates a separate and indefensible category of "infant" baptism which has a different initiatory force from that of "adult" baptism....[It] is paradoxical to admit children to membership in the body of

Christ through baptism, and yet to deny that membership in the eucharistic meal that follows.[21]

The *BEM* document draws the same conclusion:

If baptism, as incorporation into the body of Christ, points by its very nature to the eucharistic sharing of Christ's body and blood, the question arises as to how a further and separate rite can be interposed between baptism and admission to communion. Those churches which baptize children but refuse them a share in the eucharist before such a rite may wish to ponder whether they have fully appreciated and accepted the consequences of baptism.[22]

The role of the bishop in Christian initiation

The normal minister of baptism [in the early church] was the local bishop (just as he was the normal minister of all the liturgical celebrations of the local community). As the church grew and spread and the local bishop could no longer preside at every baptism and eucharist, the presidency of the liturgical celebration was delegated to presbyters. In most churches the bishop who chose to delegate his presidency of the baptismal celebration delegated the celebration in its entirety. Thus in the churches of the east, just as in the churches of Spain, Gaul, and Milan, the presbyter presided over the entire baptismal celebration and did whatever the bishop would have done had he been presiding.[23]

This primary role of the bishop in relation to baptism is obscured when the role of the bishop is narrowly conceived as the ministry of confirmation. It is now clear from historical research that this narrowing of the episcopal role is peculiar to the Roman tradition in the west. Moreover, the reservation of confirmation to the bishop has now been abandoned by that tradition. The Anglican tradition stands alone, therefore, in reserving confirmation to the bishop!

It is somewhat ironic that the reservation of confirmation to the bishop, which is the sole reason for its separation from baptism in the Roman rite, has been abandoned in the new Roman *Rite for the Christian Initiation of Adults*, and

---

[21]*Nurturing Children in Communion*, 43-44.

[22]Baptism, Commentary (14)b.

[23]*Report of the Confirmation Task Force*, 9.

in the absence of the bishop the officiating presbyter is now directed to omit the customary post-baptismal anointing of the head with chrism and to substitute the *consignatio frontis*, the anointing of confirmation. Thus, in one stroke the two distinctive features of Roman baptismal practice are abandoned: the double anointing by presbyter and bishop which goes back to *Apostolic Tradition*, and the restriction of confirmation to the bishop.[24]

The bishop's role in Christian initiation is primarily related to the whole rite of initiation, whether as the president of the liturgy or through the delegation of that presidency to a presbyter. There is no theological justification for the reserving of one element in the baptismal rite to the bishop. Theologically, the relationship of the members of the church to the bishop is through baptism, in which they are incorporated into the one body with the bishop as a sign of their baptismal unity. In the context of a *koinonia* ecclesiology, the bishop is the sign of the apostolic and catholic unity and continuity of the baptized community. This understanding of the episcopal role is clearly set forth in the *BEM* document:

> Bishops preach the Word, preside at the sacraments, and administer discipline in such a way as to be representative pastoral ministers of oversight, continuity and unity in the Church. They have pastoral oversight of the area to which they are called. They serve the apostolicity and unity of the Church's teaching, worship and sacramental life. They have responsibility for leadership in the Church's mission. They relate the Christian community in their area to the wider Church, and the universal Church to their community. They, in communion with the presbyters and deacons and the whole community, are responsible for the orderly transfer of ministerial authority in the Church.[25]

Theologically, therefore, it would be far sounder for the bishop to preside at baptisms when possible, to preach and to celebrate the eucharist, than to be seen solely as the minister of confirmation. By exercising this kind of role the bishop would come to be seen more clearly as the chief pastor and sign of catholic and apostolic unity of the baptized community.

---

[24]Leonel Mitchell, "The Western Church" in *Initiation Theology*, James Schmeiser, ed. (Toronto: Anglican Book Centre, 1978), 61-62.

[25]Ministry, 29.

Conclusions

When seismic shifts begin to take place in the pattern of Christian initiation, as they are in all the churches at the present time, we can be sure that profound changes in the relationship between church and culture are going on. Becoming Christian in today's world is very different from what it was in the past. Western societies have moved out of the Christendom period and have become predominantly secular and pluralistic. This has called into question the inherited patterns of Christian initiation in the west in fundamental ways. The churches in Africa, Asia, and Latin America are emerging from the colonial era and are exploring new relationships between the patterns of Christian initiation inherited from the western missionary movement and their own indigenous cultures. This situation is both unsettling and full of promise. It is unsettling to abandon inherited patterns, but the promise lies in a renewal of the practice of Christian initiation which has greater theological and cultural integrity.

The present paper has been concerned with the issue of theological integrity in the reform of Anglican initiation practice. If the argument of the paper is accepted, the following theological principles become fundamental for the renewal of Christian initiation in the Anglican Communion:

1. Baptism is a unity in which we are united with Christ in his death and resurrection, sealed with the Holy Spirit, and incorporated into the church.

2. Both adults and the children of Christian believers are appropriate candidates for baptism.

3. Since baptism is the sacramental sign of full incorporation into the church, all baptized persons, of whatever age, should be admitted to communion.

4. The role of the bishop in Christian initiation is primarily related to the whole rite of initiation, whether as president of the liturgy or through delegation of that presidency to a presbyter.

5. Because of the confusion between two quite distinct historical meanings of confirmation, it may be best to drop the term altogether. If provinces wish to continue the practice of re-affirmation of baptismal vows in adolescence or adulthood, this should be clearly distinguished from Christian initiation and from admission to communion.

Theological Foundations for Infant Baptism
—————— *Gordon W. Kuhrt* ——————

Unsure foundations:
Creation and Christendom approaches

There is widespread theological and pastoral insecurity about Christian baptism. There have been significantly confident developments in eucharistic theology and practice in recent decades, but the same cannot be said of baptism. Thirty years ago, the World Council of Churches' Faith and Order Commission wrote:

> since baptism encompasses the whole of Christian life, lack of clarity concerning the meaning of baptism leads to uncertainty all along the line. It is beyond dispute that in no church body does baptism have the decisive significance which the witness of the New Testament ascribes to it. Here we all have much to learn. A serious penetration into the meaning of baptism and an appropriation of the treasure given in baptism would give preaching and teaching both a centrally focused content and a new breadth, together with an insight which clarifies and unifies the whole of Christian life. The more the baptized learn to see their whole life in the light of their baptism, the more does their life take on the pattern of life "in Christ."[1]

The quality of writing on baptism, and particularly on infant baptism, by Anglicans or other pædobaptists, has not, generally, been impressive. Meanwhile, Baptists have produced major scholarly works. Throughout many parts of the world the Baptist doctrine is dominant in Pentecostal, charismatic, and "New" churches. The combination of renewed confidence in biblical theology and the experienced reality of Holy Spirit baptism/renewal has led many Anglicans to adopt Baptist or quasi-Baptist views. The WCC Faith and Order paper *Baptism, Eucharist and Ministry (BEM)*[2] was very weak on some aspects of the theology of baptism, and especially infant baptism.

Many clergy and lay people in English churches are increasingly

---

[1] *One Lord, One Baptism* (London: SCM, 1961), 71.

[2] Faith and Order Paper No.111 (Geneva: WCC, 1982).

perplexed by the regular phenomenon of parents and sponsors publicly declaring Christian faith in a baptismal liturgy but declining to receive the sacrament of holy communion because they have never confirmed their own baptism. The growth in public baptisms and of the parish eucharist as the main service has clarified the incongruity. The growing pressure for "re-baptism," or some dramatic (even "watery") form of baptismal renewal, has highlighted another consequence of indiscriminate baptism with which many clergy are at a loss to cope. The *BEM* document stated that those who practise infant baptism must reconsider certain aspects of their policy, and "must guard themselves against the practice of apparently indiscriminate baptism and take more seriously their responsibility for the nurture of baptized children to mature commitment to Christ."[3] The Lambeth Conference of 1988 agreed: "we accept the Lima judgement that indiscriminate infant baptism should not be practised. It obscures the purpose of such baptism...."[4]

The Lambeth bishops also encouraged "the development of standards and guidelines for the preparation of parents and sponsors, with a view to a common discipline."[5] In England, however, the expectations of the present canon law with regard to baptism in the main service, proper preparation, and sponsors being confirmed communicants, are not widely fulfilled.

Finally, in this catalogue of causes of insecurity, we find ourselves both at the beginning of the Decade of Evangelism but also recipients of widespread warnings against sectarianism. Which way are we to go? How seriously must we regard the "decisive significance" which the New Testament ascribes to baptism?

The *BEM* document is very clear and helpful on some aspects of the theology of baptism. It speaks with clarity of:

A. Participation in Christ's Death and Resurrection
B. Conversion, Pardoning and Cleansing
C. The Gift of the Spirit
D. Incorporation into the Body of Christ
E. The Sign of the Kingdom

---

[3] Baptism, 16.

[4] "The Nature and Meaning of Mission," Lambeth 1988 Section Report on Mission and Ministry in *The Truth Shall Make You Free* (London: ACC, 1988), para.193.

[5] "The Nature and Meaning of Mission," para.193.

and adds an entire section on Baptism and Faith. Reference to the baptism of infants, however, is kept for the section on Baptismal Practice,
and no biblical and theological justification for it is advanced.

In this century there has been little convincing biblical and theological work in this area. Three main patterns of foundation can be discerned
for the Anglican practice of infant baptism. The key theological concepts
are: Creation, Christendom, and Covenant. Each of these theological
approaches maintains a strong emphasis on the initiative of God's grace,
but they diverge when expounding how that grace is offered and then
received.

The *Creation approach* emphasizes that God made the world, loves
its people, and is continually involved in every aspect of life. God's concern is universal and without restriction; God's grace is limitless. Baptism is seen as a sacrament of this universal grace and therefore linked
to the fact of birth. The description of baptism as a "rite of passage"
is not an embarrassing one, for God made, loves, and owns every human
being. All are God's children and baptism expresses precisely that. Jesus
welcomed the little children and told his disciples not to forbid the parents' bringing them to him (Mark 10). Parents who are not publicly church
members and communicants should nevertheless be encouraged to bring
their infants to baptism. They often have a sense of the numinous when
a child is born, a feeling of a supernatural, even spiritual dimension to
their lives. Call it "folk religion" if you will, but baptism is the focus
and appropriate sacramental expression of it.

The *Christendom approach* has been expounded in England by R.R.
Osborn in his book *Forbide them not*,[6] and more recently by Dr. Mark
Dalby in *Open Baptism*.[7] These two books are both very English, but
aspects of their ecclesiological argument can be transposed to other parts
of the world. They argue that England has very significant and pervasive
Christian traditions and culture in spite of the fact that such a small propor-
tion of the population is in church on Sundays. This historic Christian
feeling means that the nation is essentially part of Christendom—a Christian kingdom. In a positive sense the community is heir to the Emperor
Constantine's conversion, the Holy Roman Empire of the European Middle
Ages, the nationalization of the Church of England by Henry VIII, and

---

[6](London: SPCK, 1972).

[7](London: SPCK, 1989).

the Elizabethan religious settlement. (This historic description could be re-written for other countries, areas, or tribal groupings.) In this theology, baptism is a sacrament of God's grace to the community that owns him as Lord (albeit in a general and often unclear way). The faith which receives the sacrament is not necessarily, or even primarily, the faith of the parents (let alone of the infant or child), but the faith of the church, which may be expressed through the role of godparents or sponsors.

These two views must be taken seriously, though I believe they are insecure foundations for infant baptism. With regard to the *Creation approach*, while it is true and important that God made and loves the world and all its peoples, our theology must do justice to both the universalistic and the particularistic dimensions of God's revelation. Within God's overall purpose of love and concern for the world there is a real theology of election, seen clearly in the stories of Noah, Abraham, and the exodus. God says to individuals, families, and nations in a special way: "I will be your God and you will be my people" and "all peoples on earth will be blessed through you" (Genesis 12:3). Though God's grace and blessings are available to all, there is a continual emphasis on the necessity of trusting obedience and the sad and devastating consequences of unbelief, disobedience, and judgement. Baptism is a sacrament not so much of creation but of redemption, of new life in Christ and especially of his death, resurrection, and Spirit. It speaks not of birth but of rebirth, not of natural but of spiritual life.

With regard to the *Christendom approach*, while we thank God for the way in which whole societies and cultures have been radically influenced by Christian faith and life, our theology must do justice to the way in which the biblical revelation both affirms and passes judgement on civilizations and cultures. The essential ministry of the prophets was to recall the people to the covenant. God's covenant of circumcision was never meant to be merely an outward sign of natural birth or racial descent. From Abraham's time onward it was a mark of God's ownership, of God's covenant promise and blessing, of God's offer of communion and friendship. The prophet Jeremiah said: "Circumcize yourselves to the Lord, circumcize your *hearts*" (Jer.4:4). The biblical theology of sacrament, both of circumcision in the Old Testament and of baptism and eucharist in the New Testament, is of grace-gifts which are set in the context of a living, obedient faith, met by faith, and worked out in believing obedience. Though there is widespread anxiety about drawing (tight) boundaries for the church, and a right concern not to make judgements on the spiritual condition of people's hearts, we must, nevertheless, take very seriously the biblical teaching on the two realms which are in dramatic and vivid contrast. As I wrote in *Believing in Baptism*:

> We may be members of the old creation or the new creation, either in Adam or in Christ, in darkness or in light, living according to the sinful nature or by the Spirit, in death or in life, belonging to the world or belonging to God. These contrasts will be found in 2 Corinthians 5.17; 1 Corinthians 15.22; Ephesians 5.8 (cf. Colossians 1.13); Romans 8.5f.; 1 John 3.14 (cf. John 10.10); John 17.6-19. However, although the conversion from one realm to the other is critical, and theologically a contrast that cannot be exaggerated, nevertheless from the human point of view, that conversion may be a long, gradual and almost imperceptible process rather than a single, dramatic event. The New Testament writers nowhere require a sudden conversion experience, but do require convertedness—"Unless you change (literally 'turn') and become like little children, you will never enter the kingdom of heaven" (Matthew 18.3).
>
> *Conversion* means to turn around, to face the right direction, to be following Christ. The significant issue is not *when* or *how* but *whether* a person is going in the right direction, i.e., is converted (Acts 3.19; 26.18). The metaphor of "being born again" (John 3) is more to do with the decisively new character of life with God than with the suddenness of its arrival in human experience.[8]

The Creation and Christendom models do not give us sure foundations for infant baptism.

A strong foundation: God's covenant

The biblical and theological concept of God's covenant provides a much surer foundation for infant baptism. I have worked through the evidence in detail in my *Believing in Baptism*. This concept is not foisted onto biblical history but emerges from it. It provides a sure foundation for at least six reasons:

1. *The covenant was in the apostles' minds.* In the New Testament letters, the writers unselfconsciously link baptism to Abraham's family (Galatians 3:26-29), to circumcision (Colossians 2:11-13), to the flood (1 Peter 3:18-21), and to the Israelites' journey with Moses (1 Corinthians 10:1-4).

---

[8](London: Mowbray, 1987), 75.

These passages are quite explicit associations of baptism with Old Testament covenant episodes. The apostolic writers move naturally to them for explanation and illustration. Baptist writers neglect this clear association because of their over-emphasis on the dispensational discontinuity between the Old and New Testaments and because of their conviction that no parallel should be drawn between circumcision and baptism (notwithstanding Colossians 2:11-13). But it is quite remarkable how other writers (Dunn, Osborn, Dalby) have avoided this key theological category. With regard to the *BEM* document, I have written:

> It is a major weakness of the report "Baptism, Eucharist and Ministry" that in its Baptism statement it makes no reference at all to this covenant context. It speaks of baptism as "entry into the New Covenant," and refers to "symbolic uses of water in the Old Testament," "salvation from the flood" and "an exodus from bondage," but nowhere are these images linked by the covenant theme.[9]

2. *The covenant expresses the unity of God's working.* In the vast canvas of history, law, prophecy, poetry, wisdom, etc., in the scriptures, it is easy to miss the forest for the trees. But the central theme is quite simply this: God wanted a people to love—children, friends, a family. When humanity refused the constraints of God's love and asserted a unilateral declaration of independence, God's love involved a plan of rescue, of salvation. This initiative of grace involves atonement, reconciliation, and a new way of life. This is expressed in God's covenant. God's covenant plan of salvation can be summarized in two words: grace (from God) and faith (by which the covenant is accepted).

The covenant principle is the central theme of the Old Testament—introduced with Noah, clarified with Abraham, developed with Moses and David, broken time and again, but renewed through the prophets' ministry. It was fulfilled in the Messiah—"this is my blood of the (new) covenant" (Matthew 26:28, etc.) But paradoxically, the terms of the "new" covenant are the same as those of the old: a) a spiritual relationship between God and God's people; b) forgiveness of sins; c) a spiritual response of trusting obedience (Jeremiah 31:31-34; also 32:40; Ezekiel 16:59-63; 37:26-28). The new covenant is new because after centuries of "promise," there is now "fulfilment" through the unfolding of the

---

[9]*Believing in Baptism*, 30.

mystery of Christ (Ephesians 3:1-13). Also, the assurance of forgiveness and baptism of the Spirit gives hope of greater faithfulness in the covenant people of God. Discontinuities there are, but the benefits remain essentially the same, as does the basis in God's grace and the means of response in faithful obedience. There is every justification for the assertion of Dr. J.I. Packer:

> The covenant is the comprehensive soteriological idea of the Bible. It is the presupposition, sometimes explicit, always implicit, of everything that is taught from Genesis to Revelation concerning redemption and religion, church and sacraments, and the meaning and goal of history. It integrates these doctrines into a single unified structure, sets them in their true mutual relations and enables the theologian to view them from a proper theocentric standpoint. It is thus the key to Biblical theology.[10]

3. *The covenant preserves the initiative of God's grace*. Baptism is now seen clearly as a sign of God's covenant. It is the sign and seal of God's grace effecting what it signifies in the context of faith. This covenant understanding integrates the two great dominical sacraments with the ministry of the word and the expectation of trusting obedience, i.e., a living faith. This issues in a godly life. The blessings of baptism are equally and emphatically the blessings of the gospel message received by faith: a) forgiveness and cleansing (Acts 2:38; 15:9); b) identification with Jesus Christ (Acts 2:38; Ephesians 3:17); c) sharing the death and resurrection of Jesus (Romans 6:3-5; Colossians 2:12); d) the gift of the Spirit (Acts 2:38; Galatians 3:14); e) new birth and sonship (Titus 3:5f.; Galatians 3:26); f) membership in the body of Christ (1 Corinthians 12:13; 1 John 1:3).

James Denney rightly said: "Baptism and faith are but the outside and the inside of the same thing."[11] The baptized life is lived through the grace of God; it is the life of trusting obedience to the word and will of the Saviour God.

---

[10]*Churchman*, June 1955, 76. There are some, however, who question whether "covenant theology is the only or controlling context" (cf. Martin Reardon, *Christian Initiation — a policy for the Church of England* [London: Church House, 1991], 19). But neither Reardon, Dalby, nor Bryan Spinks have provided a detailed critique or a biblical/theological alternative.

[11]*The Death of Christ* (London: Hodder and Stoughton, 1903), 185.

4. *The covenant gives credibility to the sacramental language of efficacy*.
The outward sign is repeatedly described in terms of the spiritual reality
it signifies: "We were buried with him through baptism"; "we were
all baptized by one Spirit into one body"; "baptism now saves you"
(Romans 6:4; 1 Corinthians 12:13; 1 Peter 3:21). It is the biblical theology of the covenant that integrates both the efficacy of baptism and the
necessity of faith. The *BEM* document claims, significantly, that:

> The necessity of faith for the reception of the salvation embodied and set
> forth in baptism is acknowledged by all churches. Personal commitment is
> necessary for responsible membership in the body of Christ.[12]

The "apparently indiscriminate baptism" of infants which is often
associated with the Creation and Christendom approaches considerably
obscures the necessity of a living faith, and leads thoughtful people to
question the theological appropriateness of sacramental language of
efficacy. The new testament uses that language without embarrassment,
however, because of the covenant understanding which is its context.

5. *The covenant makes sense of the family principle*. The family principle is closely associated with the covenant pattern. God's initiative of
grace has a special emphasis on the family unit. While each individual
stands responsible before God for disobedience and unfaithfulness to the
covenant, nevertheless there is a strong element of family solidarity running through the scriptures. Noah was called to take his whole family
with him into the ark; the promise to Abraham was also to his descendants after him. Yet we have noted that God's covenant promises were
not merely racial, tribal, or national. From the beginning there was a
universal dimension, and from the beginning the enjoyment of covenant
grace by each person was by faith.

It is covenant theology that integrates both the family principle that
justifies Christian family baptism and the requirement of individual
responsibility. This family principle does not specify the nature of the
family unit, however. The particular sociological context may well play
a determining part as to whether that unit is nuclear or extended (more
or less).

---

[12]Baptism, 8.

6. In contrast to the Creation and Christendom approaches, *the covenant model provides a coherent basis for pastoral practice, liturgical provision, ecumenical relationships, and spirituality.*

Building on the foundation

One of the important tests of theological foundations is whether they can bear the weight of the structures which have to be built on them. Four areas of church and individual Christian life must be examined.

a) Pastoral:

There is widespread anxiety among many clergy and those lay people who share in baptismal preparation and consequent nurture. The *BEM* document and Lambeth 1988 expressed this anxiety about "apparently indiscriminate baptism." The Creation model inevitably leads to a universalistic and diluted "Christian" practice. The Christendom model has the dangers of nationalism and tribalism and involves an unreal expectation of nurture. (To expect church and godparents to achieve what the parents ignore and are uncommitted about is pastoral fantasy.)

The Covenant theology model does *not* imply rigorism and harsh pastoral judgement. It does give a credible basis for baptism as a dominical sacrament and covenant sign which is meaningful only within the community of faith, and indissolubly united with trusting obedience to the word of God and participation in the eucharist. Inevitably, therefore, baptism will normally take place in a main public service, and at least one parent and the godparents will be communicant Christians. The difficult pastoral situations where there is an historic expectation of "apparently indiscriminate baptism" can be met by a gradualist pastoral response which is warm and generous but which has a clear goal for its teaching and preparation.

The other major pastoral issue is the increasing "re-baptism" of Christians originally baptized as infants. There are several reasons for this practice but the chief one is the absence of apparently Christian upbringing or nurture following the infant baptism. The Creation and Christendom models do not offer a credible basis for not seeking such a "re-baptism," but the Covenant model does. Because it stands securely on biblical theology and argues the normativeness of the faith context, we can distinguish the issues of validity and efficacy in the covenant sign. The validity is not dependent (as in Baptist baptism) on the time and the circumstances; the validity is in the nature of the sacramental action itself. The emphatic role of faith-response in the Covenant model, however, will enable the pastoral approach of expressing sadness about deficiencies in nurture, and encouragement to public renewal of baptism vows and confirmation.

b) Liturgical:

The rich variety of imagery that is in many baptismal liturgies (as is listed in *BEM*) can be both theologically and spiritually confusing. God's covenant plan of salvation is the principle of coherence around which references to the flood, the exodus, and the Red Sea can be linked and then shown as fulfilled in the manifold aspects of the work of Christ.

Further, the covenant theology integrates: i) the grace initiative and the faith response, and ii) the family dimension and the individual nurture—both of which are essential elements in baptismal liturgy for infants. The Creation and Christendom models do not provide an integration, either for the imagery or for those essential pairs of theological principles.

c) Ecumenical:

In theological and liturgical consultations with other communions, Anglicanism has been at a grave disadvantage in recent generations. This is because theologians and liturgists have often proposed separate theologies for adult and infant baptism. Clearly the Creation and Christendom models will have that likely effect. Covenant theology, on the other hand, provides an integrated sacramental theology which is coherent and unembarrassed in either the adult or infant (Christian family) mode.

The Baptist perplexity over Anglican (and other pædobaptist) doctrine and practice is often more over apparently indiscriminate practice than over a careful theology and practice of Christian family baptism. Considerable ecumenical strides could be made at this point, with the consequent reduction in the serious problem of apparently indiscriminate "*re*-baptism."

d) Spiritual:

The *BEM* document emphasizes the responsibility for the nurture of baptized children to mature commitment to Christ. Urgent questions need to be asked about the spiritual efficacy (not quite the validity) of a baptism (adult or infant) where the baptized person is subsequently unwilling to "confirm" the baptism and live a committed communicant Christian (i.e., baptized) life. Unfortunately, this is very frequently the norm where the Creation and Christendom models have major influence.

The spiritual dangers of separatism and sectarianism are very real, but the expressed hopes of Christian nurture in "open" baptism policies are nearly always optimistic in the extreme and often totally unrealistic. Covenant theology offers a genuine basis for a biblical partnership between home and church, parent and priest/pastor, in developing nurture.

It offers, too, a splendid pattern for preaching and teaching which integrates history, theology, liturgy, and spirituality. Bible, doctrine, worship, and experience will point unitedly to our children growing up in the fear and nurture of the Lord—in Christ, in the Spirit, in the Church. Can Christian baptism mean anything else? Is not baptism (like eucharist) the sign and seal of these very gospel and spiritual realities which are received and lived by faith?

Consequences of Infant Communion

Gregory Kerr-Wilson
and Timothy Perkins

The purpose of this essay is to explore some of the long-term effects of allowing small children to receive communion, and to suggest various responses to the changes in the life of the local worshipping community which may or should occur. As infant communion is a relatively recent practice within Anglicanism, there is not an extensive body of data to analyze. Some creative thinking concerning the issues involved and thoughtful reflection on the limited experience currently emerging, however, seem to indicate certain directions which may be helpful to pursue. The principal areas we see being affected are: catechetical practice (children), catechetical practice (adults), perceptions of the eucharist, perceptions of the church, and the quality of community worship.

Catechetical practice (children)

In the past (and often still today), sacramental catechesis usually has been restricted either to confirmation classes for those in their early teens or first communion classes for six- to nine-year-olds. Children's experience of worship has been basically that of exclusion, either being sent out of the liturgy early or being brought in to worship only for the communion. In many parishes, children have not attended worship on a regular basis at all. Children's sacramental *experience*, therefore, has been sadly lacking; what information they have received has been taught rather than experienced.

In his introduction to *Liturgical Inculturation in the Anglican Communion* (the papers presented at the York meeting of the IALC), David Holeton writes:

> Christians are formed by what they say and do in the liturgy. The way we conceive of God, the way we understand the nature of Christian community and the manner in which we engage the world are all shaped by our common liturgical life.[1]

---

[1] Alcuin/GROW Liturgical Study 15, David R. Holeton, ed. (Bramcoke, Notts.: Grove, 1990), 6.

Holeton is underscoring the basic principle of *lex orandi, lex credendi*. In keeping with this, the practice of infant communion shifts the direction of sacramental catechesis from information to formation. A child's first encounter with the eucharist will not be instruction about what they are going to be allowed to do, but an experience of receiving the body and blood of Christ in the context of the eucharistic community. Children will not so much learn *about* the eucharist as they will become inculturated *in* the worship life of the church. This shift in direction is important for at least three reasons.

First, such a process of formation is a more natural way of learning. One hardly needs to engage in an extended discussion of the various theories of human development to recognize that children learn family life by participating in families, that children learn table manners by sharing in meals, that children learn ways of expressing affection by living in a community in which they give and receive love.

A friend once observed that his toddler's eating habits varied depending on whether he was eating by himself or at table with his parents. When eating alone, the eighteen-month-old would play with his food, push the dishes onto the floor, and generally make a mess. When eating with his parents, the presence of the rest of the family transformed his eating habits; he became attentive to the table manners of his parents (at least as long as his young attention span would allow). In like manner, children receiving the eucharist will learn eucharistic life by living and sharing in the eucharistic community.

Second, the process of formation is a more foundational learning experience. It is foundational in that it is more akin to the way people learn their culture's particular worldview. Common attitudes and values are formed through immersion in the cultural environment, and the sharing of such attitudes and values encourages a sense of belonging. If a person has been taught an erroneous method in a math or science class, the error can be corrected rather easily by teaching an alternative method. Foundational attitudes, however, are far more deeply rooted than the methods taught in math or science classes. They are often still manifested in behaviour patterns long after a person has changed his or her mind about a particular issue.

In terms of the eucharist, the specifics of this inculturation will depend to a certain degree on the way a particular community goes about its eucharistic celebration. Fundamental to eucharistic experience, however, will be a sense of belonging which comes through participation and a sense of being fed by the body of Christ. In the long run, this eucharistic formation will establish more firmly in the consciousness of the participants the centrality of the eucharist to Christian life and Christian community.

Finally, this process of formation, far from excluding teaching, offers opportunities for making the information side of catechesis more responsive to the needs of children. Children are naturally inquisitive and tend to ask questions about whatever they experience. When children receive communion on a regular basis, the things we teach them about the eucharist can be directed at the specific concerns, attitudes, and perceptions which the children express from within the experience. Anyone who has experienced the frustration of trying to teach a young child the importance of a particular idea or behaviour when the child has no immediate context within which the information can be integrated, will understand the value of such a responsive form of catechesis.

The practice of communicating children, then, will have an obvious impact on the approach taken by those acting as catechists (priests, deacons, parents, teachers) in the children's lives. We have found a helpful analogy to this in Martin Thornton's *The Heart of the Parish*.[2] Thornton speaks of the parish priest as "coach" rather than "teacher." By so doing he draws a picture of an athlete who is already engaged in the sport, but who requires information, correction, and suggestion in the practical development of playing the game.

Children may be beginners, but they are already in the game. They are beginning Christians, growing toward maturity. Sometimes, perhaps often, they require coaching as they grow into proficiency in their lives of faith. This is particularly true of their participation in the eucharist as central and foundational to the Christian life.

Catechetical practice (adults)

Catechesis for adults will also be affected by having small children receive the eucharist, especially when it comes to parents bringing their children for baptismal preparation. Already many churches in the Anglican Communion are reforming the way in which they respond to those who come to have their children "done." If we are going to continue to claim that children are full members of the body of Christ, and that they therefore

---

[2] *The Heart of the Parish: A Theology of the Remnant* (Cambridge, Mass.: Cowley Publications, 1989), chapt. 2.

will receive the sacrament of that body from baptism onwards, that claim can only be maintained if both the assumption and goal from the very outset of baptismal preparation is that parents will bring their children to the eucharistic assembly every Sunday, and will participate with them in the ongoing learning process as their children grow. This understanding has several consequences.

First, the community, through its appropriate representatives, will need to be intentional about taking responsibility for who will and who will not be considered candidates for baptism. The deciding issue will be the parents' intentions concerning ongoing participation in the life of the Christian community. Already there is cynicism among church members concerning Christian initiation because of the numbers of infants presented by parents for baptism who then immediately disappear from the life of the community. Communicating all the newly baptized simply compounds the problem.

Second, prebaptismal catechesis will need to be far more intentional in its efforts to reinforce the parents' own sense of communicant membership in the eucharistic assembly. Many, if not most, will also require some guidance in how best to participate as parents in their children's increasing awareness of the eucharist and its significance. Only in this way can we hope to have parents taking their part in coaching their children.

Perceptions of the eucharist

As the process of learning about the eucharist changes, we must expect change in the perception of the eucharist itself. We speak of "perception" rather than "understanding" as the effects of this different catechetical process will be more cognitive than rational. The "understanding" someone has of the eucharist is based on a teaching process in which historical, theological, or biblical information is brought to bear. The "perceptions" people have of the eucharist, however (what they experience the eucharist to be), are formed through their lifelong involvement in the liturgy, and are much more deeply rooted.

Here we offer as illustration the elderly woman who, having heard an explanation for why we make peace with our neighbour before receiving communion, protested that the Peace is not necessary because the eucharist is about each individual's private communion with God. This woman's perception of the eucharist was formed through a lifetime of liturgical experience in which personal contact between the communicants was kept to a minimum rather than through any deliberate theological teaching.

New perceptions will effect significant changes in our eucharistic life. The first is likely to be in the perception of the *eucharist as communal event*. People will come to see that receiving the sacrament is about belonging in the church; or, to put it in more traditional terms, that the reception of the body of Christ (bread) is participation in the body of Christ (Church). This connection between reception and belonging to the community can be seen through some of the negative experiences children have in worship. An example of this is the encounter one of us had with a first communion class. The first session of the class was an attempt to have the children think about baptism and how baptism included them in the church. The children, aged six to eight years, were asked: "What makes you feel you belong or do not belong in the church?" Without any prompting at all, a number of the children stated quite unequivocably that not being allowed to receive the bread and wine when everyone else did made them feel that they did not belong.

This example is not an isolated one. At communion, many of us have seen very young children raise their hands beside their parents only to be refused, either by parents or priest. Or, we have heard children asking their parents: "Why can't we have some like everybody else?" We heard one child state, simply but profoundly: "I want Jesus too!" And the more children come to sense that the eucharist is special and important, the more their feeling of exclusion is heightened.

This sense of exclusion has long-term effects. Children perceive their world in concrete ways. When they are at the eucharist, it is the concrete aspects of the liturgy that they experience, and, in particular, the moment when their family and others go forward to receive the bread and wine. Anyone who has watched small children receiving communion will have noticed that, in contrast to the adults around them, the children are very aware of the communal nature of the occasion. They look at others, smile and make contact with them. They have yet to be socialized out of the very natural perception that we are doing this together, into a piety which sees the eucharist as a private matter between the communicant and God.

The impact of exclusion or inclusion during this crucial stage in a child's faith development has major repercussions. To allow children the regular experience of receiving communion, while still living within that natural perception of community, is to reinforce community as a fundamental component of what the eucharist is all about. This inclusion will have an effect on the way adults experience the eucharist as well. The infectious sociability of the children is caught by the more sombre adults around them; community begins to "rub off" on them.

A second change in perception is in the sense of the *eucharist as food*, another result of the concrete terms in which children see their world. Children tend to perceive the eucharist as food and experience the eucharist as an actual meal in a way that adults often do not. Even though the eucharist has its roots in the table fellowship of Jesus and the Last *Supper*, many adults do not see themselves as participants in a meal at which they receive eucharistic food. The reason for this is that the manner in which they first began to receive, and the catechetical emphasis on "understanding," conspired to produce a highly abstract or rationally based understanding of this religious ritual which overshadowed the fundamental aspects of eating and drinking.

The mystery of the eucharist is deepened when all facets of the sacrament are held together as a whole. While perceiving the eucharist as a communal event and as a meal is certainly not, in and of itself, a sufficient sacramental theology, it is an essential foundation on which to build. When that foundation is missing, our perceptions of the eucharist are skewed.

As young children increasingly receive communion, a third change in perception of the eucharist will be in the area of *the language of symbol*. Aidan Kavanagh has suggested that everyone understands the language of symbol at some level or other.[3] His evidence is drawn from various aspects of life: art, theatre, handshakes, hugs. But there are varying levels of openness to the language of symbol. Western society, at least in recent centuries, has tended to prefer the discursive languages of science and rationalism to the intuitive language of symbol. As a result, many of us have been socialized out of the world of symbols.

Young children have yet to suffer this loss of symbolic perception. They often retain the ability to apprehend symbols which adults seem to have lost. Children are able to receive a piece of bread on their hands, while hearing the words "the body of Christ", without suffering any kind of cognitive dissonance. They also receive the wine with the words "the blood of Christ" without wrinkling their noses and making faces as many children did when they were first communicated as early adolescents. Some might argue that smaller children, in fact, do not understand the spoken reference. That is not our experience. We have found sufficient number of children who have, unsolicited, expressed connections between the

---

[3]*Elements of Rite* (New York: Pueblo, 1982), 103.

elements and the body and blood of Christ, to convince us of their ability to apprehend liturgical symbol.

We believe that the communion of children will have a positive impact on the entire community's use of symbol and symbolic language. Insisting on a certain level of theological understanding before reception distorts the sacred mysteries by overemphasizing the importance of rationalism. With a constant exposure to the eucharistic symbols, as they grow, children are far more likely to retain their early ability to experience power and grace conveyed in symbols, and therefore to experience the *sacrament* of the eucharist.

Perceptions of the church

A third area in which infant communion will have a major impact is on our perceptions of the church itself. No longer will the body of Christ be perceived as an exclusively adult community. No matter what we may say about baptism as full initiation into the church, by not communicating children the message sent is that they are, in fact, not full members of the community. While some may draw a parallel with citizenship—children are not allowed to vote or to drive a vehicle while still being citizens and full members of the society without all of its rights and privileges—the parallel is misdrawn. These rights and privileges are withheld from children on the basis of competency. To complete this analogy, one would have to argue that children are incompetent to receive at the eucharist. To be strictly consistent, adults would also need to demonstrate their competency to receive. But such an approach would make the eucharist something which is earned rather than something which is received as pure gift.

Withholding the eucharist from children entrenches the perception of the church as an adult-only fellowship. Allowing children to receive has the opposite effect, but our exclusively "adult" attitude about the church is something which will take some time to overcome. Few things have more potential to convey a sense of inclusivity in the life of the church, however, than to have every member of the community—male and female, young and old, whatever level of education—join in the procession to the altar to receive the sacrament of the body of Christ by which the Church is constituted, week by week, as that Body in the world.

Quality of worship

One area of church life which will be immediately affected by welcoming children to the table is the quality of worship. For many Anglicans, especially those living in Anglo-Saxon cultures, worship has a particular ethos which includes a major amount of silence during various portions of the liturgy. When children are involved in worship, however, there is little chance that the familiar quiet will descend upon the worshipping community for any significant period of time. Children are children, and they are not particularly good at remaining quiet.

While the sound of infant voices may be jarring for many people in the beginning, its effect is to transform the nature of the worshipping community. This change requires a shift in expectations and some time in which to become acclimatized. Those of us who have made the transition can testify that, after a few months of initial discomfort, we no longer find the sounds of children a distraction. These sounds even contribute to the celebratory atmosphere of worship. For those who have adjusted to the sounds of children in worship, participating in a eucharist without children present, with its attendant silence, seems almost sterile. Without the sounds of children at Sunday worship to remind us of the others with whom we have gathered, the silence can at times turn people back in on themselves, privatizing the experience once again.

We do not intend to suggest that quiet for reflection and meditation is now unimportant, however. We are suggesting that the inclusion and communication of children is a priority in the worship of the church because it is consistent with our understanding of baptism as full incorporation into the life of the eucharistic community. Silence can, and does, have a place in the church's worship. It simply does not have the disproportionate claim we have allowed it to have. The daily office and liturgies for special occasions may have to provide the quiet, meditative atmosphere which is of importance to many people.

In conclusion, the Sunday liturgy must uphold what the church understands itself to be: a gathering of the whole people of God. And that includes small children. As St.Paul has written:

> The cup of blessing which we bless, is it not a participation in the blood of Christ? The bread which we break, is it not a participation in the body of Christ? Because there is one bread, we who are many are one body, for we all partake of the one bread. (1 Corinthians 10:16-17)

The eucharist is that which constitutes the people of God as the *one* Body of Christ. To accept and express this reality authentically in a church community, shifts the *perception* church members have of what constitutes full membership. This means that the character, not only of our worship but also of our whole ecclesial life, will change in ways that will reflect more accurately the nature of the church as the *whole* people of God.

II Baptism, Mission, and Ministry

Baptism and Mission
—————— Louis Weil ——————

I began my ordained ministry in 1961 as a missionary priest in Latin America. Whatever we might want to claim about the common missionary vocation of all baptized Christians, my pastoral work was undertaken with an explicit identity as an "overseas missionary." The home church sent me into another culture to fulfil a role about which more was taken for granted than had really been reflected upon in terms of a claimed theology of mission. I was a missionary sent from a national church (the Episcopal Church USA) to serve in a missionary diocese (the Episcopal Diocese of Puerto Rico).

What began as a three-year missionary term eventually became a ten-year stint. I marvel, in retrospect, at the *naïveté* of the young deacon setting forth as the representative of a cultural and ecclesiastical domination of which he was, at that time, largely unaware. To a great extent, my views on baptism and mission were shaped in the crucible of that early formative experience, as, gradually, I came to recognize the profound defects of the theology of mission upon which our presence was based, and, well-intentioned though it was, the anomaly of my presence as an agent of that model of mission.[1]

It was within that context, during the first year of my ordained ministry, that I became aware of the disastrous effects of the model of Christian initiation which, at that time, held unquestioned dominance in the pastoral practice of the Episcopal Church. It was within that pastoral/missionary context that the imperatives of the theology of Christian initiation came alive to me and led to a commitment which has continued throughout these three decades. For me, therefore, baptism and mission have been closely linked in my own pastoral experience and cannot really be considered in isolation from each other. I believe this link to be true in every context: Our models for baptism flow inevitably from our understanding of the nature of the Church as it pursues its mission in the world.

---

[1]For a useful analysis of the underlying presuppositions of this understanding of mission see Ruben Lores, "El destino manifiesto y la empresa misionera" in *La iglesia y su misión*, Vida y Pensamiento 7.1-2 (San José, Costa Rica: SBL, 1987), 13-30.

The theological and pastoral imperatives which liturgists have come to attach to the sacrament of Christian initiation during recent decades first began to claim their appropriate significance for me in an incident during the first week after my ordination to the priesthood. The incident was the first baptism which I performed. Because of the character of the occasion and the fact that it was within a missionary context, I have found it useful as a focus for reflection on these matters. I shall briefly describe the event and then make a number of comments about it.

It was the Feast of the Epiphany, a major folk as well as religious celebration in Latin America. After presiding at the eucharist at the main mission for which I had care, I returned to the nearby rectory. Several hours later, early in the afternoon, there was a knock at the door and I opened it to find a middle-aged couple holding a recently born infant. The couple were the *padrinos*, the godparents of the child whom they asked me to baptize. In retrospect, of course, I realize that I responded according to the model I had observed during my months as a deacon—the only model of Christian initiation I knew.

I told the couple to take the infant up to the church and that I would join them shortly. I put on my cassock, followed them to the church, and took out the record book to note down the usual information: name, date and place of birth, the names of the parents and of the godparents. That information fulfilled the preliminaries, according to the model then accepted in Latin America. The possibility of prebaptismal preparation did not even occur to me.

I put on my surplice and stole and began the rite, cueing the godparents for their responses, since they obviously assumed that everything to be done of any importance would be done by me. That was perhaps my assumption as well. Then came the critical moment—the moment which was a revelation to me of the total inadequacy of the model which I was perpetuating. The godmother handed me the baby. I turned to my right to pick up the shell for the affusion and to make absolutely certain of the baptismal formula in Spanish since I was still rather insecure in that language. When I turned back to face the font, I found that the baby and I were totally alone. The godparents, having completed (according to the model) their responsibilities, had gone out onto the porch of the church where, when I looked out, the godfather was lighting a cigarette.

It was a traumatic moment for me. Here I was, newly ordained a priest, having offered myself for the missionary work of the church: What on earth had I gotten myself into? Suddenly, my natural ecclesial instinct cried out within me that this model was profoundly wrong, that it was a betrayal of the sacrament which it was intended to fulfil. I called the godparents back into the church and gave them, in my halting Spanish, what I have since called a "fifteen-minute catecumenate." Within myself I debated whether or not I could go on with the rite. I could not reject this now exceedingly anxious couple who were simply following the only model of Christian initiation they had ever known.

From that day, I date the passion of my commitment to the restoration of the full integrity of the rites of Christian initiation. It is important to remember, however, that on that day in Latin America probably thousands of baptisms took place following exactly the same model for both clergy and godparents, without hesitancy on the part of either as to the full adequacy, not to mention validity, of the model. As is quite evident, the model is a clear expression of the self-understanding of the church upon which it rested. The model embodied what the church understood itself to be. And by model, I mean far more than the text of the rite. In fact, I would suggest that the non-verbal dimensions of the model are far more determinative of the popular theology of baptism generally held by the people than the theology which the text of the rite would claim to articulate.

Although the model I have described has been modified in many parts of the church in recent decades, it was not a caricature or an extreme case. It was the commonly accepted pattern throughout Latin America, and was not all that different from the generally accepted practice in the United States. We are all aware of the significant ways in which the newer rites of Christian initiation in the various provinces of the Anglican Communion have confronted this model, and called for the emergence of a norm which is more clearly expressive of what we believe incorporation into the church to mean. But the model I have described, in its essential presuppositions, carries a very long history within Christianity. It has shaped in powerful ways the manner in which great numbers of Christians—clergy as well as lay—still understand baptism. Considering, then, the example of my first baptism, what do the characteristics of that model of Christian initiation suggest to us concerning the nature of the church and its mission?

As we look with a hindsight illuminated by several decades of special attention within the church to the rites of initiation, what is most striking to me in this model is its almost total indifference, in its contextual signification, to the ecclesial nature of the sacraments. The 1928 (USA) rite spoke, of course, of the candidate being "baptized with Water and the Holy Ghost, and received into Christ's holy Church, and made a living member of the same." But the experiential context of the rite bore little indication of the corporate implications of that phrase. Popular folk theology had little understanding of that corporate meaning, which had been replaced by a highly individualized sense of the salvation signified by the rite. The rite was celebrated in virtual isolation from the outward expressions of ecclesial incorporation: It was celebrated not only without the attendance of the local assembly, but without even their awareness. It was separated from even a hint of catechetical preparation except, in my traumatic experience in Puerto Rico, for the fifteen minutes of fervent teaching which I was moved to give as a result of my sudden insight into the inadequacy of what was taking place. Further, the baptism had no implied relation to the eucharist, either as offering the framework for the completion of the rite or as an expectation for the future. In fact the godparents were among the great multitude of people who could claim *"somos Episcopales,"* (or, similarly, *"somos Catholicos"*) but whose relationship to the church was expressed in requesting baptism for the newly born and later, perhaps, marriage and eventually burial.

It is important to emphasize that I do not blame the great numbers of laity who understood the church in this way. That was the only model held up to them. The historical factors which led to this situation are well known to anyone who has read something of liturgical history and there is no need to summarize them here.[2] It is perhaps useful to point out the relationship of this model not merely to the church's self-understanding, but also to the church's understanding of mission.

When we consider, for example, the pre-Constantinian situation as represented in the *Apostolic Tradition* of Hippolytus, it is evident that there was no rush to baptism. Mission was understood as the drawing of new persons into the common life of the Christian community, and this was not undertaken precipitously. There was a long period during which such persons were kept, as it were, at the periphery of the community's life, not even attending the eucharist. During that period a process of socialization took place which, if we may judge from the text of Hippolytus, was very much concerned with the transformation of the lifestyle of these catechumens, notably with regard to the putting aside of occupations which the church saw to be in conflict with the profession of faith these persons would make at their baptism. But the arrival at baptism itself was certainly not hurried even when one was faced with

---

[2]See, for instance, Nathan D.Mitchell, ''Dissolution of the Rite of Christian Initiation'' in *Made, Not Born* (Notre Dame, IN: University Press, 1976), 50-82.

the danger of arrest "for the name of the Lord" since, as Hippolytus writes: "if he suffers violence and is killed, he will be justified, for he has received baptism in his blood."[3]

I am not trying to suggest that the church today can appropriately recreate the social context of Hippolytus's time. It is perhaps useful to note, however, the sharp contrast between this model, with its leisurely pace toward baptism—a model in which an evident transformation within the catechumen's life was expected prior to the actual baptism itself—and the model which I have described of the baptism I performed in January 1962. In this latter, we have the dregs of what has been called the "Christendom model" of the church. The significant social and political shift in the church's situation which took place in the fourth century, before very long, took a profound toll upon the model of incorporation which we see in Hippolytus. With that shift, which was undoubtedly seen as a triumph of Christian faith, there came radical changes in the earlier pattern, which continue to affect us today, living as we do in what is clearly a post-Constantinian situation in regard to the church's relationship to the larger society.

From my perspective, the most serious loss was the obscuring of the ecclesial character of baptism, with its replacement by a minimalist model of sacramental efficacy. Within the context of the Christendom model, this pattern of initiation seemed to be all that was required. With the assumption that society had been Christianized, the mission of the church in the local communities involved merely the incorporation of the newly born into what had, presumably, already been achieved within the adult community as a whole. What was not recognized was that the consequent dominance of infant baptism and the loss of the catechumenate, along with an increasing priority placed upon the ministry of the ordained, led to a situation in which a large portion of the laity often had little grounding in the fundamentals of the Christian faith. Their membership in the church was simply an aspect of their life in society. They often were, in the phrase of Louis Boyer, "Catholic without being Christian."

Ironically, when the church moved in mission outside the urban centres around the Mediterranean, and especially into the socially less civilized situation in northern Europe, it carried this minimalist model of

---

[3]*Hippolytus: A Text for Students*, Grove Liturgical Study No.8, Geoffrey J. Cuming, ed. (Bramcote, Notts: Grove, 1976), para. 19.

baptism into a social context in which the religion of the ruler became that of the people, and incorporation into the church involved little more than a sprinkling with water in the name of the God whom the king had embraced. In a society in which education was a privilege of only a few, the lack of a catechumenal framework before, or even after, baptism meant that the adherence to Christianity involved little more than the acceptance of the prescribed outward forms. As contrasted to the missionary attitude which we noted in the Hippolytan model, mission came eventually to mean little more than "getting the baby done," which is precisely the model which operated at that, at least for me, fateful baptism thirty years ago in Puerto Rico.

Significant parallels may be noted between the situation of the church today and that of the pre-Constantinian era. But we carry our history, and the memory of some form of establishment model continues to affect, often unconsciously, the expectations of those who implement the models of current practice. Attempts to restore the catechumenate are one expression of our recognized need to rediscover the relationship between a transformed life and baptism.[4] If mission may be defined as "the first encounter with the gospel," then the stewardship of the church for every aspect of baptism, including all that leads up to it and the ecclesial and eucharistic life which flow from it, must take a very high place in the pastoral priorities of the church.

[4]A perspective on these issues in the contemporary context is found in *The Baptismal Mystery and the Catechumenate*, M.W. Merriman, ed. (New York: Church Hymnal Corp., 1990).

The Catechumenal Challenge to the Church
Robert J. Brooks

Baytown, near Houston, Texas, sits below sea level and has the world's largest oil refinery. The humid air is filled with pollution from the petroleum and chemical industries; the culture is filled with violence: acquaintance against acquaintance, spouse against spouse, parents against children. Education is considered a sellout to the bosses who run the oil and chemical companies. The school drop-out rate is high as children follow parents into the refineries and continue the cycle of violence and ignorance. The message of commerce is that one's worth is based on consumption: "I consume, therefore I am; the more I consume, the more I am." The dominant religious view is that one is to accept one's place in the scheme of things and that God will bring deliverance only after death. There is no consolation, no hope, only dehumanization and violence mitigated by the opiate of consumption, producing but a transitory sense of worth.

Arriving as vicar of All Saints' parish in the early seventies, I soon felt totally lacking in the tools necessary to meet this cultural challenge. Certainly a liturgy with a twenty-minute sermon on Sundays and the occasional adult education hour were not sufficient to counter the cultural message which the local institutions reinforced seven days a week, twenty-four hours per day. Perhaps a more ambiguous setting would have made it more difficult to conclude that a radical response was needed. Whatever the response was to be, however, I knew it would have to be deep enough, profound enough, and lean enough to engage people at the level of their truest selves—to equip them not only to survive but also to triumph over, and thereby transform, the dominant cultural values of their community.

Baytown may seem an unlikely venue for the recovery of a way of being the church from that historical period prior to the church becoming a department of the imperial state. There have, however, been less likely places in Christian history where reform began. In any case, it was the catechumenal pattern of the early church which equipped the faithful of that time to make their witness to an often hostile state and culture, and to eventually transform both. Nothing less comprehensive or effective would meet the cultural challenge caricatured in Baytown, Texas.

The catechumenate is, as Henry Breul has said, "the Church's survival kit into the 21st century." To propose the restoration of the catechumenate is to acknowledge that the church lives in a post-Constantinian world which has insufficient institutions or social structures to provide a Christian ethos in society. As I discovered in Baytown, what is at stake is nothing less than the lives of the baptized. It was my pastoral duty to equip these people to survive and to flourish in their Christian witness in all of life. Indeed, the pastoral experience of those who have restored the catechumenate has so commended itself, that the Episcopal Church USA has officially adopted catechumenal rites as the normative process of preparing unbaptized adults for Christian initiation and baptized adults for the reaffirmation of their baptismal covenant.

This restoration of the catechumenate challenges the church to respond to the post-Constantinian world in a radically new (old) way. This paper attempts to outline some of these challenges.

1. *The catechumenate challenges the church to an awareness that the paschal mystery is the very centre of its life.* All else in the church is made sense of in terms of this mystery. The catechumens embody within the parish community the reality that Christians are constantly passing from death to life in Christ. Aidan Kavanagh has said that we draw our meaning of what it is to be the church by what the church says about who the catechumens are as they step into the font. According to the American *Book of Common Prayer* (1979), Christianity is a faith for adults as well as children, where Christ continually passes from death to life in the person of the catechumens who are made "christs" by baptism and consignation/chrismation and who manifest the reign of God present in the world by sharing in the messianic banquet of the eucharist. That is a considerably richer definition of what it means to be human than "I consume, therefore I am."

2. Because it knows it lives in a post-Constantinian era, *the catechumenate develops a prophetic faith to challenge the values of late twentieth-century society.* This development is in stark contrast to the initiation process of an earlier era, which tended to provide a nominal faith to meet the minimal requirements of living in a "Christian" state. So the catechumenate challenges our liturgy to be related to the actual life of the community, speaking in truth about who we are. It questions a church that regularly expects godparents and congregations to commit perjury at baptism by vowing that they will be Christian role models to a child they may see only rarely, if ever again.

Further, catechumens are brought to the font through the communal participation of the faithful in the process of evangelization and catechesis, for the faithful share a corporate responsibility for catechetical formation. Thus the catechumens receive a flesh and blood experience of church (catechists are to represent the diversity of the local congregation) rather than an exclusively intellectual assent to an abstract model of the church.

3. *The catechumenate challenges the view that baptism is an inoculation of the individual against sin and evil*, preserving the individual Christian in his or her journey through the jungle of life. Baptism is not ''religious Darwinism,'' a guaranteeing that the right spiritual survival genes will be passed on to the next generation. While the catechumenal process certainly develops personal faith, it is in the communal context that our story is joined to the great story of Jesus dead and rising, where our journey becomes part of the continuing exodus of the people of God from slavery to freedom. It is through the communal that we are saved.

So the catechumenate challenges ''program-centred'' initiation classes and ''graduation-style'' catechesis (at age twelve, after six weeks of instruction, you will be confirmed). Its use of catechetical stages culminating in the various rites gives, rather, a sense of journey. And the community is called to discern readiness in the candidates. Instead of conforming to time-frames or deadlines, as in employment or other areas of life, the entire community puts itself at the disposal of what God is doing in the catechumen, discerning that person's journey with God. As the beginning of a lifestyle with more of the same to follow (learning how to live as the church), the catechumenate challenges most conventional baptismal and confirmation practices.

3. *The catechumenate challenges the compartmentalization and fragmentation of parish life.* As the paschal mystery centres and makes sense of the various elements of Christian communal life, and is at the heart of the catechumenal process, the catechumenate requires that all aspects of parish life be in dialogue with each other. Too often in the parish, there is a bible study group, a prayer group, a social justice committee, and those who assist at worship. Often these groups are made up of totally different people. But the catechumenate challenges the church to see that scripture, prayer, social justice, and worship are all indispensable parts of every Christian's survival kit.

Scripture, prayer, social justice and worship are the four basic marks of the Christian lifestyle. They provide the faith milieu both for those coming to baptism and those seeking to reaffirm their baptismal covenant. They are the ''marinade,'' to use Aidan Kavanagh's image, in which persons are steeped as they grow in the Christian life. Christian formation consists of equipping the catechumens with an habitual lifestyle, characterized by their own unique expression of the four in combination.

Other aspects of church life are also challenged by the catechumenate. Evangelism is called to affirm that God has already been active in the lives of those outside the church and that God will direct their Christian formation within the church. The catechumenate makes evangelism concrete by encounter with the Risen One within the faith community.

Christian education is challenged to see catechumenal implications in every facet of catechesis and sacramental preparation. The fourfold catechumenal milieu will be the context for all Christian instruction, including marriage preparation and ministry to the sick and penitents. For those already baptized, catechesis is always mystagogical—the community, by its life, evoking from its members ever deeper meanings of the baptismal mystery within them. The catechumenate invites Christian education to be formation which leads to transformation, experience as well as information, lifestyle (the Beatitudes, Matthew 5:3ff.) as well as theological understanding. The catechumenal curriculum is essentially the intersection of the life of this community/nation/humanity with scripture; the catechetical methodology is that of reflection on that experience in the context of the fourfold catechumenal milieu.

The catechumenate also affects preaching. When this process forms parish life, then the preaching on Sundays is either leading towards Easter baptism or drawing out the implications of what happened in Easter baptism. The Sunday lections take on a new hue as they flow from the paschal mystery of Christ experienced in baptism.

Like preaching, the liturgical year is seen in a different light. The heart of the year becomes the Triduum. All seems to lead to, or reflect on, the Easter Vigil, the church's "New Year," in which the church is reborn out of the waters of the font through the neophytes each year. A five-year-old in All Saints' was heard telling a visitor about the vacations she had taken with her family. She dated her life in relationship to the Easter baptisms—"that was the year Michael was baptized; that was the year Judy was baptized." She instinctively knew that the Easter event has irrevocably reordered and transformed time itself.

4. *The catechumenate challenges the church's understanding of ministry.* It is centered in laypeople forming others for the ministry of the church (baptismal life). It causes both catechists and catechumens to discover gifts for ministry, and empowers them to offer those gifts both inside and outside the Christian community. Equipped with the church's survival kit, the baptized begin to see their work life and social life as an

arena of ministry. They have learned to expect that God is already working in those venues and, knowing the story of how God has acted in history, seek to discern and cooperate with God's saving activity in the present. By their lives and the witness those lives make, the baptized help others to discover their destiny and dignity as God's children.

The catechumenate is a challenge to surrogate Christianity in which the baptized remain passive out of the expectation that the "minister" will and should be Christian for them.

In conclusion, each of the four stages of the catechumenate raises a challenging question for the church. The evangelization period asks: Why does the church want more Christians? The catechumenal period asks: What should we ask of our catechumens? (This question is directly related to the obstacles to living the gospel in the local area; to equip catechumens to live the gospel we must ask gospel, rather than "acceptable," questions.) The period of candidacy for baptism asks: How do we teach one another to give all for the sake of others, as Jesus did, so that our lives are honest? The mystagogical period asks: To what will we call the neophytes so that the baptized can move again? Our answers to these questions will require us to think anew about what it means to be the church.

Ultimately, the catechumenate challenges the church consciously to surrender its love affair with Constantinian Christianity, and to reorganize its life to equip the baptized caringly and effectively to respond to the post-Constantinian culture in which they live. For the sake of the baptized, it is time to take up the challenge.

Restoring the Catechumenate in the Decade of Evangelism

John W.B. Hill with Paul Bowie

There is a tension within the work of evangelizing between proclaiming the reign of God already revealed in the resurrection of Jesus Christ, and inviting people and nations to realize that reign through the obedience of faith. In this Decade of Evangelism, the church needs to honour both aspects of the evangel: We need to learn again what it means to announce this reign, and we need to invite people into the free and conscious enjoyment of it.

As long as the church was able to promote its vision of the reign of God as the unifying vision of the established social order, that second aspect of evangelization (inviting response to the gospel) consisted of urging conformity to the symbols with which a Christian civilization celebrated the reign of God. But in most parts of the world today, the church cannot point to such a unifying social vision. Christendom is dead or dying; inviting response to the gospel means inviting people to cross over from one social order to another—to an order that is more promised than actual, more sacramental than conspicuous. Such a crossing over entails conversion on levels of perception, personal identity, habits of consciousness, social engagement, patterns of daily life, spiritual wakefulness, ritual expression, moral sensitivity, and so on. The effectiveness of the churches in inviting response to the gospel, then, will depend largely on making available a clear mode of response—a "language" of response—which enables people to accept this invitation and experience this conversion.

It has become common, in the last few decades, to claim for the contemporary church a special affinity with the pre-Constantinian church, and this appeal to the first three centuries certainly brings some aspects of our current dilemma into sharper focus. For example, it is clear that, from the time of the New Testament and until the beginnings of mass conversions to a newly established civil religion, it was baptism which served as the primary mode of signifying response to the gospel and integration into the eschatological community.[1] By contrast, Anglicans

---

[1] See Aidan Kavanagh, *The Shape of Baptism* (New York: Pueblo, 1978), 25.

have inherited a practice of baptism which generally does not signify response to the evangel; nor can it signify conformity to the comprehensive order of Christendom, for in most provinces of our Communion no such thing any longer exists. Instead, baptism has come to signify a private transaction with a temple deity, or perhaps nostalgia for the security of a lost era. The widespread assumption that infants are the normal candidates for baptism has exacerbated this degeneration. What we need to recover is precisely that pre-Constantinian use of baptism as the sacrament of response to the gospel.

This distortion of baptismal use and meaning has been further exacerbated by a distortion of ecclesiology. It has been argued that, since the Enlightenment, the church in the west has accepted the very protection which the church of the early centuries refused; namely, the protection of being classified as a *cultus privatus*.[2] This suggests that the contemporary church has relinquished the authentic apostolic identity of being a sign of a new humanity, in favour of being a religion of the private sector.

Privatization has deeply affected the understanding of baptism (and therefore of response to the gospel), and has played into the hands of our already excessive clericalization. If baptism is adoption into the household of God, then we have been witnessing an adoption procedure that fails to seek the consent or cooperation of the household and does little to facilitate social integration into the family's way of life. With respect to baptism, clergy have become purveyors of private salvation instead of leaders of a community of salvation. Such distortion of ministry inevitably causes a distortion of the gospel; defective ecclesiology results in defective soteriology.

Nevertheless, the remedy for this distortion cannot be a return to the pre-Constantinian church. When it comes to baptism specifically, we cannot wish ourselves back to a time in which people would generally request baptism only when they had: a) consciously encountered the grace of God in the witness of the Christian community, b) been persuaded that they were being drawn to welcome this grace into their own lives, and c) sought to join themselves to this community.[3] And yet, our work of evangeliza-

---

[2]See Leslie Newbigin, *Foolishness to the Greeks* (Geneva: World Council of Churches, 1986), 99ff.

[3]It has sometimes been suggested, for example, that because baptism is portrayed in the Book of Acts as being conferred immediately upon request, we should do the same. But that would not be a return to "New Testament order," for there are very few "pre-Christian" hearers requesting baptism in our "post-Christian" cultures.

tion will continue to be paralyzed by our degenerated practice of baptism; for without the apostolic rite of baptism as the fundamental signification of response to the evangel, we shall be unable to invite any response that signifies adequately the Christian vocation in a post-Christian world.

The title of this paper is perhaps hazardous, and in two ways. First, it would be naive to think of the Decade of Evangelism as ten years of concerted recruiting to regain for the church some of its lost ground. Better to think of the Decade as ten years in which to learn how to be an evangelizing church within the post-modern world. Second, in one sense it is misleading to speak of the "restoration" of the catechumenate, as if the church could find in the third and fourth centuries a pattern for our radically different time.[4] Nevertheless, the thesis of this paper is that only through the rebuilding of an ordered ministry of pastoral and liturgical catechesis can we surmount the inherited patterns of a privatized, infantilized, and marginalized baptismal practice, and restore to our ministry of evangelization this critical element of effective invitation and response.

In the last few decades, many provinces of our church have seen significant renewal in ecclesial consciousness, fostered in large measure by the restoration of the eucharist as the principal form of assembly on the Lord's Day. We have proved the wisdom of our forebears in the liturgical movement: Praying does shape believing. But now, in a number of provinces, we are facing another revolutionary liturgical experience: the recovery of a public eucharistic setting for the celebration of baptism (in some instances, the primary setting being the Great Vigil of Easter). More than anything else, it is experience such as this which has revealed to us the near bankruptcy of our baptismal consciousness and conviction. People are now moved to ask: How can these candidates (or parents) possibly mean what they are saying? Is it even possible for us who witness these vows to enter into the kind of discipleship proclaimed here?

---

[4] The importance of the fact that our most elegant models for the catechumenate derive from those two centuries, which themselves bridge the gulf of the imperialization of the church, should not be underestimated. Clearly the catechumenate served radically different purposes in those two periods: in the former it enabled people who would know virtually nothing about the Christian life (except what they might infer from the public slander of it) to discover its real meaning and power; in the latter, it attempted to screen the hordes of new applicants for membership (many of whose motives might well be dubious).

What is needed is a communal (i.e., liturgical) and pastoral ministry to those seeking baptism, which enables them to be converted to the gospel of humanity renewed in Christ, and, at the same time, enables them to transcend the defective ecclesiology implied by the inherited pattern of baptism. This is not to suggest that our churches today are unaware of these critical issues or impotent in addressing them. Catechetical formation is being offered in a great variety of fashions and with great diversity of conscious goals. A proposal to restore the catechumenate is therefore not a proposal to put in place something that is presently absent from our life, but to begin to work together to discern its fundamental character and guiding principles. Then, we shall be able to move together beyond the apparent impasse of our present defective baptismal patterns.

What follows is an attempt to identify some of these fundamental characteristics and guiding principles.

1. *Baptismal catechesis is not an excuse for clerical manipulation, but the ministry of a community providing support* for a candidate who is facing the basic issues raised by baptism itself. Clergy may indeed be gate keepers, but coercion is not part of the job. If a pastor says, in effect: "I have the power to baptize, and you want baptism; so you must fulfil my conditions to get it," no matter how excellent the catechesis offered, it will be experienced as barter. Rather, the *community* must gently but firmly insist that it is not the candidate's business to define what he or she wishes baptism to mean; it is the community's business to share with the candidate what it has found the baptized life to mean, and to provide for the candidate adequate opportunity to explore it and weigh its implications.

What are the personal questions or challenges that baptism necessarily raises for that candidate? If the community can help identify these challenges and support the candidate in beginning to deal with them, then appropriate catechetical formation will be taking place. And the ritual celebration of the crossing of these genuine thresholds can bring these questions and challenges into focus.[5]

---

[5]For example, if the first basic pastoral issue for enquirers is recognizing and strengthening those deepest desires which have drawn them to God, then it is appropriate that the celebration of admission to the catechumenate bring to a head the question: What do you seek? (as indeed that rite has traditionally done).

2. *Basic formation in the life of faith is a ministry that can properly be provided only by the community of faith*; clergy by themselves cannot provide it. The community must be allowed to resume its rightful place as the adoptive family. This means that a variety of articulated ministries can be provided from within the community: evangelizing, catechizing, sponsoring, giving spiritual direction, hosting, planning liturgical celebration, praying for the candidates, modelling life in faith, and so on. It also means that as a candidate progresses through discernible stages in entering the life of the church, such passages can be acknowledged and enacted liturgically. Accepting a Catechumen and Calling Candidates to Baptism, as well as baptism itself, can become public moments as enquirers are drawn by degrees into a life of shared faith and common prayer.[6]

3. *There are very different agenda that must be honoured* when someone is entering the Christian life. The individual has his or her own agenda; only by attending to that agenda will the church win the right to tell its own story. First, it must take seriously the individual's story. It must help the person discern the grace of God already at work in his or her life, and discover the connections with the story we call gospel. Attending to this personal agenda enables the church to help people recognize the spiritual quest which motivates them.

Once a person is persuaded that this quest must be pursued within the church and in the light of the gospel, then the church's agenda must also come to the fore. This is an agenda shaped primarily by scripture and specifically by the lectionary, for that is how the people of God place themselves under the word of God. Dealing with this agenda is not something an individual can do alone. The most common mode of support is the small group of people who together hear and pray the word of

---

[6]These moments can become genuine rites of passage provided that they bring a particular dimension of the journey of faith into focus, and thus enable a new dimension to be consciously entered upon. The liturgical celebration of these moments gives them a grounding in the communal faith and consciousness, delivering the individual from private subjectivity.

God, demonstrating how this rhythm shapes their own lives, and drawing the newcomer into that rhythm.[7]

4. *Effective catechesis moves from experience to reflection.* Catechesis does not mean filling people's heads with all the doctrinal information they will need to keep them on the "straight and narrow" for the rest of their lives, but leading them by the hand into the experience of Christian discipleship, and helping them understand and integrate that experience into their lives. It necessarily proceeds by stages: Before people learn the creed they need to see the creed in action; before they accept the calling to serve the world in the power of the Spirit of Jesus, they need to know that they are loved, and practice something of the life of loving service which will reveal to them something of their own hearts; before they are ushered into an experience of the sacraments they need an opportunity to live amongst the baptized as hearers of the Word, and discover whether that is indeed the covenant into which God is calling them. Providing for this experience and reflection requires the development of a pastoral understanding of discipline in stages.[8]

5. *Being transformed in the life of faith is a matter of responding to the Spirit of God*, not of conforming to the expectations of the church. Any ministry of catechesis which fails to take into account the response of the individual, which simply lays down a program of instruction with the implicit message that finishing the course ensures receipt of the prize, makes catechesis a demand of the church to which the individual must conform. And it makes baptism a reward for achievement. The issue for discernment, at every point, must be whether the candidate has authentically heard the call of God and found the freedom to respond.

---

[7]Formation during the period known as the catechumenate is shaped and disciplined by a scriptural agenda rather than a doctrinal or personal one. This does not exclude doctrinal or personal concerns; rather, it allows them to arise within the context of salvation-history. It also enables a person to learn and experience the fact that our relationship with God is one of covenant, and thus to prepare to face the questions of the baptismal covenant.

[8]John W.B. Hill has proposed a way of mapping this pastoral catechesis for the Canadian situation in *Making Disciples* (Toronto: Hoskin, 1991). It follows in broad outline the traditional form of the catechumenate, but interprets the four periods through questions arising out of the fundamental challenges of the baptismal rite.

This requires a ministry of discernment shared by candidate, community, and pastor. Specifically, it requires a frank recognition that the decision to baptize (or the decision to enter the catechumenate, etc.) is never automatic, and the period of time spent as a catechuman is determined by responsiveness to the Spirit.[9]

6. *The restoration of an order of catechumens is something needed not only by those seeking life in Christ, but also by the church.* We need a witness in our midst that discipleship is a journey of faith, and that growth and stages of development are the norm. Too easily our church life conveys the impression that once you are a member, you have reached a stasis which you maintain by showing up for the liturgy. Catechumens (if their journey is essentially a public one) are a living reminder to the church of its own vocation to grow up into Christ. The case is akin to that of penance and reconciliation: As long as it remains an undercover issue, as if it was none of the community's business, the faithful will never be effectively encouraged to deal with their own need for conversion and reconciliation.

7. *There is only one baptism, and adults are not the only legitimate candidates.* There seems at present to be a real danger in the Roman Catholic Church, with its Rite of Christian Initiation of Adults and its Rite of Baptism for Children, that initiation will be divided into two different statements about the meaning of membership, the meaning of church, the meaning of gospel, and the meaning of response. This development does not need to happen, for in the baptism of a young child, the parents and other sponsors must make (and continue to make) the movements of response in faith; the child can make such movements only

---

[9]It may be helpful in this regard to recognize the interplay of the two agenda referred to above: the individual's and the community's. Corresponding to the first of these is the *time-frame of the individual*, within which there must be freedom to bring personal issues to fruition before moving on. Symbolic of the community's agenda is the *community time-frame*—the liturgical seasons. There needs to be a conscious readiness when an individual passes from one to the other, a sense that the individual time-frame has been honoured, and that the community time-frame has now become one's own. Requests for baptism that seem oblivious to the community's time-frame ("My aunt will be in town next week so I would like the baptism then") may reveal unreadiness to enter the community.

through them. If parents can promise that their child will live within the covenant, they can just as truly promise to enter the child upon the path of formation in Christ. If it is they who must be catechized in order to enact this ritual authentically, then it is the child through them who becomes a catechumen. Thus any proposal for a restored catechumenate needs to take into account the fact that candidates may be of any age, and it needs to recognize the importance of discerning readiness on the part of parents, no less than on the part of adult candidates.

The Roman Catholic Rite of Christian Initiation of Adults, first promulgated in 1972, has made a decisive impact on that communion and ensured that the catechumenate will become a lively issue for the rest of the church. It could hardly be considered a rite accessible to Anglicans, however, for a number of important reasons. It was devised, needless to say, for the universal church, with provision for local adaptation. For that reason it begins not from an analysis of the local challenge of faithful initiation but from an archetype of the catechumenate modelled on that of the third and fourth centuries. This fact, together with the characteristic Roman Catholic method of imposition of rites as the starting point of pastoral reform, makes the rite appear to some Anglicans as unduly encumbered with archaisms and as a questionable expansion of the essential requirements for valid initiation into the church. As noted above, it also fails to deal with the anomaly of current initiatory practices for infants, and this has led to the curious paradox of communities which take great care in the baptism of adults while allowing indiscriminate infant baptism to continue unchallenged. Nevertheless, the experience of the contemporary Roman Catholic Church, in learning again how to be faithful and effective in evangelizing adults, has much to teach us.[10]

The challenge for us will be to find methods of developing this ministry which are authentic to Anglican experience and vision. It is, perhaps, a test case for the inculturation of the liturgy. The proposal of this paper is that each province reflect on the implications of its baptismal rites within its own pastoral and cultural context, with a view to discerning what are

---

[10] The journal *Catechumenate* (Liturgy Training Publications, 1800 North Hermitage Ave., Chicago IL 60622-1101 USA) and the work of the North American Form on the Catechumenate (5510 Columbia Pike, Suite 310, Arlington VA 22204 USA) are noteworthy in this regard. The Forum conducts workshops for developing catechetical ministries, and publishes a newsletter.

the issues with which applicants for baptism will have to deal in order to make baptism an authentic response to the gospel. If those issues can be identified, they can become the starting points for the development of an appropriate catechumenate.

It is not suggested that this be undertaken separately by parish communities, for the task is considerable and full of pitfalls. But already, in North America, considerable work has begun at national levels to provide for a truly liturgical and pastoral catechesis. Already the Episcopal Church USA and the Church of the Province of Southern Africa have authorized rituals for at least some dimensions of this ministry.[11]

In the Episcopal Church USA, the Office of Evangelism has recognized the catechumenate as the cornerstone of the Decade of Evangelism. This is a sign of things to come for the Anglican Communion. Without the development of a conscious address to the fundamentally changed relation of gospel and culture today, and of the debilitating impact of our outmoded patterns of initiation, there can hardly be effective evangelization in the years ahead.

---

[11]See *The Book of Occasional Services* (New York: Church Hymnal Corporation, second edition, 1988), 112-141, and *An Anglican Prayer Book* (London: Collins, 1989), 417-419.

Preparing Parents for Infant Baptism
Ronald L. Dowling

Over the past two decades or so there has been a flourishing of renewal in the thinking about baptism and its place in the life of the church. This has been expressed in a revival of writing about the nature of baptism, the process of Christian initiation, and the celebration of baptism in the life of the local congregation, to mention only a few areas of renewal. Revisions of the liturgy have taken seriously the baptism of adults, which once again has become a pressing pastoral concern. All of the major Christian denominations have revised their baptismal liturgies, emphasizing the place of adult candidates. Anglican liturgies have been part of this movement. However, it is still the case that, in the western provinces of the Anglican Communion, most of the baptisms that are celebrated are those of infants or young children.

Setting aside the major theological and ecclesiological questions that this practice may raise, the purpose of this paper is to examine a crucial pastoral matter: baptismal preparation when the candidates are infants or young children. It has been Anglican custom (and indeed a long-continued custom of the church at least from the time of Hippolytus) to have sponsors or godparents answer for the infants. In recent decades, parents have been included either amongst the godparents or as sponsors in their own right. When it comes to baptismal preparation, then, it is the parents (and godparents) who are the focus of attention.

The Book of Common Prayer (1662) does not recognize the possibility of preparation of parents and/or godparents. The opening rubrics of the rite for the baptism of infants state:

> When there are Children to be baptized, the Parents shall give knowledge thereof overnight, or in the Morning before the beginning of Morning Prayer, to the Curate.

It seems that it was more important to get the children baptized than to be concerned about the understanding of their parents. The rite itself was designed to provide all the instruction necessary.

Over the past few decades, there has been considerable change in the attitude of the churches concerning the preparation of parents and godparents. Some Anglican provinces now *require* that preparation take place. Canada, the USA, and the Province of Southern Africa, to name but three examples, have written this requirement into the rubrics of their revised baptismal liturgies. The American *Book of Common Prayer* (1979) provides the following rubric:

> Parents and godparents are to be instructed in the meaning of Baptism, in their duties to help the new Christian grow in the knowledge and love of God, and in their responsibilities as members of his Church.

The draft Australian revision, *Holy Baptism with the Laying on of Hands* (1990) infers that preparation will take place, and the draft new Australian canon law would make preparation mandatory. Other provinces, such as England, Scotland, and New Zealand, do not refer specifically to preparation, but it is clear that individual dioceses and parishes make their own guidelines to ensure that preparation takes places as a matter of priority.

Principles

Three principles for preparation of parents emerge from a renewed sacramental theology, the rediscovery of lay ministry, and new insights in Christian education and nurture. These are:

1. The sacraments are the celebration by, of, and for the gathered Christian community.

2. Preparation for parents and godparents of infants is essential.

3. The responsibility for the entire baptismal process, including preparation, belongs to the whole church.

Recent developments in sacramental theology have led to a change in understanding of how the sacraments work, and who is the focus of the sacramental action. Individualism is passing away and being replaced, more and more, by a corporate understanding of the sacraments. No longer are we solely concerned about what a sacrament effects in the individual, but what the sacrament effects within the gathered community and the church as a whole. As far as baptism is concerned, the focus is no longer entirely on the candidate, but on the Christian community as well. This has led to at least three developments: a) returning the celebration of baptism to the main Sunday liturgy; b) seeing baptism as a springboard for all Christian ministry; and c) appreciating once more the important role of the local congregation, both in the celebration of the liturgy and in the bonding of new members into the faith community.

Our forebears, the Anglican reformers, were deeply concerned about understanding and faith in the entire sacramental economy. Consequently, many of their liturgies were full of didacticism. This result applied to baptism as much as to the other Prayer Book liturgies, with lengthy exhortations and prayers full of teaching. In our own time, liturgy has been moving away from this approach. Symbolism is used far more today, and the symbols and symbolic actions are allowed to convey many of the meanings that were previously expressed in words alone in the rite. As a consequence, texts are often less verbose and shorter in length. Thus the text of the baptismal liturgy is less inclined to do "on the spot" teaching about the meaning and responsibilities of baptism. Current insights into the nature of catechesis and Christian formation have served to promote this situation. It is more often the case today that preparation takes place before celebration.

Because baptism is a corporate event, it is very important, whenever and wherever possible, that the celebration take place with groups of infant candidates. This inclusion emphasizes the corporate nature of baptism in a striking way. Many revised rites suggest particular occasions for these group celebrations. The new Australian draft rite states, for example:

> Certain times in the Church's year are particularly appropriate for the celebration of baptism; Easter Day and the whole Easter season to Pentecost, our Lord's Baptism and the Epiphany season, All Saints'tide, and the bishop's visit.

Pastoral experience has shown that set times throughout the year may be initially resisted, but soon become very much part of the parish cycle of celebration.

If the celebration of baptism is corporate in nature, so too is the preparation. The days when the priest interviewed each individual set of parents in the study for the "statutory half-hour" are passing. In many places the entire preparation process is conducted in groups, each group preparing for the next corporate celebration. Once again, this emphasizes the corporate nature of the process and also opens up the process for "church" involvement and responsibility. In many places lay people are involved as teachers as well as sponsors.

Baptismal preparation is not just preparation for the liturgy, but also preparation for growth in Christian living. This development has come about not only from of the need to prepare recently converted but unchurched adults for baptism, but also from the need to graft lapsed parents back into the church after some considerable time away from meaningful involvement. Further, the focus of this preparation has not simply been the candidates or their parents or godparents. The diocese and the local congregation also has needed (or needs) preparation, if the initiation process is truly to be renewed. (It is still the case that in many places baptism has barely made it into the main Sunday liturgy, let alone into the living consciousness of regular worshippers.)

Given the principles stated earlier, any attempt to prepare parents for the baptism of their infants must begin with preparation of the local congregation. The reality in the western churches (at least) is that most parents who bring their infants for baptism are not regular worshippers. How often at a baptismal eucharist do no members of the family (or at best a few) come to receive communion? The focus of preparation must be the parents, and the most important aspect of that preparation is to bond them into the local Christian community. But this preparation cannot be left to the clergy. It is essential that the congregation take this ministry very seriously, not least because this ministry is at the forefront of evangelism and mission.

The "process" of baptism

Throughout this essay, the "baptismal process" has been referred to a number of times. We turn now to that process which involves: inquiry, instruction, celebration, and integration.

Inquiry:

In many parishes or Christian communities there are regular, committed members who wish to discuss the matter of the baptism of their infants. This request may happen during the period of pregnancy or soon after the birth of the child, and could simply involve discussion about godparents, the system of preparation, and the date of the next appropriate celebration of baptism in the parish.

For those parents who are not active members of the congregation, the inquiry is usually made by telephone or, with any luck, after attendance at the Sunday liturgy. In some parishes, these parents are simply informed about the same matters as are the active members. This way is not always the most successful, however. In some parishes where there are many inquiries about baptism, inquirers' classes (or sessions) are held at regular times. Those parents not actively involved in the life of the congregation are invited to join one of these sessions first. Discussion at these sessions might include clarification of what baptism is and what baptism is not (i.e., a naming ceremony, a divine insurance policy). The system of preparation can be explained, and parents asked to think seriously about what it is they want and what commitments they are prepared to make. Then, they may be invited to join in instruction classes.

Instruction:

For many years, baptismal preparation, where it was done at all, had minimal content. Parents were instructed about their duties and responsibilities (part of the 1662 rite). They were perhaps taken through the rite, and possibly had items like the Apostles' Creed explained briefly. Often the instruction involved not much more. In the catechumenal pattern offered in the American *Book of Occasional Services* (1979), however, the content of instruction is outlined as follows:

> During the period of the catechumenate, the context of catechesis is a continual reflection on Scripture, Christian prayer, worship, and the catechumen's gifts for ministry and work for peace and justice.

If these are the requirements for an adult candidate's formation, should the church require any less from parents who are taking on the nurture and Christian formation of their children? The methodology of this approach is that of experience first, followed by reflection. Baptism is an extremely important event. The church is right to expect that those who come for baptism, or those who bring their children, will prepare seriously for Christian living and not just for the baptismal event itself.

How this can be done in a relatively short time is a matter of question. There are those who argue that it cannot be achieved in a short time at all, and that, at the very least, it should take a number of months. Local congregations will need to work this schedule out to meet their own situations realistically, but should not shirk this responsibility.

Celebration:

If the parents have been formally introduced in the congregation (see appendix to this essay), have attended the liturgy on the intervening Sundays, and have been prayed for by name during this period in the general intercessions, then the day of the baptism will most likely be an occasion of communal celebration and joy rather than a situation of "them" and "us," with absolutely no interaction between the "regulars" and the baptismal families. In those places where a member of the congregation has been chosen as a sponsor, there are already close ties.

Some of those who have participated in the preparation program should also take part in the liturgy: as readers and intercessors (within the baptismal rite), but also in other ways such as leading the "welcome" or giving the candle. Not only does this continue to make connections, but it is also the liturgical expression of the continuity of the baptismal process and the corporate responsibility taken by the whole congregation.

Integration:

Reflection on significant experiences is a vital part of the baptismal process. If this applies during the preparation period, it also might apply to the period after the baptism. Some places gather parents together again to share their reflections on and reactions to the liturgy in which their children became members of the church. This can be a very useful way of continuing the connection with the congregation. It can also demonstrate that the baptism is not the end of the story or a one-shot event, but an initiation into a life journey.

The parents can be encouraged to continue on that journey. Pastoral care is a fundamental part of this encouragement. It is often the case that the moment the families leave the church premises on the day of baptism, they are forgotten. Pastoral visiting by lay persons, now common in many parishes, should make particular effort to include these parents, and so try to integrate them into the on going life of the community. Some parishes visit with a small gift (such as a copy of the scriptures) and invite parents to join various appropriate groups within the parish.

Integration also involves the infants themselves. In a number of provinces, the infant may be welcomed to communion immediately. Such children will grow up knowing that they are always included in the full eucharistic life of the community. Other provinces do not allow this inclusion to happen until a later age (often the magical age of seven years). These children will grow up knowing that they are not yet full members despite what we say about baptism being full initiation. If it is true that baptism is complete initiation, then all the arguments against early admission to communion are also arguments against early baptism. As a communion, we Anglicans still have a lot of work to do in this area.

The parish Christian education program (whatever form that takes) can help the child reflect on her/his baptism and place in the church, as the years go by, and maturing happens. Programs will be geared to each level of the child's development and thus be appropriate for this process. In due course the growing and maturing young person will be expected to renew her/his baptismal stance within the whole congregation at a time of corporate renewal such as the Easter Vigil. It might also be the case that each individual will make a personal profession before the bishop and receive the laying on of hands.

Further concerns

The process outlined above has its roots in the catechumenal model. One very important question that needs to be addressed, if we are to use this pattern for parents, is the matter of choice about whether to proceed to baptism or not. In the catechumenal model, this point comes after most of the period of instruction has been completed. The 'election' involves a decision both by the candidate and the Christian community. In the case of parents, this moment of choice is often made far too early. Parents come to inquire but, in fact, have already decided that they will do whatever is required to get their child into the water. The decision to *seek* baptism has been the real moment of choice.

Yet many of these parents do not know what they are choosing. There is a real disparity between what the parents want and what the church is offering. There is a real challenge here. If the moment of choice is to take place after most of the instruction, then considerable work will need to go into helping parents understand that they can choose only *after* they have received instruction. In this way the choice will be a realistic one, based on real knowledge and actual experience.

In many parts of the church effecting this understanding will be quite a challenge. Many parents come with an expectation of immediate satisfaction. This is especially true in those provinces where baptism is often seen as part of the ''civil religion'' of the culture. To put in place the pattern outlined, with the moment of choice delayed, will take time. Parents (and grandparents) may become anxious; dates for baptism may come and go. But it would seem that we must strive to inject real integrity into this process, both on the part of the parents and on the part of the church. Anything less would simply continue all the myths about baptism and infants.

Another aspect of this matter of choice is the possibility of choosing to delay the child's baptism for a number of years. The older child would then be able to participate fully in her/his own preparation, baptism, and communion. In some places, infants are accepted as catechumens, with an appropriate liturgical rite, and the process of preparation then continues for several years. At a later stage, the choice is made, final preparations begun (the child sharing in the preparation in an active way), and (hopefully at the Easter Vigil) the child participates fully in her/his baptism. There is much to be said for this alternative.

When baptism is to be delayed, it is important for the child to be admitted liturgically as a catechumen, or for a liturgy of thanksgiving for birth to be celebrated. Liturgical recognition of the child's place within the community is of paramount importance. Where parents choose to go on with instruction and possibly baptism, it can be useful to have a liturgy of welcome or blessing (see appendix). Such a liturgy has the advantage of introducing child and parents in the community and beginning the community's care and prayer for this family. This not only marks the passing from inquiry to instruction but also is a significant way of connecting the child, the parents, and the Christian community.

It may appear to some, that the above suggestions will create a very rigorist process of baptismal preparation. All this will depend on how the local congregation owns the process, and how lovingly members of the congregation enter into building relationships with those families who come seeking baptism. Clearly, in every parish situation, there is a real tension between being open, welcoming, and responsive to those parents seeking baptism for their children (for whatever reason), and the need of the church to take seriously the formation of new Christians and the parents of new Christians. This formation must go beyond minimal instruction and minimal connection with the Christian community. The church must maintain its own integrity of faith and practice, while encouraging baptismal inquirers to explore with the same integrity their own faith stance and practice. Continuing the often watered-down approach of the past will do nothing to help pass on the faith!

Whatever patterns of preparation are adopted by any given diocese or parish, they must be flexible as far as local need and custom are concerned. I am reminded of a country priest in my own diocese who has six small isolated towns in his parish, most of which he visits only once each month. Baptismal preparation in these circumstances is extremely difficult. He is presently trying to train one lay person in each centre to take on this task. It is creative approaches like this that make the process possible.

The preparation of parents and godparents of infant baptismal candidates is not simply an important pastoral concern. It is fundamental to the entire baptismal process, and, thereby, to the nature, life, and continuity of the church. When each Christian community owns the baptismal process and takes active and enthusiastic responsibility for it, preparation will become accepted as essential and normative. Holy baptism will then become a true celebration of the Church.

Appendix

For those bringing a child for preparation for baptism.

[*The parents (and sponsors) of the child bring him/her to the altar step.*]

Priest: What do you seek?

Parents (and sponsors): New life through baptism for our child N.

Priest: Will you be regular in attending the worship of God, and in receiving instruction?

Parents (and sponsors): We will.

Priest: Will you pray for N. and help him/her grow in the knowledge and love of God by your own example.

Parents (and sponsors): We will.

Priest: Let us pray —
    Eternal and loving God,
    you have promised to be faithful to a thousand generations of
    those who love and revere you:
    + bless this child N. and preserve his/her life;
    receive him/her and enable him/her to receive you,
    that through the sacrament of Holy Baptism he/she may become
    your child in Christ and a member of your Church;
    through Jesus Christ our Lord,
    who lives and reigns with you and the Holy Spirit,
    one God, now and for ever. *Amen.*

(*to the congregation*)

    People of God,
    it is our intention to present N. for Holy Baptism on (*date*).
    I commend N., his/her parents and sponsors, to your prayers
    and your loving support.

[*The Prayers of the People follow.*]

III Confirmation and the Renewal of Baptismal Faith

Confirmation
Colin Buchanan

Introduction

Confirmation is either centre-stage or only slightly off-stage throughout modern Anglican discussions of initiation. Even the decisive removal of confirmation from the sphere of initiation, of which the Toronto Statement is but one example, nevertheless requires a careful consideration of the nature of sacramental initiation. Moreover, the Toronto Statement offers one or two further unexpected twists about confirmation.

I have written elsewhere an ordered account of the development of the rite of confirmation, both as it emerged before the Reformation and as it was shaped by the Reformation and subsequently by the Anglican liturgical tradition.[1] In preparing this paper for the Toronto Consultation, then, I had to ask myself: At what point should I pick up the story in order to provide sufficient background for this discussion? In answer, I found a convenient centenary being completed in 1991: the publication of the second and definitive edition of A.J.Mason's *The Relation of Confirmation to Baptism*. This will serve to mark the beginning of the paper.

Two-staging: its rise

Mason's book is a landmark in the history of Anglican writings on confirmation. There is no doubt about the theological stance of its author: He is the archetypal "two-stager." To be accurate, we ought to call him the "two-stages-in-one-rite-er," but I hope that the simpler "two-stager" will suffice. The proper expansion should be borne in mind, however, when the shorthand version is used.

Mason was not actually first in the field. Indeed, if you follow his argument, you must agree that the apostles themselves were the first in the

---

[1] *Anglican Confirmation*, Grove Liturgical Study No.48 (Bramcote, Notts.: Grove, 1986).

field, and it was the *denial* of two-staging which was a later innovation.[2] But even if you do not accept his argument, you can see his antecedents. They derive in the west from Tertullian and Hippolytus and in the east (though less certainly) from the postbaptismal anointing in the *Apostolic Constitutions* and Cyril of Jerusalem's *Catechesis*.

Mason's Anglican predecessors were relatively few, though Jeremy Taylor and his *Chrisis Teleiotike* are usually listed among them.[3] The antecedents which led more immediately to Mason's 1891 publication were:

1. The provision in 1662 that those baptized in "Riper Years" should also be confirmed as soon as possible afterwards. This gave a framework in which episcopal confirmation was in principle required of all, whether they had received baptism in infancy or in adulthood.

2. The general *tendenz* of the high sacramental teaching of the Tractarians. This, in itself was, however, for the first fifty years, somewhat thin on confirmation.[4]

---

[2]This is, of course, a wildly perverse view; neither the scriptures nor the authorities writing about the scriptures give any substantial ground for taking such a view. It is almost as though Anglican writers who value confirmation for extra-biblical reasons then go looking for any shred of evidence that might be alleged to point towards it in the scriptures.

[3]In *Anglican Confirmation*, I had reason to comment on S.L. Ollard's essay "Confirmation in the Anglican Communion" in the book by various authors, *Confirmation: 1.Historical and Doctrinal* (London: SPCK, 1926). Ollard was trying to establish from sixteenth-century precedents a somewhat twentieth-century "two-staging" view. My comment was that "he has to dub author after author, exceptional—and his normative authors live in nooks and crannies" (p.19, n.2).

[4]Thus Pusey, for instance, made virtually no mention of it (cf. *Anglican Confirmation*, 31), and we may add here R.M. Benson, whose undated but presumably mid-century definition of "Puseyism" began as follows:
1. High thoughts of the two sacraments.
2. High estimate of episcopacy as God's ordinance.
3. High estimate of the visible Church as the body where we are made and continue to be members of Christ.
4. Regard for ordinances...such as daily public prayers....
(quoted in David Edwards, *Christian England* [London: Fount, 1989], vol.III, 181). Clearly, if confirmation ranked *anywhere* in the basic sacramental system of the Puseyites, it would have received mention in this list. If it had been part of sacramental initiation, surely it would have had to have been mentioned.

3. The ever greater availability of confirmation in practice (in England—I dare not make statements here about New Zealand or the USA in the nineteenth century, let alone about PNG or Central Africa). During the years from 1830 to 1891, four different factors made for this greater availability in England:

(i) the division of dioceses, giving diocesans a smaller area;
(ii) the provision for retirement of bishops, giving diocesans a way of escape when they could no longer cope physically;
(iii) the addition of suffragans, giving extra chance of providing an itinerant, confirming, episcopal ministry;
(iv) the spread of the railways, giving quick and easy access to distant corners of a diocese.[5]

Thus "Soapy Sam" Wilberforce was (incorrectly) credited with pioneering "pastoral" confirmation services when he was Bishop of Oxford, 1845-69. By "pastoral" was meant services with hymns and preaching, and a controllable number of candidates. Several centres were nominated in a diocese and the bishop started to appear at them annually. And so, from the mid-century onwards, the sheer possibility of *getting* confirmed provided a context in which a very "high" view of the rite could begin to flourish. The reverse had certainly been true previously: Where confirmation could *not* be had, it had been difficult to view it as an integral necessity for full initiation. That in itself sets the silence of the early Tractarians on the subject into context. Correspondingly, the nineteenth-century change in pastoral practice was a natural preparation for Mason and his school.

4. In the 1870s the anglo-catholic movement sorted out to its own satisfaction the absolute requirement of confirmation as the basis for admission to communion (a basis virtually unknown in Anglicanism before).[6]

---

[5]See P. Jagger, *Clouded Witness: Initiation in the Church of England in the mid-Victorian Period 1850-1875* (Allison Park, Penn.: Pickwick, 1982), 101ff.

[6]Of course the American colonies in the seventeenth and eighteenth centuries, and many other parts of the Empire in the nineteenth, had no bishops. Anglican incumbents in those parts had perforce always to do what rural clergy very often did in England at that time, that is, admit to communion without episcopal confirmation.

This clarification of minds was precipitated by the "Revisers' Communion" at Westminster Abbey in 1870, a date which neatly coincided with a sensing by anglo-catholics that they could now make the running in the Church of England. They did so make the running that within fifty years or so it was almost entirely gone from common memory that dissenters had once received communion in the Church of England without benefit of confirmation. This pressing of the "confirmation rubric" inevitably pushed minds towards a high understanding of confirmation as integral to sacramental initiation. The role of confirmation was ceasing to be a kind of certificate of having been catechized and thus of being *prepared* to receive communion, and was becoming a non-negotiable completion of sacramental initiation, totally requisite ritually for admission to communion.

5. Mason was, in the event, preceded by Fr. Puller, whose *What is the Distinctive Grace of Confirmation?* was published in 1880 (the advance herald of the major thrust to come—the "Mason-Dix" line!)

In *Anglican Confirmation* I stated that, in broad terms, the two-stagers were in the ascendancy for eighty years, from 1890 to 1970. Here it will be helpful to see the characteristics of that school of thought, note its deflation, and trace out its continuing effects.

Two-staging: its characteristics

Doctrinally the heart of the two-staging position is that there are two *inward* stages in initiation, denominated, represented, and conveyed by the two outward stages: a re-birth in water, and a baptism with the Holy Spirit. This reference to baptism in the Holy Spirit was not a phenomenological statement, however; anglo-catholics never traditionally expected confirmation candidates to speak in strange tongues or otherwise go ecstatic. So the assertion of either re-birth or the coming of the Holy Spirit, more or less without visible effect in the candidates' lives (even without anything much in the way of faith), was a problem to evangelicals. The assertion that the two effects came *separately* in two different stages of a rite, whose parts might be divided by a period of ten, fifteen or even fifty years, only compounded the problem. Though I am not going to explore it at this point, that side of the issue must be understood and noted, for it is a part of the backdrop to other sacramental disputes.

Biblically, there is little to be said for the two-staging view. The two-stagers, however, had four great strings to their bows:

   (i) they went to town on the Samaritan episode in Acts 8;

  (ii) they asserted that references in the scriptures generally to *bap-tisma* referred to a complex rite of initiation which included the laying on of hands;

 (iii) they laid great weight on the tradition of the church, in which the *Apostolic Tradition* of Hippolytus in Dix's hands underscored and reinforced the case of Mason (who had not had the benefit of it);

 (iv) they were unopposed by evangelicals as there was virtually no evangelical scholarship worthy of the name in the first half of this century (the biggest querying of them came rather from Pusey-like anglo-catholics such as Wirgman and Darwell Stone).[7]

Liturgically the 1662 rite looked fairly denuded if it were to be taken seriously as a main service in this period (1890 to 1970).[8] Accordingly most attempts at revision tried to incorporate the Acts 8 passage into the preface, whilst the 1922 Canadian book even added Acts 19 *and* Hebrews 6 as well. These passages, if they were relevant at all, taught almost too much: Acts 8 appears to record the initial (indeed Pentecostal) coming of the Holy Spirit, whereas the texts only wanted to say that "a special gift" of the Holy Spirit was imparted. Other liturgical touching up of 1662 was that the renewal of baptismal vows tended to get articulated

---

[7] As a check on this I referred to the only evangelical exceptions I could easily identify. W.H. Griffith Thomas, in his *The Principles of Theology: An Introduction to the Thirty-Nine Articles* (1930), gives a page and a half of his 540 pages to "those five commonly called sacraments." In a few lines only he expounds confirmation more or less as Cranmer would have done, simply to make the (not very easy) point that Anglican confirmation is "a state of life allowed in the scriptures," whereas Roman Catholic confirmation is "the corrupt following of the apostles" (third edition, 1945, 353-355). He nowhere even mentions Mason (nor, of course, Dix). The same author, in his *The Catholic Faith* (1920 edition), gives a pastoral interpretation of the rite. On "after the example of thy holy apostles" he comments (without giving biblical references): "We thus retain the exact form of the apostolic action, but with a different purpose" (181).

[8] It *was* a main service, of course, though one without scripture, hymnody, sermon, presentation, welcome, or communion as it stood in its 1662 form. The great English precedent was for it to happen mid-week and to be followed by a special "first communion," as likely as not at 8 a.m. on the Sunday following. (It must be remembered that large parts of the Anglican Communion observed fasting for communion until about 1970—the Pope relaxed *his* rules in the 1950s, but it took some time to get through!)

in full in this period, and there was a strong tendency to sing *Veni, Creator Spiritus*, all kneeling, before the bishop's confirmation prayer.

Later liturgical priorities do not obtrude into the pre-1970 rites. Confirmation, as noted in an earlier footnote, is, in these rites, still a separate service from baptism and still admits to communion. First communion is still a separate event on the first Sunday following confirmation.[9] In England the popular tendency still brought considerable numbers of 12-year-old children from unbelieving homes to join confirmation classes in the pre-1970s.

Psychologically, confirmation looked important, demanding, and possibly even promising (Acts 8, if read on such occasions, is full of misdirected, if not actually spurious, promise of experiential results). But the importance came as much as anything from the sheer pomposity of an episcopal occasion. Episcopacy has a religious romanticism woven around it (a romanticism from which the occupants of the office are not always themselves immune), and the very scarcity value of a bishop seems to give great significance to the occasion. It will be recalled that the Puritans objected at Savoy, that the provision that only a bishop could confirm "seemeth to put a higher value upon confirmation than upon baptism or the Lord's supper; for…every deacon may baptize, and every minister consecrate and administer the Lord's supper, but the bishop only may confirm."[10] To this the bishops replied:

---

[9]A marginal exception to this would be the coming of fully "two-stage" rites in the Church of England's experimental series near the end of the period. The mind of Dix can be seen here. Draft services were produced in 1959 and, in a heavily amended shape, these were then authorized as "Series 2" services in 1967 and 1968. They originated from the Mason-Dix theory that water and the laying on of hands *together* make up sacramental initiation. The groundwork for them had been done in the various convocation reports (sometimes in minority reports) on initiation from the period 1944 to 1954 (see *Anglican Confirmation*, 23, including n.4). They also included the celebration of the eucharist (and thus first communion) as a norm, and in this too they were pioneering (though *permission* for the eucharistic context had been provided in the Church of South India in the late 1950s). It is somewhat anomalous that the *ASB* rites today run on in this 1950s mold, and the difficulty of breaking the mold in England is enormous. Apart from the Church of England, I cannot find any pre-1970 provision for uniting baptism and confirmation in one rite except in the Canadian 1959 book, and that makes no provision for the eucharist.

[10]Edward Cardwell, *Conferences on the Book of Common Prayer* (Oxford: OUP, 1840), 329.

The reserving of confirmation to the bishop doth argue the dignity of the bishop above presbyters, who are not allowed to confirm, but does not argue any excellency in confirmation above the sacraments. St. Hierom argues the quite contrary....[11]

I offer as a contemporary English analogy the suggestion that this is like comparing Maundy money with ordinary currency. From the point of view of scarcity, and of the royal occasion at the presentation of it, Maundy money has enormous value. No one, however, could live on Maundy money or hope to exist solely on dole-outs from the Queen; the necessities of life come in ordinary currency terms. This analogy, I think, preserves the emphasis in what the bishops were saying, though whether their answer was accurate or credible others must judge. What is clear is that the importation of a bishop (cope, staff, mitre, outriders, and all) for the event threatens to turn it into a royal debutantes' ball (and, traditionally, the girls were dressed accordingly). If to that pomp is added the Acts 8 passage, let alone a sermon from a bishop schooled in the two-staging era, then the recipients can be forgiven if their expectations are pitched very high—and if they feel let down when "nothing happens."

On the other hand, the bishop is far from let down. Confirmation is his special outing and feeds his wanting to be needed. Whether he holds to a two-staging view or not, he becomes very sure of the necessity of episcopal confirmation in the life of the church and, indeed, the necessity of it looking and *feeling* in accordance with existing expectations. There is an episcopal conservatism in relation to episcopal services which corresponds to the much-vaunted lay person's conservatism in relation to great festivals. I retain a strong suspicion that, just as all biblical hermeneutics must take into account the context of the reader as well as that of the writer, so attempts to evaluate (and perhaps to restructure) existing Anglican confirmation patterns are up against the experiential loading of the evaluation made by existing bishops.[12]

---

[11]Cardwell, 359.

[12]For instance the present Bishop of Coventry (Simon Barrington-Ward), in his speech in the General Synod of the Church of England in July 1991, said:

"I would like to speak very much from experience.... [In] the whole discussion of this

Ecumenically, the upshot of a two-stage view of confirmation is that Christians in denominations which do not practice episcopal confirmation have been viewed by Anglicans as only half-initiated.[13] So the pressure is often upon other denominations to insist on a laying on of hands as well as water-baptism for "full" sacramental initiation. Meanwhile, the matter may be relieved marginally by rites in some of the new prayer books of the Anglican Communion for receiving Christians from other denominations, rites which are avowedly not to be called "confirmation," though they confer the same canonical status as confirmation.[14]

---

issue there has been a gross undervaluing of confirmation itself as an aspect of initiation, yet this is one of the things that I have come to value enormously in my experience as a bishop.... I have had a very different sense [from that of the Bishop of St. Edmundsbury and Ipswich], from my own experience of confirmation.... My experience has certainly illustrated that sentence in 1 Corinthians chapter 6 verse 11.... That experience has become meaningful to me in confirming and in experiencing this as a gift of the Spirit, and as the true completion of baptism and entry to communion for many, many people...." (General Synod *Report of Proceedings*, July 1991, 319). This was a statement of enormous sincerity, springing from services which had been most carefully planned and conducted under the most careful and sensitive episcopal leadership; this is a statement by a bishop whom I hold in high esteem. I officiate in such confirmations myself, so I both thrill to them and honour all that the speaker is investing in these rites. And yet I still believe we should not give confirmation a higher place in the economy of the Holy Spirit than scripture would warrant. No amount of high experience—even for bishops—should distort our hermeneutics.

[13]The same is of course true of the view taken of others (including Anglicans) by the Orthodox, and sometimes by Roman Catholics. The Orthodox give the "seal" to Protestants who become Orthodox, and are irretrievably two-staging themselves. In the very course of writing this paper I came across the essay on "Chrismation" by the Orthodox writer Cyrille Argenti in *Ecumenical Perspectives on Baptism, Eucharist and Ministry*, Max Thurian, ed. (Geneva: WCC, 1983). Argenti's article includes a solemn citation of the Acts 8 and Acts 19 passages, though even he reveals that crucial lacuna when he goes on to say: "anointing or chrismation administered immediately after emerging from the waters of baptism, and conferring the gift of the Holy Spirit, is solidly attested in the Universal Church from the third century of our era...." (p.53). This is a sharp-edged (and probably non-negotiable) view, and makes it astonishingly clear that the coming of the Holy Spirit is sacramentally distinct from baptism in water.

[14]These are the American *Book of Common Prayer* (1979), the Canadian *Book of Alternative Services* (1985), *A South African Prayer Book* (although the rite in this book appears to be giving episcopal confirmation *de novo* to those from non-episcopal denominations), and *A New Zealand Prayer Book* (1989). Such rites do *not* appear in the Church of England's *Alternative Service Book* (1980), nor in the Church of Ireland's *Alternative*

The collapsing of the view

Those who propounded a two-stage view might have had some difficulties in the New Testament texts but, in accordance with their own principles, they had at least to locate the view in the practice of the early church. Indeed, the plea was that they were driven by the practice of the early church. In recent years, however, they have run into problems on both fronts, i.e., in both the New Testament and the early post-apostolic church; it is these problems which expose their methodologies as special pleading with the evidence.[15]

I have offered 1970 as a symbolic date for the end of the two-staging ascendancy. One major factor was the passing from the scene of the heavy-weight two-staging scholars which, in England in the post-war years, included Gregory Dix, Lionel Thornton, Arthur Couratin, Edward Ratcliffe, J.D.C. Fisher and Michael Ramsey.[16] Fisher was still writing in the 1970s whilst Couratin and Ramsey lived into the 1980s, but the impetus was gone. No new "Mason-Dix" authors have appeared, and this theological oddity has perished at the age of fourscore years. Certainly, it simply ran out of steam, but this was hastened by a series of "one-stage" findings which helped to bring its era to an end.

Prayer Book (1984). They are, however, in view in the Church of England and the Liturgical Commission has done some initial work on them (thus the General Synod asked in July 1991 for such rites to be produced). At Toronto, the section handling "Renewal of Baptismal Faith" said clearly that drawing a distinction between those who have previously received episcopal confirmation and those who have not "is no longer appropriate" (para.3.22).

[15]See the Toronto Statement, 1.15-16; 3.1-2; 3.15-18.

[16]I include Michael Ramsey, referring to his famous *The Gospel and the Catholic Church* (1936). In the course of a major discussion of baptism in Chapter V, he simply lets slip, in passing, his two-staging view: "Baptism, therefore (with the laying-on-of-hands as its normal completion*) is the first significant fact about a Christian...." (second edition, p.59). The asterisk in the quotation refers to a footnote: "Cf. Acts 8.14-17, 19.1-7, Titus 3.5, and probably 2 Tim.1.6." This almost passing comment suggests, however, that the covert implication of all his references to baptism is that they need the "completion." Curiously, when, forty years later, Ramsey in retirement wrote a book entitled *Holy Spirit*, I could find no reference in it to the "completion" of baptism, or to the coming of the Holy Spirit through the laying on of hands or anointing. Had Michael Ramsey himself emerged from the pre-1970 era? (Certainly the conversation the authors of *Growing into Union* had with him in May 1970 suggested he was well aware of a changing question in the church.)

First came Geoffrey Lampe's *The Seal of the Spirit* (1951). This established, at the very least, that the two-stage case could be contested historically, and undertook the task from the very patristic evidence that was supposed to teach the two-staging position.[17]

There was then, in June 1966, a slight advance shock in an area where no Church of England authority had even realized there was a problem. The House of Laity, which had been elected in autumn 1965, denied to the 1928 confirmation service the two-thirds majority it needed if it were to be authorized as "Series 1," making it clear that it was the citing of Acts 8 which was central to the objection.[18]

Then came in 1970: a) J.D.G. Dunn, *The Baptism of the Holy Spirit*; b) *Documents of the Baptismal Liturgy*, E.C. Whitaker, ed. (second edition, but with a new introductory essay); c) the beginning of admission of unconfirmed children to communion in New Zealand; d) *Prayer Book Studies 18* in the USA (though it was equivocal on this issue); e) and a tiny extra weight added by the above-mentioned *Growing into Union*. Immediately after came the "Ely Report," *Christian Initiation: Birth and Growth in the Christian Society* (CIO, 1971). This affirmed the central principle that "sacramental initiation is complete in baptism," and recommended not only that unconfirmed children should be admitted to communion on the basis of their baptism, but also that confirmation should not be required for all of those baptized as adults. In 1971–72 in England, there was also a change made by General Synod in the canons which thereafter gladly and unambiguously welcomed baptized communicants of other denominations to receive the sacrament at our eucharistic celebrations.

---

[17]It is fascinating now to read the review comment of Cyril Pocknee (a lesser "Mason-Dix" man) on *The Seal of the Spirit*. Pocknee termed it: "the last and most skilful rearguard action on the part of the more conservative element of the Church of England who are now in retreat" (quoted in Leonel Mitchell, *Baptismal Anointing*, Alcuin Club Collections No.48 [London: Alcuin/SPCK, 1966], 188).

[18]I was myself helping out on the Church of England Liturgical Commission at the time, as we were engaged in re-touching the aborted 1959 proposals for a new attempt at authorization. Acts 8 was not being cited; but other suggestions that the laying on of hands is the candidate's Pentecost were. The Series 2 services were much improved in the process, and, when they were completed, I included merely a note of dislike (see my *Liturgy for Initiation: The Series 3 Services*, Grove Booklet on Ministry and Worship No.65 [Bramcote, Notts.: Grove, 1979]).

Since the early 1970s, the practice that would allow (sometimes only just allow) the continuance of a two-stage theology has continued on previously acquired momentum (sustained virtually till the present day by an episcopate "formed" prior to 1970), but its momentum has been slowed by various braking forces. Among them, I draw attention to the following:

1. The growth of treating baptism as the sole sacramental prerequisite for receiving communion, along with statements on the subject such as the Boston Statement (1985) and the "Knaresborough Report" in England (1985). Even in the month before I originally drafted this chapter, both the Church in Wales Governing Body and the Church of Ireland General Synod had been showing a lively interest in this practice.

2. Similarly, episcopal confirmation has generally not been required of guests at Anglican eucharists, over which the post-1870, anglo-catholic reading of the "confirmation rubric" had previously run rampant (cf. the row over the "Kikuyu Communion" in 1913).

3. Whilst the finally authorized American Episcopal *BCP* in 1979 (following the "Zebra Book" of 1973) retained the laying on of hands on all at baptism (even on infants), the separate "confirmation" service was placed not with initiation but instead in the section entitled "Pastoral Offices."

4. In the Canadian *Book of Alternative Services* of 1985, the laying on of hands was *not* required of those baptized as adults, they being admitted to communion without this ceremony.[19] The separate service of confirmation for those baptized as infants was placed not in with baptism but in the section entitled "Episcopal Offices."[20]

5. The Lima text (1982) is ambivalent (and actually not fully entitled to all the praise heaped on it). Under "II," "III" and part of "IV"

---

[19]See the Toronto Statement, 1.18: "...the administration of confirmation at or following adult baptism is unnecessary and misleading, and should be discontinued"; also the "Ely" recommendations cited previously.

[20]See the Toronto Statement, 1.19: "Confirmation therefore stands as a pastoral office in its own right, and not as a part of the initiatory process." (Note the contrast with the Church of England's texts and proposals.)

(paras. 2-13) the whole discussion is based upon baptism *being* baptism, a single, once-for-all act. All the discussion of faith, conversion, of the gift of the Spirit, apparently relates to such a single act; and all the references to the scriptures are of baptismal and "one-staging" passages. So all thus far appears univocal and clear on that particular issue. But it is all contradicted in paragraph 14. Suddenly the text lapses into "Christians differ in their understanding of where the sign of the gift of the Spirit is to be found. Different actions have become associated with the giving of the Spirit...." And in paragraph 20 there appears worse still: "Some churches consider that Christian initiation is not complete without the sealing of the baptized with the gift of the Holy Spirit...." This kind of inflation of a postbaptismal ceremony in turn casts doubt upon everything said in such an apparently unqualified way about baptism itself in paragraphs 2-13.[21]

The first International Anglican Liturgical Consultation in Boston in 1985 (the findings of which were re-endorsed by the Toronto Consultation in 1991) included in its recommendations: "vii. That each Province clearly affirm that confirmation is not a rite of admission to communion, a principle affirmed by the bishops at Lambeth in 1968."[22] In this, as in various other reports, the centre of attention is baptism, and admission to communion springing from baptism. Once these landmarks have been established, confirmation becomes something handled more or less in passing. It is treated not as something vitally important to a scriptural and principled ordering of the church, but more as something which has

---

[21]In *Ecumenical Perspectives on Baptism, Eucharist and Ministry* (1983), David Holeton contributed a learned, panoramic, pastoral, and phenomenological essay on confirmation. For what it does, it is marvellous. This reader could not help wishing, however, that: a) he had been more dogmatic about what positions were credible and what not, and b) he had addressed himself to the Lima text in relation to confirmation which, as far as I can see, he did not do, and thus it escaped his dissectory processes. (It is perhaps unfair to complain of Homer nodding, and it is certainly the more notable for being so rare. But how his scalpel might have exposed the fudge on this occasion!)

[22]For the Boston recommendations see *Nurturing Children...*, Study No.44, Colin Buchanan, ed. (Bramcote, Notts: Grove, 1985), 49. These are repeated in *Christian Initiation in the Anglican Communion*, 25. The Boston Statement itself wrote an epitaph on "Mason-Dix": "The foundation upon which the 'Mason-Dix' approach was ostensibly based, historical enquiry, proved to be its weakest dimension."

a negotiable pastoral role within the life of the church; it is not of com-mandment, and ranks as important *only in the sense that it must not be allowed to become too important*. The emphasis is, therefore, often upon what confirmation cannot and must not do or be thought to secure, as a corrective to the appalling over-bidding of the "Mason-Dix" era.

7. Also in 1985 came the Church of England's report, *Communion before Confirmation?* (CIO, 1985). This working party, under the chairman-ship of the then Bishop of Knaresborough, unanimously found that bap-tism alone is the basis for admission to communion. Its treatment of confirmation closely paralleled the Boston findings. It expressed, more-over, a broad hope that, if its provisions for admission to communion long before the existing age of confirmation were brought into use, then the age of confirmation would move upwards and the rite would become a genuine occasion for mature decision, and that it would be by confir-mation that Anglican Christians would be enfranchised within the church structures. The General Synod "took note" of the report in November 1985, and it then lay with the House of Bishops until July 1991.

8. The 1988 Lambeth Conference Report included a statement on liturgy in its "Mission and Ministry" section, and I was myself secretary of the group which compiled the statement. In paragraph 192 we said: "Bap-tism by water is the scriptural sacrament of once-for-all initiation into Christ and into his Body."[23] Later paragraphs reassert this uniqueness and completeness of baptism whilst not totally escaping, though certainly minimizing, a fudge in relation to confirmation. In particular, the group was pressured by the Mission and Ministry sub-plenary section not to air the Canadian *BAS* pattern of adult initiation. (Some bishops in the sec-tion who were not on our Group did not want to know what was actually happening in Canada, and it had to be suppressed.[24])

---

[23]See *The Truth Shall Make You Free* (London: ACC, 1989), 70.

[24]The "experiential" factor was again at work. Bishops show extreme nervousness about anything which might appear to touch confirmation, and it was easy in the section, which was surveying drafts from our Group very summarily, to appeal to that nervousness. The Conference revealed a triple difficulty about making points which might vary or alter confirmation when bishops are running the discussion: a) bishops are usually over 50 (or over 60) and so have imbibed some "Mason-Dix" virus in their own training; b) the "experiential" factor is week by week reinforcing their position about confirmation;

9. The Toronto Consultation itself became the next major place of inter-Anglican theological proclamation about Christian initiation, and it is extensively surveyed and portrayed in this volume of essays. It consciously echoed the findings of the Boston Consultation of six years earlier. It will suffice here to collect a *catena* of materials relating to confirmation.

The Recommendations

(only two of the seven mentioned confirmation):

c. Baptism is complete sacramental initiation and leads to participation in the eucharist. Confirmation and other rites of affirmation have a continuing pastoral role in the renewal of faith among the baptized but are in no way to be seen as a completion of baptism or as necessary for admission to communion.[25]

g. The pastoral rite of confirmation may be delegated by the bishop to a presbyter.

The Statement:

...There is little warrant in Scripture, the Reformers, or in the Prayer Book tradition itself, to support the notion that the imposition of hands somehow completes baptism and concludes the process of Christian initiation... (1.16).

...With this...understanding of baptism [that it admits to communion], the pressure for early confirmation is relieved so that the rite may actually express a *mature* ratification of baptismal faith (1.17).

...Given this understanding of the rite [that those baptized as infants may ratify their baptismal faith as adults], the administration of confirmation at

---

c) they are rarely reading the literature on the subject as the teachers of liturgy must (and very few liturgists ever become bishops—and no one was ever made bishop *because* of his liturgical knowledge).

[25]Four members of the Consultation dissented from this recommendation, and their names are recorded in the published edition. They proposed an alternative text which would have kept the substance of the recommendation finally approved. The Consultation members voted this out by a majority, however, and the four were left to dissent. But they had very nearly got there.

or following infant baptism is unnecessary and misleading, and should be discontinued... (1.18).

Confirmation therefore stands as a pastoral office in its own right, and not as part of the initiatory process. If the title "confirmation" is retained, the status of the rite as a pastoral office must nevertheless be clearly understood (1.19).

(In addition there is a brief historical outline in 3.1 to 3.5, largely clearing away misapprehensions, a survey of the whole spectrum of possible current views in 3.15 to 3.18, and a mention of confirmation in connection with reception from other denominations in 3.22.)

Whilst much assimilation is still to come and some division of opinion still clearly exists, and whilst Anglican ecclesiastical inertia remains most awesome, yet the directions appear well set. Indeed, if this were another field of reform, it is likely that the term "reception" would be invoked; that is, that we (undefined) *know* what is right, and we are sure that as others come to a right mind also, so the doctrine will be duly "received." It is distrust of the mischievously altered use of the term "reception" which inhibits me from using it (here and elsewhere), and not any lack of conviction as to the direction in which we are going.

Residual (and virulent) two-stage elements

The present situation, however, still involves division; consequently, we must address the continuing two-stage features. The momentum acquired in those eighty years of theological ascendancy has not all disappeared at one breath. In some places, in fact, two-staging has acquired some minor, new impetus, even whilst its old momentum was running down. I list a series of influences upon the situation:

1. The first is the power of the concept of an originally "integrated rite" which in later years "disintegrated" and is now being "reintegrated."[26]

---

[26]The historical assertion being made here is open to investigation and, of course, tends to fall at the first fence (see *Anglican Confirmation*, 6-17, and the Toronto Statement 3.1-3). But the terminology of "disintegrated" and "reintegrated" has had a further subtle effect, for there is a subliminal moral judgement conveyed by these words. "Integrated" tends to be seen as a positive word, "disintegrated" as a negative one.

This concept (which was not popularized much earlier than Dix, and reached its zenith well after Dix's time) still runs strong. *In the beginning it was not so*, however, and the first and second centuries must be viewed as the *primitive* church, not the early third century.[27]

2. A second influence is the persistence of ceremonial which is less-than-a-sacrament. Not only do Anglicans generally still expect those baptized as adults also to be confirmed (though for what purpose is wholly unclear, unless it be "Mason-Dix" ideology), some also show signs of wanting to add anointing to both baptism and confirmation.[28] This situation can quickly bring us back to the old problems with the signing of the cross after baptism. The Puritan issue (met in the American *BCP* of 1790) was that a secondary ceremony which was *of commandment* purported to be part of the dominical sacrament, which it is not. It is well attested that since then many have thought that the sign of the cross *is* the sacramental sign in baptism; and a rationale which teaches that a ceremony is not requisite before God, but is enforced by the church, gives out a very uncertain sound.[29]

(The reverse effect is achieved if we discuss how baptism during the early centuries become "cluttered" with other ceremonies [negative], and later became "uncluttered" [positive], before being "recluttered" in Anglican history.)

[27]See, for instance, the citation from Argenti in an earlier footnote, where he claims "...from the third century of our era." That to an Orthodox (if it is true history, and there are some muddy spots here) is decisive as autonomous tradition. To an Anglican, however, that is not so.

[28]I confess I am also astonished to encounter rites, such as have just been approved in Wales, where an ecumenical provision includes a *mandatory* imposition of hands immediately after baptism.

[29]It was delightful to me at Boston and Toronto to probe a little at the position of Leonel Mitchell, who some time ago wrote the major work *Baptismal Anointing*. To this day, he strongly advocates anointing at and with baptism, but limits his advocacy and argues that: a) baptism is baptism, even without anointing (his illustration is that a eucharist even without a reading of the gospel is a eucharist, though he does not like to think of such a defective rite); b) such anointing belongs in, with, and to baptism itself, and is the lesser part of a single rite which cannot be separated from it to become a kind of confirmation, nor be treated as a second half of baptism giving "completion" to an otherwise incomplete sacrament. Mitchell is therefore a signatory of the Boston and Toronto recommendations and Statements. I stick to my own caution about rubrics which require ceremonies which scripture and sound theology do not require, however. Such rubrics easily become the basis of a changed theology by those less sophisticated than Leonel Mitchell (as, for instance, happened with the 1662 requirement of confirmation for those baptized in "Riper Years").

3. This effect is increased where vast claims are made for the chrism of confirmation. In the Church of England such chrismation is allowed by an opening note in the rite, but that small gap has since had to accommodate a coach and horses. There are prayers around the dioceses for use at the Maundy Thursday rite for new oils (largely drawn from Rome) which apparently teach that the anointing at confirmation is *the* great time of the coming of the Holy Spirit. Yet the use of chrism only occurs in about one parish in twenty, and when it is used it has no liturgical accompanying prayer or declaratory formula whatsoever. The congregation in general, therefore, would hardly know it is there. (The Canadian *BAS* makes a slight and slightly ambiguous bow in the direction of chrism in the provision for blessing oils, but allows for its use at baptism alone.)

4. The matter is not helped by the episcopal concern about "the bishop's role in initiation." I would urge that Anglicans, and especially bishops, look hard at this, and see if there is anything of substance in it.[30] In biblical terms it is very doubtful, and a new convert would only think episcopally if told to do so by those receiving him or her. To enter into the life of the church through one sacrament of baptism, and to become, thereby, participants in the other sacrament at the Lord's table, *is* to be fully in communion with the church and, *ipso facto*, with the bishop.

The Toronto Statement examines closely (in paras. 3.33-40) the claims being made, and concludes in broad terms that the role of the chief pastor is in no way endangered if functions are delegated by him or her. Hence it is that Recommendation (g) can open the idea of confirmation itself being exercised by presbyters, a practice well established in the Roman Catholic Church but sufficient to cause the sky to fall in the Anglican.

---

[30]Quite apart from anything else, it is in many situations highly inconvenient. There are two alternative ways of administering adult initiation in a consistent way. One is to give baptism "on the spot," wherever a new convert is found (but bishops are not usually ready to drop everything in their schedules and come up to 1000 miles to give baptism); the other way is to move toward Easter baptisms everywhere (but, again, the bishop is not able to be in many places at one time). Either of these possibilities, then, is self-defeating. It is clear that, if bishops are persuaded that their touch, given either at or after baptism, is somehow crucial to the standing of young Christians within the life of the church, then we are very nearly back at a covert "two-staging" rite.

5. I suspect also that we may be in some danger from the *RCIA* lobby (though I write with the greatest of admiration for the pastoral concerns of the philo-catechumenate school). The "stepped" approach to adult initiation runs risks in its liturgical drafting and the message of its structuring of not only ascribing separate, further, postbaptismal benefits to confirmation (which the Roman Catholic Church does attempt to do), but also of doing so in a "polarized" way, where (as in that *fons et origo* in Acts 8) the two stages are far separated from each other.

6. There are also problems to work through in the growing notion that the laying on of hands may not be a once-for-all-life ceremony, but may be repeatable. That is fully in line with the flexibility of scripture in this area, but it will be no gain if *either* one of the times of laying on hands proves on inspection to be *the* "seal of the Spirit" or, alternatively, if it is not defined which one is vital. However, it is certain that a minimum of one such administration is necessary for the recognition that confirmation has somewhere been given. A *program* of theoretically repeatable rites will do nothing but confuse if its proponents or chief practitioners still use once-for-all-life sacramental terminology. If the once-for-all-life concept is abandoned (along with "character," etc., terminology), then it will be no longer possible to describe any Christian as "confirmed" (any more than it would currently be possible or desirable to distinguish the "anointed" or even the "blessed" from the "unanointed" or "unblessed"). And conversely, whilst the status of "confirmed" remains, then some once-for-all-life rite must bear that title.

7. Next we have the old rite with yet a further rationale. Aidan Kavanagh has propounded a theory that the laying on of the episcopal hand is in fact the "coming to the bishop's hand" of the newly baptized, or, to use his more rigorous term, a "dismissal." Thus, it is a ceremony illustrative of baptism and properly going with it—not the *locus* for the illapse of the Spirit but a liminal ceremony ushering the newly baptized from the fountain to the table. Kavanagh writes that if we restored the ancient significance, "it might then become possible for people to hear what confirmation has to say, namely that baptism and eucharist are the premier sacraments of Christian initiation, and confirmation itself nothing more nor less than the Roman Catholic Church's way of linking the two."[31] This appears to be very close to declaring the rite to be con-

---

[31]*Confirmation: Origins and Reform* (New York: Pueblo, 1988), 111.

tingent, domestic, and negotiable. However, the effect is to bind confirmation more closely into the baptismal initiatory process, and Kavanagh can even suggest that first communion should *never* be allowed to precede confirmation.[32] Thus whilst he evades any historical connection between the laying on of the hand and the coming of the Spirit,[33] he appears to fall back into the trap of a *necessary*, secondary ceremony following baptism. His thesis has had a certain appeal for those romantics who, nevertheless, recognize that a full-blown "Mason-Dix" is no longer sustainable, but want confirmation to be around and to mean at least something.[34]

8. The last bastion of resistance to change is to be found in the Church of England and most notoriously in the public response of the House of Bishops to the Knaresborough proposals. Whilst diocesan synod after diocesan synod were passing resolutions calling for the implementation of the so-long-delayed Knaresborough proposals, the House of Bishops finally compiled the following resolutions to bring to the General Synod in July 1991:

That this Synod

(a) affirm the traditional sequence of baptism-confirmation-admission to communion as normative in the Church of England;

(b) accept that within this sequence confirmation can take place at an early age when this is deemed appropriate by the parish priest and the bishop;

---

[32]Kavanagh (p.110) is drawing out a parallel with the Orthodox "seal." This is, of course, very unlike the developed Roman Catholic practice of the last one thousand years.

[33]Whilst fully aware of Tertullian, for instance, he nevertheless finds a propaganda purpose behind Innocent I's citation of Acts 8:14-17, the first recorded dependence upon Acts 8 for episcopal handlaying (Kavanagh, 57). But *why* did Tertullian associate the handlaying with the illapse of the Spirit? I am sure there is a reason which will easily allow us to treat Tertullian's account as historically conditioned and therefore not binding. Kavanagh, however, is so determinedly unpneumatic in relation to the handlaying that he does not even discuss the significance of an allegedly pneumatic instance.

[34]See, for instance, David Stancliffe in his chapter on confirmation in the recent *Liturgy for a New Century*, Alcuin Club Collections No.70 (London: SPCK, 1991). The Kavanagh view gets aired, with attribution, in the Toronto Statement at 15.6, thus completing the spectrum of views (likely and unlikely) from which, if there is to be confirmation, the best candidate must be chosen.

(c) agree that experiments of admission to communion before confirmation should be discontinued at a rate which gives due regard to the pastoral difficulties in the individual dioceses and parishes;

(d) ask the Liturgical Commission to prepare a series of rites...for the renewal of baptismal vows, for the reception of members of another Church, and for reconciliation and healing;

(e) [this concerned patterns of nurture].

Whilst the House of Bishops was not corporately bound by this composite motion, the Synod was somewhat thrown by it. The House of Bishops had done a full reverse-turn, disregarding recent scholarship, diocesan motions, the Boston findings, overseas experience, Knaresborough, and the lot. In the event, the Synod did three things of consequence: i) it removed the back-tracking clause (c) from the motion; ii) it added a new clause after (d) above to "ask the Liturgical Commission to prepare a rite of Adult Commitment..."; iii) having then passed the composite motion, it voted on the Rochester diocesan "following" motion:

That this Synod request the House of Bishops to prepare draft regulations that enable children to be admitted to Holy Communion before confirmation, so that discussion can take place within the Church and conditions for such admission, if any, can be considered.

This motion went to a count by Houses, where the upshot was:

	Ayes	*Nays*
Bishops	7	34
Clergy	112	105
Laity	116	102

It was thus defeated heavily in the House of Bishops and, as a result, fell just short of an overall majority. Perhaps a marker had been put down.

So how fares confirmation itself in all this? A large part of the debate seemed to be handling the question: How can confirmation as we know it be defended?[35] Indeed, the Knaresborough proposals have been treated

---

[35]This was more or less explicit in the speech of the Bishop of Coventry, quoted in a previous footnote, and in various other episcopal speeches. But no scriptural or patristic evidence was adduced for that which was being defended.

by the House of Bishops as first and foremost an attack on confirmation. It is clear in (a) and (b) of the main motion that the bishops of the Church of England did not particularly object to lowering the age at which baptized children would be first receiving communion, so long as they could still confirm such children as the means of admitting them. The upshot is, of course, that the minimum age of confirmation might well go down to seven or some such age. The concept of confirmation as a mature ratification of baptismal faith would be further off than ever, and the amendment to bring in a ''Rite of Adult Commitment'' was openly intended as a corrective or supplement to an immature confirmation.

The complexities of all this defy the imagination, and, as a way of preserving the common traditional discipline (which is how it was presented), it is wholly absurd. In addition, there was a cheerful ignoring of all the rest of the Anglican communion.[36] The crucial conclusion (very obvious in the voting on the Rochester diocesan motion) is that the House of Bishops must have confirmation. Yet the Synod debate did not close the door entirely to reform, and particularly the excision of that clause to end all ''children in communion before confirmation'' parish projects was significant. The great hope must be that the Toronto Statement will itself be taken seriously in England, particularly as it was signed by so many official members of the Church of England Liturgical Commission.

So there are many obstacles to progress in England, and quite a confused undergrowth of ideologies, policies, and practices to encounter in order to effect change. The big hope must be that the Toronto State-

---

[36]It was of course alleged that confirmation of twelve-year-olds and of older teenagers also had almost ceased in some parts of the world where they had been admitted to communion early. To that extent it *might* be said that the pastoral role for confirmation envisaged in Knaresborough and Toronto would not work out. Certainly we need more surveys of the sort the Archbishop of New Zealand is providing. But meanwhile the Church of England has to ask itself: a) how many children of twelve years and under are coming to confirmation nowadays? b) how many of them are still regular communicants at age sixteen or seventeen? c) if teenagers are going to lapse, is it better that they should have been confirmed prior to lapsing or not? and d) are we in fact *sure* we ourselves have a pastorally successful (as well as biblically impeccable) discipline in place? We might also ask ourselves whether, if there do happen to be those in New Zealand or the United States who grow up baptized, believing, and communicant, but do not, as it happens, ever get confirmed, there is any great loss to the individual or the church. *Does* confirmation have any revealed and commanded status or not?

ment will itself facilitate the process. If it provokes Anglicans to have a worldwide view and thus to escape from a provincial parochialism, then clearing the undergrowth will at least come onto the agenda.

On the worldwide scene itself, despite all the contrary factors listed above which slow down the process, the direction is clearly set. The theological changes since 1970 move on securely, and Toronto takes its place in that ongoing march, setting signposts for confirmation which the practice of the provinces will surely follow in due course.

Summary

I conclude that the Thirty-Nine Articles and the 1604 catechism had it right: There are *two* sacraments of the gospel—baptism and the Lord's supper—and the outward sacramental sign in baptism is solely the administration of water (in the appropriate liturgical context). Toronto (and I) would want to go further and then assert that admission to baptism in principle *is* admission to the Lord's table, and that infants and children can qualify for admission to both sacraments as members of the body of Christ in believing homes.

Where, then, is confirmation? It is excluded, or excluded at least as being a requisite component of initiation or a completion of baptism, or as in any way the necessary door of admission to communion. It cannot have these initiatory roles; to create them is to place upon it a weight it cannot sustain.

There is a case for a pastoral ceremony (even an episcopal one) for the candidate's ratifying and the church's recognizing baptismal faith at the age of discretion for those who have been baptized and become communicant in younger years. The laying on of hands would be wholly appropriate here. There may also well be a case for restoring the lapsed, renewing baptismal vows, and even welcoming the newcomer who is "joining" the Anglican church, with a similar ceremony. But such ceremonies have no standing as scriptural and catholic sacraments; they have no promise of "inward grace"; they must not be a necessary (as opposed to illustrative) part of sacramental initiation; they must not be wished on those who do not need them (particularly on those baptized as adults); and they must not be made a *sine qua non* in reunion negotiations. And at each and every point in this conclusion, the Toronto Statement points in the right direction.

There is in this statement a very explicit program for hard reform. It has been part of the glory of Anglicanism to be able to reform its tradi-

tions in each generation, and often to be able to do so country by country as the vision has grasped bolder spirits in one land than it has so far
done in another. The Toronto Statement at large, and its handling of
confirmation in particular, provides a good instance of this capability.
The thin edge of the wedge had been driven far into the practice of some
provinces since 1970, and Toronto now furthers the reform by driving
a theological wedge into the thinking of us all. Certainly, much existing
Anglicanism is characterized by soft-headed romanticism, mindless conservatism, theological muddling, or knee-jerk defensiveness, and our confirmation inheritance is no exception. Yet the Toronto Statement is urging
us into hard-headed, clear-eyed, critical engagement with this received
traditional inheritance. Province by province, step by step, there should
be a God-given critical response.

IV   Rites of Initiation

Liturgical Tradition and Recent Anglican Liturgical Reforms
Thomas J. Talley

The process of becoming a Christian preoccupies contemporary liturgical reform, as does study of the tradition of what liturgical literature in
this century has generally called "the rites of Christian initiation." The
Liturgical Commission of the Church of England has observed that, in
the early centuries, this term, "though not unknown, was neither normal nor common."[1] That is true if we are thinking of just that phrase,
but the idea of initiatory ritual, and the broader terminological vocabulary that was employed regarding it, is more evident in the early literature, than the Liturgical Commission suggests.

A recently published collection of selected works by Pierre-Marie Gy
includes an essay on the Christian notion of initiation that traces the use
of the idea of initiation in relation to baptism from the apologists to the
post-Vatican II era.[2] It is interesting to note that reference to baptism
as initiation disappears in the medieval period and is rare in the period
of the Reformation. Even now, to speak of rites of Christian initiation
is likely to seem problematic in some parts of our communion. This situation was reflected at the second International Anglican Liturgical Consultation at Brixen four years ago. There, in the course of an extensive
plea for liturgical indigenization, Professor Elisha Mbonigaba of Uganda
said:

> New liturgies have used the title "Initiation" for the rite of Christian bap-
> tism, which is the rite of naming and incorporation into the Christian church.
> Initiation in most African societies refers to circumcision and other rites that
> come at the age of adulthood. This comes after other rites of incorporation
> that are done at and after birth, like naming and weaning. I am not quite

---

[1] *The Alternative Service Book: A Commentary by the Liturgical Commission* (London:
CIO, 1980), 105.

[2] "La notion chrétienne d'initiation," *La liturgie dans l'histoire* (Paris: Editions du Cerf,
1990), 17-39. This essay originally appeared in *La Maison-Dieu* 132 (1977), 33-54.

sure whether they would be called initiation, and yet they are very important. An indigenous liturgy of baptism would therefore need to use all symbols of incorporation before and after birth, including naming.[3]

Those familiar with the Prayer Book tradition back to 1552 will not, of course, find it surprising that the sacrament of holy baptism can be seen as a naming ceremony. From the second book of Edward VI to the Prayer Book of 1662 (and in much more recent revisions in many provinces), it is at the point of baptism itself that the priest first demands of the godparents: "Name this child." It has been the naming at the very point of baptism that has given rise to the rather bizarre custom of referring to the ceremonial naming of warships and other such vessels as their "christening." Even if the champagne bottle breaks on cue, the battleship is not thereby made a member of Christ!

Earlier than 1552 the English liturgy retained at least the vestiges of the mainstream tradition that distinguished the rite of baptism from preliminary enrolment *by name* in the catechumenate. In the first *Book of Common Prayer* (1549), while the Sarum Manual's separate title *"ad faciendum catechumenum"* had been dropped, it was well before the baptism itself, and at the door not the font, that the priest asked by what name the candidate would be known. Then, addressing the child by that name, the priest signed its forehead and breast reciting the formula that from 1552 onward, in a revised text without the name, replaced the chrismation formula following the actual baptism.

In 1549 the naming of the child was not, therefore, at the baptism but at what can still be recognized as enrolment in candidacy, the final stage of the catechumenate.[4] It was followed by a prayer, exorcism, and the *traditiones* of the gospel, Lord's prayer, and creed, features of the major lenten scrutiny of baptismal candidates in the west in documents dating back to at least the late sixth century. By that time, of course, the catechumenate was already in serious decline and those enrolled as candidates for baptism were commonly small children. That fact only

---

[3] "Indigenization of the Liturgy," *A Kingdom of Priests: Liturgical Formation of the People of God*, Alcuin/GROW Liturgical Study 5 (Grove Liturgical Study No.53), Thomas J. Talley, ed. (Bramcote, Notts.: Grove Books, 1988), 44-45.

[4] Here, as in the medieval Latin books, a much longer process has been conflated. Ambrose insisted that those to be baptized at Easter give in their names at Epiphany.

underscores the importance attached to the process of formation in faith leading to baptism, exemplified in the retention, however vestigial, of these catechetical materials in the sixteenth century.[5] Even when infant baptism became virtually universal, it remained an exception within the tradition, or, as Aidan Kavanagh has characterized it, "a benign abnormality."[6]

Curiously, however, the assignment of the giving of the name to the moment of baptism itself, and the effective obliteration of the catechumenal rite, had the effect of reducing the liturgical *function* of baptism to enrolment in the catechumenate, the theology of baptism to the contrary, notwithstanding. If catechesis was not required before baptism, it was now required after baptism and before confirmation; in England it was confirmation, not baptism, that admitted to the eucharist. The giving of the name, the important and ancient commitment to candidacy for baptism, was now to many eyes the significant moment of the baptismal rite itself. Baptism was now, as Professor Mbonigaba observed, a rite of naming, whereas initiation into the full life of the church was now available only to those who had come to faith through catechesis consummated in confirmation.

That pattern, familiar to Anglicans for four hundred years, came under critical scrutiny with the flowering of liturgical studies in this century; such studies have had an important impact on many reforms of the baptismal liturgy. The most important of these, surely, was the Roman Catholic *Rite for the Christian Initiation of Adults* drafted by Professor Balthasar Fischer of Trier, in which the normative character of adult baptism became once again manifest in liturgical patterns that reach through admission to the catechumenate and enrolment in candidacy, to the initiatory mystery of baptism, confirmation, and communion, and conclude in the *mystagogia* that reveal the initiatory mystery as paradigm of the life in Christ now begun. Here baptism, confirmation, and

---

[5]In the sixteenth century we have only compressed vestiges. The maintenance of the full lenten scrutinies, however, (noted by John the Deacon, c.500) was of great concern still in the Carolingian period, as has been shown recently by Pierre Riche, "Faut-il baptiser les enfants?" *Rituels: Mélanges offerts au Père Gy, O.P.*, Paul de Clerck and Eric Palazzo, eds. (Paris: Editions du Cerf, 1990), 449-53.

[6]*The Shape of Baptism* (New York: Pueblo, 1978), 110. At the Canterbury Congress of the Societas Liturgica, Kavanagh used the somewhat softer expression, "a benign anomaly."

communion are viewed as inseparable dimensions of one ritual process, and a simple presbyter who baptizes an adult is required (not merely allowed) to confirm the initiate immediately. The Roman Catholic Church, at least, is now prepared to say that the bishop is only the "original" minister of confirmation, not, as was formerly the style, the "ordinary" minister of that rite.

This means that, of the major Christian Communions, the Anglican stands alone in believing that only a bishop can confirm.[7] Even if it were true that Anglicans are agreed that only a bishop can be the minister of confirmation, that would seem to be about the extent of our agreement regarding that rite. Whether confirmation is an aspect of Christian initiation, whether it is a sacrament, what (if anything) it has to do with the Holy Spirit, whether it is requisite for admission to communion: all these and other questions have failed to find consensus among us, even though such questions would seem to be considerably more fundamental than the question of who, if anyone, is going to perform the act.

Still, such uncertainty regarding confirmation is by no means unique to Anglicanism. Western scholastic sacramental theology, with conciliar authority since at least the *Decretum pro Armenis* at the Council of Florence (1438-45), has sought to obscure the peculiarity of occidental episcopal confirmation by identifying it with the postbaptismal chrismation performed by presbyters who baptize in the oriental rites (although Latin-rite presbyters also anoint with chrism after baptism). Confirmation, in fact, is a western peculiarity whose emergence as a "sacrament" has been traced with admirable clarity and precision by Gabriele Winkler.[8] We now recognize that the Pseudo-Isidorian Decretals, attributed to Miltiades, Bishop of Rome c.310-314, are parts of a sermon on confirmation preached in Gaul in the fifth century by one frequently identified as Faustus of Riez. These False Decretals were incorporated into the *Decretum* of Gratian and so found their way into the *Quatro Libri Sententiarum* of Peter Lombard, the twelfth-century text that was the basis for all scholastic theological education. Lombard's *Sentences* was also the text that first

---

[7]Attempts to defend this purely Anglican oddity by appeal to the episcopal consecration of the chrism employed after baptism by presbyters of other communions are simply embarrassing and approach superstition.

[8]"Confirmation or Chrismation? A Study in Comparative Liturgy," *Worship* 58 (1984), 2-17.

postulated the familiar catalogue of seven sacraments, confirmation among them.

Central to scholastic discussion of whether confirmation was a distinct sacrament was the supposed authority of Miltiades. The exposure of the False Decretals by the Centuriators of Magdeburg was not sufficient to challenge Lombard's list, by that time canonized at Trent. The fifteenth century had seen the introduction among the Bohemian Brethren of an imposition of hands on those children who had attained a sufficient age to make personal confession of the faith. This confession became the core concern of confirmation in the sixteenth century, even though Roman Catholics continued to speak of this rite as one of seven sacraments, and England continued the thirteenth-century insistence that it precede admission to communion.

Although the scholarly debate regarding confirmation has been carried on primarily among writers in the Church of England (Mason, Dix, Thornton, Lampe, Buchanan, among others), that debate seems thus far to have had little impact on liturgical patterns there. In the *Alternative Service Book* 1980 (*ASB*), at least, confirmation is still listed among "Initiation Services," and there is no indication that baptized persons, of whatever age, will be admitted to communion without it. As for baptism, the consignation (with optional anointing) may either precede the baptism in the old Syrian fashion or follow it as in early North Africa. Eschewing the *Apostolic Tradition*'s combination of those patterns, continued in the Latin rite to the Reformation, *ASB* is relieved of the need to distinguish two oils, and describes that used at either place as simply "oil blessed for this purpose."[9] Although the evidently normative rite unites in one service baptism, confirmation, and communion, the presuppositions of the English *Book of Common Prayer* regarding access of the unconfirmed to communion, the age of confirmands, and the minister of the rite, seem to remain largely undisturbed.

In North America the picture has been somewhat different. Already in the mid-1960s, the rubrical requirement linking confirmation to

---

[9] A similar provision for anointing at confirmation specifies that the oil was previously blessed by the bishop; but whether that applies to baptism as well is not clear. Although it is probably too early to rely on it as definitive, it is worthy of note that *Patterns of Worship* (London: Church House, 1989), in a sample service (no.13), refers only to the consignation before baptism, and there is no mention of anointing.

admission to communion was set aside in the United States; but that was the sole innovation to survive, in 1970, a first attempt to reunify baptism, consignation (optionally with chrism), and admission to communion.[10] A second proposal retained this unified initiatory rite but added a further order for episcopal "confirmation" of those baptized communicants prepared to make a mature public affirmation of their faith, an imposition of hands extended as well to those being received into communion from another church and to any seeking to return to the practice of the faith after having fallen away. Although in the final recension of the Prayer Book separate forms were provided for these three categories, later canonical definition gives assurance that any who have received the imposition of the bishop's hands with any of these forms are considered to be "confirmed" for all canonical purposes. Here, it is clear, we have to do not with an indelible sacrament but with a rite that gives formal expression to the bond between each communicant and the chief pastor of the local church (the bishop), whose blessing expresses his ratification of the already completed initiation.[11]

A rubric at the beginning of the baptismal rite declares: "Holy Baptism is full initiation by water and the Holy Spirit into Christ's body the Church." The candidates are individually presented by their sponsors by name and the initial supposition is that they will answer for themselves, those unable to answer being presented by name by their godparents (of whom special promises are required). There is no consignation before baptism but only the renunciations, promises, and credal confession (in which the entire congregation joins). After the baptism, follows the consignation/chrismation with that prayer of thanksgiving that, in one form or another, preceded the episcopal chrismation from the *Apostolic Tradition* through the Gelasian Sacramentary, to the medieval pontificals, and the rite of confirmation in the Prayer Books. Its transfer to the point of postbaptismal consignation (and optional chrismation)

---

[10]*Prayer Book Studies 18* (New York: Church Pension Fund, 1970), reprinted with the limitations imposed by the General Convention of 1970 in *Services for Trial Use* (New York: Church Hymnal Corp., 1971).

[11]That confirmation grew out of something like this has been argued by Aidan Kavanagh in *Confirmation: Origins and Reform* (New York: Pueblo, 1988). For the application of his argument to the Anglican situation see David Stancliffe, "Confirmation and its Future," *Liturgy for a New Century* (London: SPCK/The Alcuin Club, 1991), 71-81.

in this American rite is intended to identify that action with whatever postbaptismal consignation or chrismation has been regarded in the tradition as belonging to the initiatory sacrament. In effect, this baptismal rite follows general eastern tradition since the Jerusalem rite of Cyril's day.

A form for the episcopal consecration of chrism is provided following the thanksgiving over the water; but if the use of chrism is optional here, it was no less so in the rite of *Apostolic Constitutions* VII.22.3.[12] The eucharist resumes at the Peace and, while not specifically ordered, nothing hinders the first communion of all the baptized, of whatever age, at that service.[13]

The Anglican Church of Canada followed closely the developments in the United States, participating in the discussions at various points. It should not be surprising, then, that *The Book of Alternative Services* of the Canadian church, authorized in 1983, presents a baptismal liturgy very similar to that arrived at by the neighbour to the south. Here, too, confirmation, reception from another communion, and reaffirmation of baptismal responsibility are distinguished by the condition of the subject rather than the relation of those rites to the sacramental economy. As in the American book, these rites can be combined with the baptismal liturgy; they are also given separately in a section entitled "Episcopal Services." In neither the American nor the Canadian case, in contrast to that of the Church of England, is provision made for anointing at confirmation.

With apology to other possible solutions that have not been considered here,[14] we can say that the reforms seem to follow rather closely the presuppositions of the 1552/1662 Prayer Books, with their strong emphasis on confirmation as mature profession of faith and admission to communion, or, by contrast, we can give up confirmation as a dimension of Christian initiation and build instead a rite of baptism-consignation-communion along lines not unlike those common (although with

---

[12]Also optional there was a prebaptismal anointing with oil, with which was associated the gift of the Spirit.

[13]Directions for the communion of children not yet weaned are given in the Second Edition of *The Book of Occasional Services* (New York: Church Hymnal Corporation, 1988), 157.

[14]My best source for other provinces, I must confess, remains the excellent essay by David Holeton, "Christian Initiation in Some Anglican Provinces," *Studia Liturgica* 12.2/3 (1977), 129-150.

with significant variations) in east and west from late antiquity to the high Middle Ages (perhaps even at Rome, depending on our interpretation of John the Deacon).

What has not yet received focused attention in many parts of the communion is the possibility that conscious profession of faith is critical to normative baptismal commitment (although recognition of adult baptism as primary rather than exceptional is much more evident in all the new rites than it was in the past). In the Episcopal Church USA, a supplementary *Book of Occasional Services* provides the ritual forms for a catechumenal process inspired by the Roman Catholic *Rite of Christian Initiation of Adults*, and this has drawn significant attention.[15] The General Convention of 1988 mandated the revitalization of the catechumenal process as an evangelistic priority. To effect that mandate, an expanded edition of the *Book of Occasional Services* was published, offering, in addition to the process for unbaptized adults, adaptations of the catechumenal process for those preparing to return to the practice of the faith by reaffirmation of vows, and for parents of unbaptized children. In addition, the Office of Evangelism Ministries has issued a detailed manual entitled *The Catechumenal Process: Adult Initiation and Formation for Christian Life and Ministry*.[16]

It is interesting to note in the rubric of the second edition of the *Book of Occasional Services*, an acknowledgement of the possibility of an informed determination by parents to defer baptism, and provision for a ritual process, begun at the discovery of the pregnancy, leading not directly to baptism but to the admission of the newborn to the catechumenate.[17] That rite of admission includes the promise of the sponsors to support and guide the catechumen toward baptism, prayer for the catechumen, and the giving of the name with consignation, both celebrant and sponsors signing the catechumen with the sign of the cross on the forehead. With that possibility opened, parents may face more squarely what it is they seek in the baptism of their children and how they understand baptism to relate to regular communion. One suspects

---

[15](New York: Church Hymnal Corporation, 1979), 112-125.

[16](New York: Church Hymnal Corporation, 1990), the basic text prepared by Ann E.P. McElligott.

[17]*The Book of Occasional Services* (second edition, 1988), 158. For the rite of admission to the catechumenate, see p.115.

that many who bring infants to baptism continue to view that most powerful sign as only a naming ceremony at which godparental bonds are
instituted and the church's responsibility for the child's nurture is established. The possibility of the accomplishment of these ends by admission to the catechumenate will at least invite sober reassessment of the
nature and meaning of holy baptism and its relation to holy communion.

Radical solutions are rightly suspect, and we should perhaps aim for
no more than opening the possibility of recovering the main lines of the
patristic tradition which our liturgical studies have led us to respect more
than we do the scholastic formulations that accompanied such a tragic
decline of the tradition. The sixteenth century should have taught us that
in a time of ferment, liturgical reforms should seek to remove obstacles
to the movement of the Spirit, not to get it exactly (albeit locally) *right*
for all time. That movement of the Spirit in our history is what we call
"the tradition"; and quite apart from the varieties of practice insinu-
ated by local circumstances or by errors or failures of communication,
that tradition possesses a common, ritual core to the knowledge and
embrace of which the ecumenical imperative draws us, just because there
is one Lord, one faith, one baptism, one God and Father of us all.

Patterns of Christian Initiation
Kenneth W. Stevenson

In an important paper read at the 1977 meeting of the Societas Liturgica, Pierre-Marie Gy of the Liturgical Institute, Paris, drew attention to the way in which, during the nineteenth century, the term "initiation" entered the Christian vocabulary as an acceptable word, covering the way in which a new Christian was washed, anointed, and fed for the first time at the Lord's table.[1] The word "initiation" had, before then, a rather muddled application, sometimes referring to one or other of the sacraments in question, sometimes (as it still is) being used in a wider sense, in a context nearer that of Comparative Religions. It is remarkable that, in a century that has seen such an advance in this latter kind of study, "Christian initiation" has emerged as a proper term, to be applied without equivocation to the whole sweep of rites whereby new Christians are made.

It is the purpose of this paper to look at this "whole sweep" as it occurs in three quite different contexts: first, in historic Anglicanism, second, in the time of debate and adjustment since, and finally, in what is emerging today. As is always the case in liturgical study, what fascinates is not what is going on (apparently) on the surface of a new rite, but what is (actually) happening underneath.

Historic Anglicanism

The Book of Common Prayer (1662)[2] contains, grouped together, the following services, in sequence:

---

[1]Pierre-Marie Gy, "The Idea of 'Christian Initiation,' " *Studia Liturgica* 12 (1977):172-5. An expanded version of this paper appears as "La notion chrétienne d'initiation" in *La Maison-Dieu* 132 (1977):33-54 (= Pierre-Marie Gy, *La Liturgie dans l'histoire* (Paris: Cerf, 1990), 17-39).

[2]See comparative texts in F.E. Brightman, *The English Rite* II (London: Rivingtons, 1915), 724ff.

Infant Baptism (Public)
Infant Baptism (Private)
Baptism "of those of riper years"
Catechism
Confirmation.

Although the list is something we take for granted (whether we happen to like it or not), the very fact of this list contains some hidden lessons that need to be drawn out immediately. First, the two forms of Infant Baptism are distinguished by the social rather than the pastoral context of their celebration. It is a question of the new "public" versus "private" liturgical description, as opposed to the distinction made, for example, in the late eighth century *Gelasian Sacramentary of Gellone*, between the *Ordo baptisterii* and the *Ordo ad infirmum caticumenum faciendum sive baptizandum*.[3]

The contrast is even sharper when we note that the third order of baptism was only introduced in 1662 (the other forms being already present in 1549), and the very use of that curious expression "of riper years" reflects another pastoral sensitivity, as if it were a problem to formulate a satisfactory title for the service in question! "Riper" in late medieval English, when applied to persons, meant "fully developed in body or mind," "mature," "marriageable." It is still a moot point whether the arrival on the scene of this third order was motivated by a desire to baptize those unbaptized after insidious Anabaptist influence, or those unbaptized whom the empire-building English encountered in the colonies and plantations. Motives in Christianity are always, one senses, rather mixed!

That the Catechism should be placed between the third order of baptism and the order of confirmation is probably both accidental and intentional. It has to go somewhere, after all. It followed Private Baptism and preceded Confirmation in 1549 and 1552, and so it probably fitted best into the pastoral context of the average English parish of Restoration times, if it was closely linked with confirmation, a rite (be it noted) that now, for the first time, included the renewal of baptismal vows. Confirmation

---

[3]See texts in A. Dumas, *Liber Sacramentorum Gellonensis*, Corpus Christianorum, Series Latina CLIX (Turnolti: Brepols, 1981), 47ff., 312ff., 339ff.

had received its seal of approval, in articulating what Michael Ramsey once described as "conscious and intelligent faith."[4]

Such a cluster of rites, by its very nature, indicates that the Anglican reformers had not solved the problems of the medieval Catholic pattern. Under the supposed security of such a novelty as a book of *common* prayer lay history's unsolved dilemmas, a sort of residue of historic and new pastoral needs. Just as the aforementioned *Gelasian Sacramentary of Gellone* contained three patterns of baptism (the classic one—through Lent and Holy Week, culminating at the Easter Vigil; the ordinary form; the baptism of the infirm), so the Prayer Book puts together its own formulations, with new names and titles which indicate (perhaps) new pastoral perspectives; then it adds, at the last minute, the rite for "those of riper years," as if it were a reminder of an issue that would not go away, namely, that Christian initiation is not something that can be neatly packaged, as if it were a Christmas hamper ordered from Harrods.

It is worth pondering the Prayer Book pattern further by comparing it with the patterns of antiquity. Historians of the liturgy have delighted for more than a generation in seeing in the patristic pattern the genius of *phasing*[5]: the new Christian is admitted to the catechumenate, at the end of which comes baptism, confirmation, and the eucharist in one single liturgy, which is followed by mystagogy. The medieval pattern, retained in essence but adapted by the Anglican reformers, baptizes infants as an implied norm, catechises them later, after which they are confirmed, after which they receive communion—and all these actions, from baptism on, are phased throughout life's rich pattern, determined by the simple fact of getting older and growing up in the church. The phasing is still there, but it is of a different sort. The "riper years" order serves a threefold function: It asserts that the Prayer Book implied norm was already not functioning; it points back to the memory of a different way of making new Christians (just as the *Gelasian of Gellone* did, with its patristic norm sandwiched through the Lent-Holy Week-Easter liturgy); and (what is important for us), it points forward to an age in which,

---

[4]Review of Gregory Dix, *The Theology of Confirmation in Relation to Baptism* (London: Dacre, 1946) in the *Journal of Theological Studies* 47 (1946), 256.

[5]The classic treatment of this theme is in Aidan Kavanagh, *The Shape of Baptism: The Rite of Christian Initiation*, Studies in the Reformed Rites of the Catholic Church 1 (New York: Pueblo, 1978).

whether by the perils of Anabaptism, the proliferation of colonies, or the sheer fact of post-Christendom, a new and more ancient pattern has to emerge.

Highlighting the ambiguities of the Prayer Book pattern is not intended to heap praise upon it, least of all upon the "riper years" order which Frere himself wanted rewritten so that it spoke more directly to someone who *was* of "riper years."[6] I am simply using the tricks of the historian's trade to show that the primal Anglican system of 1549 could not carry the day and, by implication, that no one initiatory system can do so in any case.

Non-Juror neglected experiments

The Prayer Book of 1662 did not end the debate about how Christian initiation should be celebrated. The Non-Jurors, for instance, were known to be interested in enriching both the rites and the patterns of initiation. For want of a more accurate category, I want here to regard experimental Anglican rites of the eighteenth century as (broadly) Non-Juror.

John Henley,[7] eccentric that he was, produced a liturgy along pseudo-primitive lines which contained a lengthy anaphoral intercession, taken from *Apostolic Constitutions* VIII, in which prayer is offered for "the catechumens, the penitents, and those who are vex'd...." And that is not the end of the story. The 1734 Non-Juror eucharistic liturgy is more explicit, borrowing more directly from the same source but making the prayer optional, only to be used when the persons being prayed for actually existed:

Father, we pray unto thee
for the Catechumens of the Church,
that thou wouldest perfect them in the faith.[8]

---

[6]W.H. Frere, *Some Principles of Liturgical Reform* (London: Murray, 1911), 199ff.

[7]See text in W.J. Grisbrooke, *Anglican Liturgies of the Seventeenth and Eighteenth Centuries*, Alcuin Club Collections 40 (London: SPCK, 1958), 269.

[8]Grisbrooke, 312.

Thomas Rattray, the Scottish liturgiologist, in his own form of the eucharist, produces a similar petition similarly optional:

> Remember, O Lord, the Catechumens, and
> perfect them in the faith.[9]

It is hard to tell, when faced with such grandiose petitions with their impeccable liturgical antecedents, whether John Henley, the Non-Jurors, or indeed the godly scholar Rattray had congregations bulging with catechumens, queuing up for baptism at the Easter Vigil. One suspects not. But prone as we are these days to making the intercessions "relevant," we would be much the poorer without liturgies which prayed anachronistically, such as the Roman Rite which right up to the eve of the reforms of Pius XII prayed on Good Friday for catechumens who did not (yet) exist and for a Holy Roman Emperor long since dead and buried. Henley, the Non-Jurors, and Rattray may have been indulging in what Rowan Williams has eloquently called "liturgical hobbitry,"[10] but they kept alive a memory which was to become important in our own day.

The story of these off-beat creativities is incomplete, however, without taking note of the Catholic Apostolics. It really is amazing that long before the twentieth century churches started enthusing about one single Sunday eucharist at which all would communicate, and the revival of the catechumenate, both these themes should appear in the middle of the nineteenth century. The principal English editions of the *Liturgy and Other Divine Offices of the Church*[11] start in 1843, and move from then on through 1847, 1851, 1853, 1856, 1863, 1869, and (definitively!) 1880. It is clear that different patterns for initiation were being worked upon in the late 1840s; and in 1851 there appears a cluster of rites which has a very post-Vatican II hue, if one makes certain ecclesiological somersaults:

---

[9]Grisbrooke, 326.

[10]"Imagining the Kingdom: Some Questions for Anglican Worship Today," *The Identity of Anglican Worship*, K.W. Stevenson and B.D. Spinks, eds. (London: Mowbrays, 1991), 12.

[11]See K.W.Stevenson, "The Catholic Apostolic Church—Its History and Its Eucharist," *Studia Liturgica* 13 (1979), 21-45; see also an essay forthcoming in *Coena Domini II*.

The Order for Receiving a Catechumen

The Dedication of Catechumens previously to their Baptism

The Order for the Administration of Holy Baptism

The Order for Receiving in the Church such as shall have been Privately Baptized

The Benediction of such as, having been fully instructed in the Faith, are about to be Received to the Holy Communion

The Form of Committing to the Pastorship of the Church those who have been under the Instruction of the Evangelists

The Renewal of Vows and Dedication of those about to Receive the Laying on of Hands

The Order for the Laying on of Apostles' Hands.[12]

Not everyone would go through this maze of material; what is offered is a maximum rather than a minimum. For example, children would normally be baptized, receive the benediction at the age of eleven years before receiving communion regularly (it was at festivals only from infancy), and then receive the laying on of hands at the age of eighteen or more. Those brought into the church from outside would, by contrast, have to undergo the more elaborate scheme, which would be tailor-made to suit the individual's particular situation.

Since the Catholic Apostolics had worldwide aspirations as early as 1847, it is not incongruous, with the creative use of antiquity that is apparent in their liturgy as a whole, that they should attempt to enrich the somewhat stale Reformation inheritance of Anglicanism, as actually practised at the time, in order to produce a pattern of Christian initiation in keeping with their own reception of tradition and their changing perceptions of pastoral needs. The opening prayer in The Order for Receiving a Catechumen is a subtle blend of Cranmerian prose and a thoroughly patristic grasp of the catechumenate:

Almighty God, who willeth not that any should perish, but that all should come to the knowledge of the Truth, even of His Son Jesus Christ, who is the Way, the Truth, and the Life; And who hath given unto thee to believe His Word to desire instruction in the Faith, and to seek for His grace in Baptism; Of His great mercy grant unto thee all thy desire, and fulfil in thee the good pleasure of His Will.[13]

---

[12]*Liturgy and Other Divine Offices of the Church* (London: Pitmans, 1880), 363ff.

[13]*Liturgy and Other Divine Offices*, 363.

I have described the Catholic Apostolic liturgiography as a "creative use of antiquity." Another of its aspirations was to heal the divisions of historic Christianity. Although it has disappeared from the scene, the legacy is still with us. History may place that liturgiography as a strange offshoot of Anglicanism; my own suspicions, however, are that it has much in common with modern revisions in the way it followed their methods, though perhaps less critically. They were part of a family of liturgies whose creators saw the inadequacies of 1662, were in a position to use resources either inaccessible or inappropriate to the Caroline Restoration divines, and could see the seeds of a shift away from Christendom Christianity towards a world truly pluriform in its style and witness.

The Catholic Apostolics, strangely perhaps, do not mention the catechumenate in their (lengthy) eucharistic intercessions, even though mention is made (along eastern lines) of penitents and the possessed. In this respect they differ from the eighteenth-century antecedents cited earlier. But whatever their actual norm in Christian initiation (which one suspects was the traditional path of infant baptism through to adult membership), the fact that they had such a flexible cluster of rites, embodying a catechumenate, marks them off as, once again, a prophetic movement.[14]

One cannot leave the nineteenth century without taking note, in passing, of the important work of A.J.Mason, *The Relationship of Confirmation to Baptism*,[15] which was published in 1891 and dedicated to Edward Benson, Archbishop of Canterbury. In terms of the history of thinking about initiation, Mason begins the movement to restore the unity of baptism and confirmation, as the title suggests, a theme taken up with more force by Dom Gregory Dix in our own century.[16] It is a mine of information, for example, concerning Pacian of Barcelona and Zeno of

---

[14]See, for example, their *General Rubrics* (London: Strangeways, 1878), 78: "It is an ancient and godly rule of discipline, but by no means a necessary antecedent to baptism, that the candidates should be solemnly dedicated at the Altar a short time previously to their baptism." For a more detailed treatment of the Catholic Apostolic initiation rites as a whole, see Paul J.Roberts's Ph.D. dissertation, University of Manchester, England, 1990.

[15](London: Green, 1891).

[16]See Michael Ramsey's review of Gregory Dix's *The Theology of Confirmation in Relation to Baptism* in the *Journal of Theological Studies* 47 (1946), 253-6.

Verona. Although the ancient authors he cites deal repeatedly with the catechumenate, Mason does not discuss it, for the simple reason that it does not figure in his priorities. Because of the influence of his book and the learned tradition in which it stands, the fact that Mason does not deal with the catechumenate is of significance in itself.

The twentieth century

What will our own century look like from the perspective of a future generation? Whose doctoral dissertation will examine patterns of initiation as they have shifted over the years? In looking back at the nineteenth century and its close relationship with the twentieth in so many ways, Père Gy wrote of Romantic liturgists (thinking of men like Guéranger):

> ...the return to tradition which they set in motion was so deep, and in the event so authentic, that with the passage of time it led, by its fidelity, to a liturgical renewal which was so real that to refuse liturgical reform actually seemed like a departure from that tradition.[17]

When one reads W.H. Frere[18] on the need for a revised rite of adult baptism "to be modelled on the primitive services" (as we know the 1662 order was not), and his insistence on the importance that "ought to be laid on the immersion," that the rite ought to begin at the church door "with the reception of the candidate," that the renunciations should be made facing west, that the use of oil should be reconsidered—when all of this is considered, Gy's analysis of the momentum of looking at the tradition afresh takes on a poignant meaning.

The Anglican revisions of the 1920s took little notice of this, however. The antiquarian pattern of the Non-Jurors does recur in the 1920 *Eucharist in India*,[19] drafted by E.C. Ratcliff, in a more recognisably Eastern form,

---

[17]Pierre-Marie Gy, "The Liturgist's Task" in *Liturgy Reshaped*, K.W.Stevenson, ed. (London: SPCK, 1982), 12.

[18]*Some Principles of Liturgical Reform*.

[19]See text in J.C. Winslow, D.R. Athavale, J.E.G. Festing, E.C. Ratcliff, *The Eucharist in India: A Plea for a Distinctive Liturgy for the Indian Church with a Suggested Form* (London: Longmans, Green, 1920), 82ff.

on the model of St. James, with the dismissal of the catechumens in its historic position, but this was only optional.

The next step comes with the Second Vatican Council's *Constitution on the Sacred Liturgy* (1963) which contains the momentous words:

> The catechumenate for adults, comprising several distinct steps, is to be restored and brought into use at the discretion of the local ordinary.[20]

At the same time an adult rite for Christian initiation was to be drawn up, both on its own and also with the infrastructure of a catechumenate. It is needless here to chronicle the steps which led to the new initiation rites which ensued or the anomalies which remain inherent, both in terms of the relationship between the catechumenate and the infant rite, and the relationship of the bishop to these liturgies. Nonetheless, it is interesting to note the pressure that was building for the restoration of the catechumenate, for example in France in 1960—a sign of things to come.

How did Anglicans respond to this scene, where so much was shared both in a common desire to renew the liturgy by going back to its roots, and in a common world in which the notion of Christendom was on the wane? At first sight the picture looks as muddled and confusing as any attempt to formulate a worldwide Anglican policy about anything! *The Book of Common Prayer* (1979) of the American Church adheres to one rite of initiation, and bravely attempts to provide for a form of confirmation that "stretches" in different "directions" to include personal renewal as well as reception from other Christian churches. (This lead has been followed by Canada in 1985 and by other provinces.) On the other hand, the *Book of Occasional Services* (1979) of the American Church adapts the Roman Catholic catechumenate rites as a possible prelude to the rite of baptism, a provision both optional and imaginative. Another adaptation is to be found in *An Anglican Prayer Book* (1989) of the Province of Southern Africa.

At the other end of the scale, *The Alternative Service Book* (1980) of the Church of England provides a massive cluster of rites, richer than 1662 could ever be (but hardly as pluriform as the Catholic Apostolic Liturgy!). The list is formidable in length and for the sheer breadth of

---

[20]See *Vatican Council II: The Conciliar and Post-Conciliar Documents*, Austin Flannery, ed. (Collegeville: Liturgical Press, 1975), 21.

pastoral context: Thanksgiving for Childbirth, Thanksgiving after Adoption, Baptism and Confirmation with Holy Communion, Baptism and Confirmation without Holy Communion, Baptism and Confirmation at Morning or Evening Prayer, the Baptism of Children, the Baptism of Children at Morning or Evening Prayer, Confirmation with Holy Communion, Confirmation without Holy Communion, Readings, and the Renewal of Baptismal Vows on Various Occasions, ending with Conditional and Emergency Baptism. It seems likely that the revision of the book, projected for the year 2000, will adopt a different outlook, attempting to reflect a pluriform church that has taken greater account of the changes that have been going on in other Christian churches.

Are there some underlying lessons in this tale?

First, it needs to be noted that, if one looks under the surface, there are significant shifts in perspective. The mixture of scholarship, the possibility of liturgical change, and the needs of a new kind of world have all exerted pressures on the churches. The Anglican prayer books of the 1920s barely altered an iota in the basic thinking about initiation. The rites produced in the 1960s and 1970s, on the other hand, demonstrated a shift in two directions. One was towards a twofold provision of an "adult" rite of baptism-confirmation-eucharist alongside the Christendom model; the other is exemplified by the *ASB's* proliferation of pastoral rites around the time of birth, and the need for personal renewal. (The 1989 *New Zealand Prayer Book* reflects this even further.) Finally, there is another era, heralded (for Anglicans) by the 1979 American *Book of Occasional Services* and officially blessed by the 1989 book for Southern African which envisages, however optionally, a full catechumenate to provide a fuller context from which Christian initiation can be brought into the life of the church. It is clear that such rites provide for, in the first instance, "adult" candidates for baptism, but it could well be that these will also include an annual lenten program involving the entire local community.

Second, there is a potential conflict inherent in the fact that personal renewals are provided for in some of the books, whereas in others a catechumenate is favoured. Is it possible, one must ask, that such a pragmatic development is not altogether desirable? Are we once again victims of that bugbear of well-intentioned Anglican innovation: "It works, therefore it must be right"? History tells us repeatedly that new rites can be fashioned for the church of one age only to be discarded as liturgical debris by the next.[21] Those who want the chance to make personal,

---

[21]See Kenneth Stevenson, "The Pastoral Offices" in *The Identity of Anglican Worship*, 103-15.

public renewals often have need of powerful symbolism, and here we encounter that thorny question of whether or not baptismal water should be used, and how much of it, and where. It is conceivable that a church that becomes collectively convinced of the value of a liturgical catechumenate might well dispense altogether with such renewals.

Third, the question of *phasing* does not simply affect the way in which Christian initiation is celebrated. It also affects the possible future paths of penitential rites, and also of marriage rites. We have argued elsewhere for betrothal as a ''catechumenate for marriage,''[22] and others have done so for the sacrament of reconciliation.[23] It is hard to marginalize such thoughts as the mere dreams of twentieth-century pastors who fantasize patristically. It would seem that the very momentum to which Père Gy referred in speaking of nineteenth-century renewal has yet more surprises in store for us, as a combination of sound historical scholarship, pastoral sensitivity, and social forces together exert pressures on the churches to move forward into the next century. It would even appear to be the case that such a development would itself constitute a renewal, rather than a dispersal grudgingly given in to.

Conclusion

Anglicanism has always had a strong sense of public worship being relational, consisting of president and community, both of whom operate, as it were, under authority. Phased rites are bound to throw into relief the way in which other types of ministry (deacon, catechist, pastoral assistant, etc.) have a part to play in public liturgies. We have in the past been so good at encouraging the genesis of such rites, and so bad at thinking through the full liturgical and ecclesiological implications. Without having recourse to the whole tired, sagging tale of medieval sacramental ''magic words,'' we need, nonetheless, to distinguish between those parts of the rites which are, in some sense, ''performative,'' and those which are subsidiary, supportive, interpretative.

---

[22]See Kenneth W.Stevenson, *To Join Together: The Rite of Marriage*, Studies in the Reformed Rites of the Catholic Church 5 (New York: Pueblo, 1987).

[23]See Joseph A.Favazza, *The Order of Penitents: Historical Roots and Pastoral Future* (Collegeville: Liturgical Press, 1988).

Then there is the question of sacramental theology. Article XXVII (of the XXXIX Articles) speaks plainly about baptism:

> ...it is...a sign of Regeneration or new Birth, whereby, as by an instrument, they that receive Baptism rightly are grafted into the Church...

Each age, we are often told, needs to reformulate historic truths according to its own needs. But are we not in danger of allowing a well-intentioned consumerism to cloud our theology of what baptism is supposed to *do*? The Article in question states in bold terms the classical Anglican position—that baptism effects regeneration—but holds out the need to appropriate that grace by a life which is open to the promises of God in the future.[24] This, position it would seem, lies at the heart of what "phased rites" can do and be. They can enable that adverb "rightly" to become a reality in the life of the church. To be "rightly grafted" is not merely to be a fully paid-up member of the ghetto of the doctrinally sound—the holy huddle of the saints—but to be part of the leaven in the lump of the real world, where Christ goes before.

Finally, there is a crying need, along with such "phased rites," for a much deeper sense of baptism at the heart of the life of the church.[25] The American *Book of Common Prayer* (1979) bravely steps out of line from the popular and almost obsessively paschal view of baptism by suggesting that baptism is appropriate at the main festivals: Baptism of the Lord, Easter, Pentecost, and All Saints'. Here one encounters potential difficulties with a catechumenate that is exclusively lenten. Could it not occasionally be celebrated in Advent, culminating in baptism at the Baptism of the Lord, so that the paschal/Romans 6:3-11 baptismal spirituality of *anamnesis* can be appropriately counterbalanced by the epiphany/John 3:3-6 baptismal spirituality of *epiclesis*?[25]

Such a phased view of the baptismal process is so deeply traditional

---

[24]See Stephen W. Sykes, " 'Baptisme doth represente unto us oure profession' " in *Thomas Cranmer: Essays in Commemoration of the 500th Anniversary of his Birth*, Margo Johnson, ed. (Durham: Turnstone Ventures, 1990), 122-43.

[25]See Paul J.Roberts, "Initiation into Christian Life" in *The Identity of Anglican Worship*, 80-88; also Daniel B. Stevick, *Baptismal Moments, Baptismal Meanings* (New York: Church Hymnal Corporation, 1987).

that it could go one step further and give rise to liturgical texts—prayers as well as hymnody[26]—that bring baptism into the life-consciousness of the whole people of God. To put it at its bluntest: we are in dire need of it, and we need to find means of selling it far and wide.

---

[26]See the parallels drawn between the Byzantine tradition and the hymnody, for example, of N.F.S. Grundtvig in nineteenth century Denmark, in Kenneth W.Stevenson, ''The Byzantine Liturgy of Baptism,'' *Studia Liturgica* 17 (1987), 185.

Marked As Christ's Own Forever
Leonel L. Mitchell

At the first International Anglican Liturgical Consultation (Boston, 1985) I presented a paper entitled, "The Place of Baptismal Anointing in Christian Initiation."[1] It offered a rationale for the use of chrismation in the American *Book of Common Prayer* (1979) and the similar usage of the Canadian *Book of Alternative Services* (1985). In the American rite, following the water baptism, the bishop or priest prays for the sevenfold gifts of the Spirit using the traditional prayer going back to the Gelasian Sacramentary, and then:

> ...places a hand on the person's head, marking on the forehead the sign of the cross (using chrism if desired) and saying to each one:
> N., you are sealed by the Holy Spirit in baptism and marked as Christ's own for ever.[2]

In the Canadian book the prayer for the sevenfold gifts of the Spirit follows the signing, and there is no direction for placing a hand on the person's head. The formula is:

> I sign you with the cross, and mark you as Christ's own forever.[3]

Other Anglican provinces

The initiative of North American Anglicans in this regard does not seem to have been widely followed in the recent revisions of the baptismal liturgy of other Anglican provinces. *The Alternative Service Book* (1980) of the Church of England permits the sign of the cross to be made "in oil blessed for the purpose," either immediately following the renunciations or

---

[1] See the *Anglican Theological Review* 48 (1986), 202-211.

[2] *The Book of Common Prayer...According to the Use of the Episcopal Church* (New York: Church Hymnal Corporation, 1979), 308.

[3] *The Book of Alternative Services of the Anglican Church of Canada* (Toronto: Anglican Book Centre, 1985), 160.

immediately following the baptism, as well as its use by the bishop at confirmation[4] (although there is no reference to it in either rubric or prayer in the rites themselves). There is no mention at all of chrism in *The Alternative Prayer Book* (1984) of the Church of Ireland nor in *The Book of Common Prayer for use in the Church of Wales* (1984), although the optional use of chrism had been mentioned in a statement of the Welsh Doctrinal Commission in 1971.[5]

An Anglican Prayer Book (1989) of the Province of Southern Africa follows the custom of the earlier South African Prayer Book in permitting the bishop to sign confirmands with chrism,[6] but does not mention its use at baptism. Chrism is not mentioned in *An Australian Prayer Book* (1978), but the Liturgical Commission of the Anglican Church of Australia published a new rite in 1990 for experimental use, *Holy Baptism with the Laying on of Hands*, which unifies "the three principal liturgical ministries of the Church: Word, Baptism, and Holy Communion." This service includes the optional use of chrism to sign the newly baptized on the forehead following the water baptism, the formula being:

Name, I sign you with the sign of the cross to show that you are marked as Christ's own for ever.

The introductory liturgical notes explain the meaning of this chrismation:

The optional use of oil (chrism) restores an ancient baptismal ceremony. It evokes a rich variety of biblical images: the anointing of kings (1 Samuel 16:13), the royal priesthood (1 Peter 2:9), the seal of the saints (Revelation 7) and is traditionally associated with the Holy Spirit. Its relationship with the name *Christ*, the anointed one, reminds us that each baptism is related to the baptism of Jesus.[7]

---

[4]*The Alternative Service Book* (Oxford: University Press, 1980), 226, 241.

[5]*Christian Initiation* (Church in Wales Publications, 1971), 26, quoted in David Holeton, "Christian Initiation in Some Anglican Provinces," *Studia Liturgica* 12 (1977), 143. [The 1990 Welsh rite provides for an optional chrismation after the water baptism of children. In the alternative order for baptism and confirmation, however, the chrismation takes place at confirmation after the imposition of hands. This information was not available to the author when this paper was written. Ed.]

[6](Collins, 1989), 376.

[7]*Holy Baptism with the Laying on of Hands* (Sidney: Anglican Information Office, 1990), 6,10.

A New Zealand Prayer Book (1989) does not mention the use of chrism within the baptismal rite, although immediately before it there is a short section entitled "The Use of Oil" which permits its use for the sign of the cross after baptism. The oil is to be set apart for this purpose by the bishop or a priest and a formula is suggested for doing so:

> God of all creation, at baptism your Son was anointed by the Holy Spirit; in Christ's name we set apart this oil. Grant that those who are signed at their baptism with the cross of their Saviour in this holy oil, may be sealed by your Spirit as yours for ever, and share in the royal priesthood of your Church, for you live and reign one God for ever. *Amen.*[8]

Neither the Australian nor New Zealand rite follows the American and Canadian books in using the prayer for the sevenfold gifts of the Spirit at the consignation, rather retaining it for the laying on of hands at confirmation. Both clearly represent, however, a new (and in my view commendable) thrust in their understanding of consignation and its relationship to anointing. In the case of New Zealand, Archbishop Davis, the Primate, pointed out to the present writer the influence of the Boston Consultation on the decision to include chrismation in the rite.

One of the purposes of this essay is to commend to other Anglicans not only the American and Canadian use of chrism at the postbaptismal signing with the cross, but also the substantial theological and historical discussion of the meaning of chrism which has accompanied the rite's development.

The Lutheran Book of Worship

Chrismation has become a part, at least optionally, of the baptismal liturgies of two other North American communions. In 1978, the *Lutheran Book of Worship* included in the baptismal rite, immediately following the actual baptism, a version of the traditional prayer for the sevenfold gifts of the Spirit, to be accompanied by the laying on of hands and followed by the signing on the forehead of each person with the words:

---

[8]*A New Zealand Prayer Book* (Auckland: Collins, 1989), 382.

(Name), child of God, you have been sealed by the Holy Spirit in baptism and marked with the cross of Christ for ever.[9]

The sign of the cross may be made with "oil prepared for the purpose" and, in the companion *Manual on the Liturgy*, a brief explanation of the meaning of anointing and directions for preparing the oil by adding balsam or other fragrant oil to olive oil are included.[10]

What I consider most significant about the Lutheran postbaptismal rites is the clear assertion in the notes to the baptismal rite in the Minister's Desk Edition of the *Lutheran Book of Worship* that the inclusion of the laying on of hands "signals a return to the liturgical fullness of the ancient church which was lost when confirmation became a separate rite." The notes go on to state that:

> Signing each candidate with the cross is a principal part of the rite for Baptism, traceable to its beginnings in the ancient church.[11]

The new Presbyterian order

In 1985 the Presbyterian Church USA issued its own revised baptismal rite, also containing a postbaptismal anointing. After the water rite, the minister lays hands on the head of the person being baptized while saying a prayer for the sevenfold gifts of the Spirit. Then:

> As the MINISTER says these words, the sign of the cross may be marked on the forehead of the person baptized, using oil prepared for this purpose:

> _____, child of the covenant, you have been sealed by the Holy Spirit in baptism, and marked as Christ's own forever. Amen.[12]

---

[9]*Lutheran Book of Worship*, Minister's Desk Edition (Minneapolis: Augsburg, 1978), 311.

[10]Philip H. Pfatteicher and Carlos R. Messerli, *Manual on the Liturgy: Lutheran Book of Worship* (Minneapolis: Augsburg, 1979), 185ff.

[11]*LBW*, nn.13 and 14, 31.

[12]*Holy Baptism and Services of the Renewal of Baptism*, Supplemental Liturgical Resources 2 (Philadelphia: Westminster, 1985), 31.

The influence of both the Anglican and Lutheran forms is evident. In the commentary which is part of the published text, the anointing is discussed for over a page:

> Some contemporary baptismal rites evidence a movement to restore the laying on of hands and anointing with chrism to the baptismal rite. In these rites, the gift of the Holy Spirit in baptism is once more signified by these ancient signs. While baptism with water needs nothing to complete it, the laying on of hands and anointing help to convey the richness and abundance of the Holy Spirit and to demonstrate that Christian baptism is a baptism of water *and* the Holy Spirit. The early church developed this ritual based upon the baptism of Jesus, on whom the Holy Spirit descended as he emerged from the waters of baptism.[13]

The "contemporary rites" alluded to clearly include the Episcopal and Lutheran rites as well as the Roman Catholic *Rite for the Christian Initiation of Adults*.[14] The analysis of the relationship of these postbaptismal rites to the central ritual act of water baptism seems to me to sound exactly the right note. To go down into the baptismal water is to enter with Christ into the grave and to pass with him through the gate of death. To come up out of the water is to be reborn, to be raised with Christ from death to life. This is the primary sacramental symbol. The ritual pattern is that of the baptism of Christ in the synoptic gospels:

> And just as [Jesus] was coming up out of the water, he saw the heavens torn apart and the Spirit descending like a dove on him. And a voice came from heaven, "You are my Son, the Beloved, with you I am well pleased."[15]

As Jesus received the messianic anointing of the Holy Spirit at his baptism, so Christians are anointed with the same Spirit at their baptism. The outward anointing with chrism becomes the sign of the inward unction of the Holy Spirit. We are temples of the Holy Spirit, anointed with spiritual oil at our baptism.

---

[13]Presbyterian *Baptism*, 56-7.

[14]See the Study Edition (Washington: United States Catholic Congress, 1988). This is the official American edition of the text. The Latin text appeared in 1972, however, and ICEL's interim translation in 1974.

[15]Mark 1:10-11 (NRSV).

The Presbyterian commentary goes on to speak of the scriptural symbolism of anointing in both Old and New Testaments and of the close linguistic relationship between "Christ," "Christian," and "chrism" (they could have added "christen"):

> The anointing of new Christians emphasizes their union with Jesus the Christ and their claim to the name "Christian." ...The act of anointing is therefore particularly illustrative of one's "taking the name of Christ" in Baptism.[16]

This is a clear and concise description of the meaning of anointing. We are anointed into the Anointed One, Christians into the Christ. Therefore the anointing is Christic. Christ was anointed with the Holy Spirit, therefore our anointing too is pneumatic. Finally, the Presbyterians point out that this is not an additional rite but a part of baptism itself:

> It should be understood that the laying on of hands and anointing with oil are part of a single action and, with the prayer and the washing, express the fullness of the biblical teaching about baptism.[17]

The meaning of anointing

The admirable clarity thus far exhibited by the Presbyterian rite is somewhat mitigated, however, by its optional use of consignation and anointing in several services for the renewal of baptism, one of which is confirmation. The formula used at baptism is not repeated, but the signing may accompany the laying on of hands with the words:

> O Lord, uphold _____ by your Holy Spirit. Daily increase in (*him, her*) your gifts of grace; the spirit of wisdom and understanding, the spirit of counsel and might, the spirit of knowledge and the fear of the Lord, the spirit of joy in your promise. Both now and evermore.

Or, the even more Anglican:

---

[16]Presbyterian *Baptism*, 57.
[17]Presbyterian *Baptism*, 57.

Defend, O Lord, your servant _____ with your heavenly grace that (*he*, *she*) may continue yours forever, and daily increase in your Holy Spirit more and more, until (*he*, *she*) comes to your everlasting kingdom.[18]

Roman Catholic chrismation

In this multiple use, the Presbyterians appear to have directly copied the Roman Catholic rites which have anointing as a part both of baptism and confirmation. The Roman double chrismation is one of the principal sources of confusion about the meaning of postbaptismal anointing, and has been so since the Middle Ages.[19] In the present Roman Catholic rite the priest precedes the postbaptismal anointing by praying:

The God of power and Father of our Lord Jesus Christ has freed you from sin and brought you to new life through water and the Holy Spirit. He anoints you with the chrism of salvation, so that, united with his people, you may remain for ever a member of Christ who is Priest, Prophet, and King.[20]

Obviously this anointing is Christic. The newly baptized is anointed as a member of the royal and priestly people of God in Jesus Christ. Although this prayer is said regularly at the baptism of children, it is omitted at the baptism of adults to avoid the ritual confusion of its juxtaposition to the anointing which is a part of the confirmation which follows immediately, "unless some serious reason stands in the way."[21] The anointing at confirmation is accompanied by the traditional prayer for the sevenfold gifts of the Spirit and the Byzantine anointing formula: "N., be sealed with the Gift of the Holy Spirit."[22] There is more balance

---

[18]Presbyterian *Baptism*, 75-6.

[19]See Marion Hatchett, "The Rite of 'Confirmation' in The Book of Common Prayer and in *Authorized Services 1973*," *Anglican Theological Review* 56 (1974), 294ff. See also the discussion of Rabanus Maurus's attempt to explain the double chrismation in J.D.C.Fisher, *Christian Initiation: Baptism in the Medieval West*, Alcuin Club Collections 47 (London: SPCK, 1965), 64ff.

[20]*RCIA*, n.227, 143.

[21]*RCIA*, n.214, 125.

[22]*RCIA*, n.234, 146. For a discussion of the theological questions raised by the practice, see Aidan Kavanagh, *The Shape of Baptism* (New York: Pueblo, 1978), 138ff.

in the prayer for the consecration of chrism in the American *Book of Common Prayer*:

> Eternal God, whose blessed Son was anointed by the Holy Spirit to be the Saviour and servant of all, we pray you to consecrate this oil, that those who are sealed with it may share in the royal priesthood of Jesus Christ.[23]

Ecumenical perspectives

I have chosen to comment in such detail on the rites of Lutherans and Presbyterians to remind us that the question of postbaptismal consignation and chrismation is not uniquely Anglican, but is a part of the recovery of the richness of symbolic action associated with the ecumenical and liturgical movements. Anglicans have often tended to see the practice solely in terms of the practices of eighteenth-century Non-Jurors and nineteenth-century Anglo-Catholics.[24] The 1982 Lima document, *Baptism, Eucharist and Ministry*, provides a more ecumenical basis:

> God bestows on all baptized persons the anointing and promise of the Holy Spirit, marks them with a seal and implants in their hearts the first instalment of their inheritance as sons and daughters of God.[25]

It is this scripturally based conviction which stands behind the use of consignation and anointing. Its ritual form, as we have said, is traditionally based on the biblical accounts of Christ's own baptism. The Lima document returns to this theme in its section entitled ''Baptism-Chrismation-Confirmation'':

> In God's work of salvation, the paschal mystery of Christ's death and resurrection is inseparably linked with the pentecostal gift of the Holy Spirit. Similarly, participation in Christ's death and resurrection is inseparably linked with the receiving of the Spirit. Baptism in its full meaning signifies and effects both.

---

[23] American *BCP*, 307.

[24] I have discussed the Anglican use of baptismal oil through to 1960 in *Baptismal Anointing*, Alcuin Club Collections 48 (London: SPCK, 1966), 177-187.

[25] (Geneva: WCC, 1982), Baptism, 5.

Christians differ in their understanding as to where the sign of the gift of the Spirit is to be found. Different actions have become associated with the giving of the Spirit. For some it is the water rite itself. For others it is the anointing with chrism and/or the imposition of hands, which many churches call confirmation. For still others it is all three, as they see the Spirit operative throughout the rite. All agree that Christian baptism is in water and the Holy Spirit.[26]

Here both the agreements and differences, not only between but also within churches, are clearly stated. To separate participation in the Easter experience of dying and rising with Christ from the Pentecost experience of receiving the Holy Spirit is not really possible. We cannot be united to Christ without receiving also the Holy Spirit. This union is something which all Christians experience in their baptism, whether or not their rite contains anointing, consignation, or the imposition of hands. We must agree that water baptism in the name of the Trinity is itself sufficient.[27]

But what is sufficient for the validity of the sacrament may not be adequate for what the Lima document calls a "comprehensive order of baptism." The rite for emergency baptism in any of the Anglican Prayer Books, for example, contains all that is "necessary," but it is not an adequate rite liturgically.[28] Lima continues:

As was the case in the early centuries, the gift of the Spirit in baptism may be signified in additional ways, for example, by the sign of the laying on of hands, and by the anointing or chrismation. The very sign of the cross recalls the promised gift of the Holy Spirit who is the instalment and pledge of what is yet to come when God has fully redeemed those whom he has made

---

[26]Baptism, 14.

[27]See the quotation from the Welsh (1971) and South African (1972) reports in David Holeton, "Christian Initiation in Some Anglican Provinces," *Studia Liturgica* 12 (1977), 139.

[28]"To do sacramental theology by inquiring how little is necessary for validity is seriously to impoverish both liturgy and theology and leads to a dangerous minimalism. Few would contend that the reading and preaching of the Word, for example, were actually *necessary* for the validity of a eucharistic celebration, but even fewer would approve of a rite that did not contain such a proclamation of the Word of God. At the very least, we would consider such a rite seriously defective" (L.L. Mitchell, "Place of Baptismal Anointing," 206).

his own (Ephesians 1:13-14). *The recovery of such vivid signs may be expected to enrich the liturgy.*[29]

Vivid signs

Bryan Spinks has commented on the anointing in these contemporary rites: "It is highly questionable as to whether any can be viewed as making the sign 'vivid.'"[30] There is certainly a sense in which he is right. His own recommendation is for a form used in the ecumenical chapel at Churchill College, Cambridge:

> Jesus the Anointed One anoints you with grace, and signs you as one of his flock. You are a member of a chosen race, a royal priesthood, a holy nation, God's own people. May the Holy Spirit which is poured out upon you sanctify and preserve you. N., you are signed with the oil of Anointing in the Name of the Father, and of the Son, and of the Holy Spirit. Amen.[31]

This text has many advantages over those which we have discussed. It certainly touches all of the appropriate scriptural bases. It makes clear that the anointing is a sign of the royal and priestly messianic anointing of Christ with the Holy Spirit; our sacramental participation in it is baptism and is therefore both Christic and pneumatic. Of course in one sense it has an unfair advantage over the forms actually adopted by national or regional churches: It was prepared for a single academic congregation and had to undergo neither the political and theological machinations of a provincial liturgical commission nor the similar vicissitudes of adoption by a general synod or convention.

I am familiar with the actual use which may be made of this text. I cannot imagine it being recited at the Great Vigil of Easter over each of fifty neophytes. Practically, what is needed is a prayer to be recited once over all of the newly baptized and a much briefer formula to be used with each individual. This combination could be accomplished with

---

[29]Baptism, 19, emphasis mine.

[30]"Vivid Signs of the Gift of the Spirit? The Lima Text on Baptism and Some Recent English Language Baptismal Liturgies," *Worship* 60 (1986), 237.

[31]Spinks, "Vivid Signs," 239.

the Churchill College form (and perhaps is) by using the first part of
it only once and repeating the sentence beginning "N., you are signed..."
over each person.[32]

Spinks points out, with good reason, that Lima's call for the use of
vivid signs is addressed not only to those churches which do not use chrism,
but "to many churches, East and West, where chrism is used, but its
accompanying formula makes it an obscure or ambiguous sign."[33] It is
small wonder that more vivid signs are difficult to introduce.

The problem of a more vivid sign, I believe, is a part of the larger problem of the confusion of the meaning of baptism and of confirmation.
In David Holeton's words, "Confirmation as it has been traditionally
practiced by the Western churches has inherent and insoluble problems."[34]
Peter Hinchcliff has described well the practical problem faced by liturgical committees and commissions:

> In the field of initiation-rites the experts are attempting to reduce the confu-
> sion by producing forms which express a coherent understanding of the mean-
> ing of baptism and confirmation.... The committee is able to produce a rite
> which is neat, consistent and capable of being explained logically. The com-
> mittee, however, seldom has the power to authorize the use of the rite. Modifi-
> cations are introduced by those who have that power but not the expertise;
> the pattern is destroyed once more.[35]

Practical problems

The practical problems facing any revision of the liturgy include getting
the appropriate synodical body to authorize it, and then getting the

---

[32]The first two sentences, of course, are not a prayer but a declaration addressed to the
neophyte. They could easily be recast as a prayer, however, or at least be placed in the
subjunctive after the model of the third sentence: "May Jesus the Anointed One anoint
you with grace and sign you as one of his flock, a member of a chosen race... May the
Holy Spirit, who is poured...."

[33]Spinks, 239.

[34]"Confirmation in the 1980s," *Ecumenical Perspectives on Baptism, Eucharist and Ministry*, Faith and Order Paper No.116, Max Thurian, ed. (Geneva: World Council of
Churches, 1983), 86.

[35]"Initiation: The Modern Period," *The Study of Liturgy*, Cheslyn Jones, Geoffrey Wain-
wright, Edward Yarnold, S.J., eds. (New York: Oxford, 1978), 137.

bishops and parish clergy who preside at baptismal liturgies to use and teach it so that it becomes alive to the people of God. Symbols which have to be explained have lost their power, and anointing can easily fall into that category. But as Spinks reminds us:

> The community of the Anointed One ought not to need an explanation of the significance of anointing. If the ceremony needs explanation, then it will be because catechesis, preaching and bible reading have been deficient.[36]

The Hebrew practice of anointing kings and priests was known even to the Christians of the third and fourth centuries only through a reading of the Old Testament; it corresponded to nothing in their daily lives. Those whom Ambrose, Cyril, or John Chrysostom anointed were as unfamiliar with the practice as our people today, but their catechesis had taught them that Jesus was *Christos*, the Anointed One, and by their anointing they knew themselves to be united with him as *Christianoi*.

This concept is readily understandable by contemporary Christians as well, as long as their rites and the teaching which they receive reinforce the liturgical act. Spinks contends that, in spite of the explanation of the meaning of the anointing in the American form for consecrating chrism, the optional chrismation in both the Episcopal and Lutheran rites is essentially without meaning. He finds even more meaningless and nonsensical the use of oil in the English *Alternative Service Book*, which permits the sign of the cross to be "in oil blessed for the purpose" either immediately following the renunciations or immediately following the baptism, as well as its use by the bishop at confirmation:

> However, there are no rubrics mentioning it within the rite, nor any prayer or statement which refers to it, and therefore its use has not the slightest significance.... Far from a "vivid" sign we have here an example of what the English Puritans called a "dumb ceremony." Any meaning has to be imported from historical liturgical usage, or the usage (and formulae) and theology of other denominations.[37]

While this criticism is certainly well said and qualifies as a stinging rebuke, it is also overkill. Certainly the reason why people choose to

---

[36]Spinks, 235.

[37]Spinks, 237.

perform ritual acts is because they consider them to be meaningful. In one sense this is even more true of optional acts. As far as I am aware, no Anglican baptismal liturgy requires the use of oil; when it is used, therefore, it must be in order to convey meaning. That it often fails to do so is beyond dispute and *ASB* does appear simply to have inserted rubrics permitting the use of oil at all three places in which it occurred in the Sarum rites of baptism and confirmation. If the purpose of using oil at any or all of these places—oil of the catechumens at the renunciations and chrism after the water baptism and at confirmation—is simply to be medieval or "Catholic," that may well be the message communicated to the people. And it will not be surprising if many decide not to avail themselves of the option.

If, however, anointing is presented as a scriptural symbol, signifying our union with Christ in his baptism and anointing by the Holy Spirit, we may find that the signs will be vivid indeed.

Chrismation and consignation

Although baptismal rites exist in which oil is poured over the head or rubbed on the body of the newly baptized, all of the contemporary rites with which I am familiar use the oil to make the sign of the cross. This is not simply a modern phenomenon. There is an ancient inscription in the catacomb of Callistus in Rome which shows a dove holding a paint brush painting a chi-rho cross.[38] The reference is clearly to the marking of the newly baptized with the cross by the Holy Spirit. The fourth-century Syrian doctor St. Ephrem wrote:

> Through oil the Spirit signed priests and kings. The Holy Spirit through oil imprinted the seal upon his sheep, as a ring which impresses its seal in wax. Even so the Spirit impresses the hidden seal upon the bodies through oil when they are anointed in baptism and signed in baptism.[39]

---

[38]The illustration is reproduced in L.L. Mitchell, *Baptismal Anointing*, 94; from Cyril E.Pocknee, *Cross and Crucifix*, Alcuin Club Tracts 32 (London: Mowbray, 1962), 17, Plate I.

[39]St. Ephrem Syrus, Hymns on Virginity 7.6 (trans. in L.L.Mitchell, *Baptismal Anointing*, 35).

painted on Christ's sheep with the holy oil by the Spirit. The two symbols are closely intertwined. As long as we insist on the theological unity of the baptismal rite and do not fall into the trap of seeing it as a series of discrete ceremonies, each of which has a different meaning, then we can deal with the fullness of the rite. Washing, signing, anointing, handlaying comprise a single sacramental action.

This has been said over and over again in different ways by the various provinces of the Anglican Communion. As Louis Weil pointed out in 1977, the famous debate between the followers of Gregory Dix and those of G.W.H. Lampe, or more recently between Charles Whitaker and John D.C.Fisher, over whether Christian initiation is complete in baptism or needs to be completed by some other rite: "was an interesting theological diversion for those addicted to ecclesiastical polemics."[40] In the words of the Doctrinal Commission of the Church in Wales: "Baptism is baptism of water and the Holy Spirit, whether it is enriched by the traditional post-baptismal ceremonies or not. Nothing further is required for the full validity of Christian Initiation."[41] If signing and sealing have any theological meaning it is only in the context of the baptismal liturgy. As the Presbyterians remind us:

> It should be understood that the laying on of hands and anointing with oil are part of a single action and, with the prayer and the washing, express the fullness of the biblical teaching about baptism.[42]

---

[40]"Christian Initiation in the Anglican Communion: A Response," *Studia Liturgica* 12 (1977), 127.

[41]See D.Holeton, "Some Anglican Provinces," 139, 142f.

[42]Presbyterian *Baptism*, 57.

Reflections on Baptismal Symbolism and Baptismal Identity
Philip May

A story about water

Several years ago my father helped prepare a television commercial for a swimming pool company. The commercial was quite effective: it opens with a shot of a house in a North American, suburban neighbourhood. The house is neat and unremarkable, but everything gives the impression of oppressive heat. The air looks hazy; there are summer noises in the background.

A car pulls into the driveway and a man gets out slowly. He looks rumpled, tired, hot. Making his way in by the front door, he drops his jacket on the floor and walks past his wife and children. Slowly he makes his way to the back door. He opens the door and walks, step by step, toward the swimming pool. The camera switches to water level: we see the man pause for a moment, sweating in his suit. Then, with all his clothes on, his tie still tied, and his shoes still done up, he dives into the pool. A moment later he re-emerges, a changed being.

The children look at each other, and jump into the pool. Eventually even mother joins in. The commercial ends with a picture of a happy family splashing around with their clothes on, and a sonorous voice tells us where to get the best buy in swimming pools.

Obviously, the commercial is tied to the experience of a particular class of people in a particular social setting. Its effectiveness, however, turns on several truths which may well be universal. First, excessive behaviour invites shared experience; second, water is a good medium for excessive behaviour.

Excessive behaviour has not been a feature of our baptismal practices for a considerable length of time. In certain cases, in fact, we have gone so far in avoiding excessive behaviour that we seem even to have left moderation behind. We call our actions "symbolic," by which we mean that they have no meaning in and of themselves, and so allow them to degenerate into minimalism.

This essay is an attempt to spell out some of the contradictions we create for ourselves when we allow baptismal symbolism to become minimalist. When we trace these problems to their source, it becomes clear that we are dealing with fundamental issues of meaning and Christian identity. We are dealing with a profound neglect of the radical nature of baptism for the individual and for the baptizing community. We are dealing with a failure of nerve: a fear of allowing ourselves truly to be formed by baptism, rather than by some rational/verbal reconstruction of "what baptism really means." I believe that this is basically a confusion between "symbol" and "code."

Baptismal symbol: some healthy examples

To begin, we shall look at several positive examples of excessive baptismal behaviour. The first took place in a university chapel in western Canada. During my first year there, a woman who had been inquiring into Christian faith for some time became a candidate for baptism. She was baptized during the Easter Vigil in a font constructed especially for the event. The font was low and quite shallow. The candidate sat on the edge; the presider put his hand over her face, cradled her shoulders in his other arm, and immersed her head and torso three times. When asked about her experience afterwards, the newly baptized person said: "At first I was afraid of drowning; and then I realized that I was!" Everyone present understood what she meant.

When baptismal actions are subdued and minimalist, we are expressing to ourselves something profoundly false about baptism. We are expressing that this is not a major event, that nothing really significant is happening here. In the television commercial, when the man jumped into the pool with all his clothes on, he entered a new state of being. The suit, undoubtedly expensive and a symbol of his place in the world of commerce, was transformed into a ludicrous set of wet clothes. Upon jumping into the pool, as his body broke the surface of the water, he left the oppressive heat of the business world behind; as he broke the water's surface again upon re-emerging, he rose from the depths a new person. There is something profoundly important about breaking the surface of water, about being dead to the world if only for a few brief moments, re-emerging as a changed being with a radically altered relationship to self, world, the people around us, and to God. We drown that we might live! Only in abandoning baptismal minimalism will this truth truly be enacted in what we do.

The second example took place in a seminary as part of a pastoral liturgy class on baptism. Our make-believe candidate was a class member. Everyone present knew what to expect: an exercise with comments on technique and some more-or-less helpful criticism from our peers. But something quite different happened!

Once again, the font was improvised for the occasion. It was quite shallow but large enough for the candidate to stand in. A pitcher and very large bowl were borrowed from the college refectory. The chrism was improvised, using baby oil and oil of balsam. Fifteen to twenty people were present, gathered around the font. The candidate was presented, wearing only tennis shorts. At each clause of the baptismal formula the pitcher was filled with water from the bowl and poured over the candidate's head. Oil was poured over his head and shoulders and the smell of balsam filled the air. People who had come expecting an exercise only, from which they could remain detached, found themselves drawn into the action. Despite our awareness that this was only practise, the scale of the action in relation to the size of the gathering drew us into a truly shared experience.

When you watch an uncomfortably warm person dive into a pool fully clothed, you can identify with the experience. When a person only a few feet away is drenched with a considerable quantity of water, you can feel that as well. And when cedar boughs are dipped into the baptismal water and used to sprinkle all the people, the identification is reinforced. But when the relative scale of action to the size of the gathering is out of balance, when fonts are small and distant, amounts of water meagre, the use of oil minimal, the event of baptism is confined to the experience of the individual being baptized. Everyone else is forced into the role of witness only, and not allowed the possibility of participating with the one being baptized. Every sign, every action seems to say: This is a private moment, this has no effect on the rest of the body of Christ.

In our exercise we used more water than was strictly necessary for a valid sacrament, and certainly we used more oil. But it was this excessive behaviour which made the event large enough to accommodate everybody, and thus to accommodate the full significance of baptism. The baptism was "opened up," and we were all able to dive in.

Fortunately, this sharing of experience does not depend on small spaces and low numbers. Our third example took place in a large parish church in an affluent Toronto suburb. Once again the Easter Vigil was the setting and there were between 120 and 150 people present. Obviously the sense of community and feelings of intimacy with the candidates take on a different form in such a setting. But solidarity with the candidates was enabled by adjusting the scale of the actions so that what was happening around the font was easily visible and audible to all.

The church was illuminated only by the candles people held. A significant amount of water was used so the entire space was filled with the sounds of pouring and splashing. Again, fragrant chrism was employed. This interplay of light, sound, and fragrance was powerful enough to draw together that large community and involve them intimately in what was happening.

Without overshadowing the importance of water, it is interesting to note the positive role of the use of chrism in creating the shared experience. We are aware of the power of smell and how closely it is associated to memory. As the baptizands circulated throughout the worship space during the course of the Vigil, the fragrance of their anointing accompanied them. Many in the congregation commented afterwards that, from that time onward, the smell of the chrism would be for them the smell of baptism. The next day, when the community had gathered again, others remarked how the newly baptized still "smelled" of their baptism, and how the scent of the perfumed chrism made them aware of being in the presence of those who had so recently experienced new birth through water and the Spirit.

Here again, despite the size of the setting, the baptismal actions became shared experiences—events which drew people together and held them in unity. In a very vivid way this shared experience showed the mutuality of baptism. This kind of baptism could not be mistaken for a service provided by clergy to people who had "fulfilled the requirements." All were involved and the newly baptized were clearly gifts to the community. They were present because of God's grace and, through their presence, God's grace created something new in the community.

This point becomes even more important when the newly baptized are infants. We must avoid being sentimental about babies. But even the most realistic among us can see that very young children embody acceptance of grace and surrender of self as they are being baptized. This recognition initiates a wonderful cycle of changes. Adults present at the baptism of an infant, or receiving communion beside a young child, cannot help being changed. The unconditional nature of God's grace played out before us challenges our stubborn conviction that we have earned a place in Christ's body by our supposed "ability to understand." When we adults become a little more generous in our sense of what constitutes membership in the body, when we give up some of our control and trust grace more and our own standards of understanding less, we become a much richer medium for Christian nurture. Strong baptismal symbols reinforce this cycle, by reminding us that the newly baptized are gifts to the community.

Learning from our examples: a philosophical excursion

The three baptismal experiences I have described underscore the three most vivid effects of robust baptismal symbolism: 1. abundant water emphasizes the radical nature of baptism, the submerging and re-emerging that speaks directly of death and rebirth; 2. lavish baptismal actions—actions which can be felt, smelled, heard, and seen by everyone—create the unity of which they speak; 3. baptismal extravagance allows the candidates to be gifts to the community rather than passive consumers of ritual. I am convinced that, as we take baptismal symbolism more seriously, a new image of baptism will begin to impress itself upon the popular mind. I believe this new image will do more to promote a healthier understanding of baptismal discipline than any number of rules, regulations, or mandatory preparation classes.

What was happening in those two university chapels and in that larger parish church? In each experience, symbol had been liberated from its job of *describing* reality and allowed its more important role of *creating* reality. Symbol was allowed to reclaim its power to be something that *forms* us rather than a passive text presented for us to decode.

This distinction between symbol and text is a crucial one. The twentieth-century philosopher Ludwig Wittgenstein devoted most of his later work to clarifying this distinction and to pointing to the problems which arise when we ignore it. Wittgenstein was concerned to demonstrate that there was a particular ''picture of meaning'' hidden in our notion of text: Language, or any other system of symbols, comes to be treated as an abstract, formal construct. Language attains meaning, therefore, when some mental process allows us to make a ''bridge'' between that abstract, symbolic realm and the world of real stuff.

Wittgenstein's earlier view of symbol and language provides an ideal example of the type of view he later came to criticize. All meaningful symbols, Wittgenstein argued, are essentially pictures. A picture consists of elements arranged in a particular configuration of relationships. For instance, a topographical map consists of symbols arranged in spatial relationships on a sheet of paper. The map is given meaning through a mental process which links the symbols to items in the landscape and the relations between the symbols to spatial relations between those items. Maps are one of the simplest forms of picture, but Wittgenstein argued that the propositions of a language are essentially no different from those of a map. Maps are spatial pictures, relying on spatial relationships between basic elements; propositions are logical pictures, relying on logical relationships between basic elements. A proposition has meaning when its basic elements correspond to discrete ''pieces'' of the world, and the logical interactions of those elements indicate relationships between those items in the world. We understand meaning when we know the correspondence between the elements of the proposition and the elements of the world and when we understand the logical relationships among the elements of the proposition. According to Wittgenstein's early thinking, all truly meaningful symbols share this pictoral character. Meaning is a matter of decoding the text.

In his later thinking, Wittgenstein severely criticized his earlier views. He described himself as having been transfixed by one particular picture of meaning.[1] An account of an interchange between Wittgenstein and one of his pupils illustrates the problems he had come to see in his earlier work. The interchange took place in a music store in Cambridge, England. The student had been listening to some recordings of classical music. Wittgenstein asked if they were "any good." The student, a true philosopher, answered: "It all depends on what you mean by "good." Wittgenstein impatiently responded, *"I* mean what *you* mean!"[2]

Given a pictoral theory of meaning, or any theory which treats symbol abstractly, the student's response makes perfect sense. In fact analytical philosophers, influenced to some degree by Wittgenstein's earlier work, were attempting to clarify the limits of meaningful language, either by showing how a predicate such as "good" could stand for a definite relationship between elements in the world, or arguing that we must do without such predicates in an ideal pictoral language. Understanding the meaning of "good" is a matter of seeing the relationship between that symbol and states of affairs in the world. If the relationships we see differ, there will be no definite answer to the question, Is *x* any good? There may even be no definite meaning to the word "good" at all.

Wittgenstein's response, however, illustrates one of the basic principles of his later philosophy: Language does not obtain its meaning from a relationship between symbols and the world; language obtains its meaning from relationships between the people who use it. The meaning of

---

[1]See especially Ludwig Wittgenstein, *Philosophical Investigations* (Oxford: Basil Blackwell, 1953), paras.110-115. Wittgenstein's terse, epigrammatic style can be difficult. The most thorough and helpful secondary source is G.P.Baker and P.M.S.Hacker, *Wittgenstein, Meaning and Understanding* (Oxford: Basil Blackwell, 1983); see especially chapters 1, 3, 16.

[2]As related in Theodore Redpath, *Ludwig Wittgenstein: A Student's Memoir* (London: Duckworth, 1990), 68.

a word such as "good" does not depend on its ability to form abstract pictures of reality. Its meaning comes from the way it is used in inter-actions between speakers of the language, from the role it plays in the economy of communication. In this case, the word "good" plays a vital role in the human need to discuss value. We understand the meaning of the word when we are able to use it in accordance with the standards of our linguistic community. Its use is governed by rules, and if some of the rules can be stretched a little, if they have slightly vague bound-aries, that vagueness is itself part of the word's meaning.

An important corollary of this is that it expands our idea of "language" considerably. Though this is not the place to delve into Wittgenstein's distinction between linguistic and non-linguistic behaviour, it seems clear that actions and gestures play a role in our economy of communication as effectively as printed or spoken words. In Wittgenstein's view, it is perfectly proper to speak about the meaning of certain actions in exactly the same way we speak about the meaning of words.

Now, it may well be that language is sometimes used to create pre-cise, descriptive pictures of reality. But this is clearly not the only way language is used. In fact, it is not even the most important way language is used. As his remark on the meaning of "good" suggests, Wittgen-stein felt that we create our worst misunderstandings when we try to force all language into a descriptive mold.

"Text" is any portion of a language which is used in a purely descrip-tive way. We decode text by aligning it with referents in the correct way and so understand the message of the text. A map could be treated as a text in this sense. Baptismal symbol, however, must not, for texts rely on something more basic, some more fundamental language which will allow us to express the results of our decoding work. If we push text far enough, we reach a realm where further decoding simply misses the point. At this stage, asking what something "stands for" indicates, in fact, a lack of understanding. As Wittgenstein said: "At some point we reach bedrock."[3]

It is this "bedrock" which is the realm of true symbol. It is a realm of action and sign. But these do not obtain their significance through their ability to "stand for" something else. They have significance because they are the foundations of the entire economy of communication within

---

[3]See *Philosophical Investigations*, para. 116.

a community. In the realm of symbol, we are no longer describing reality as much as we are setting the grammar, laying the foundations for communication. By doing this, we are helping to form the community itself.

Problems occur whenever we try to treat symbols as if they were text; and this problem is especially acute with baptismal symbols. The reason for this is simply the fundamental place of baptism within Christian identity. In a catholic church, where our identity is communal, symbols which form this community are truly basic. Baptism is this sort of symbol. It is not a coded description but an event creating the possibility of Christian life. Baptismal symbol helps create the grammar of Christian language and dialogue. In our examples we saw baptismal symbol creating the death and rebirth of a new Christian; we saw baptismal symbol forming the community which makes Christian life possible; we saw baptismal symbol effecting the changes in the body of Christ which come with the addition of each new Christian.

The importance of being lavish

This role as symbol means that baptism cannot be "decoded" and re-expressed in some more basic form of language. But when baptismal symbols are meagre, that is precisely what we are encouraged to do! If we use tiny amounts of water, that communicates to people that it is certainly not the actual action with water which is important, but some other thing which that action "stands for." And each person retreats into his or her own mind to try to decode what is happening.

To break this spell of text and to bring all the gathered people into the realm of symbol, the actions of baptism simply must be overwhelming. It must be obvious that these actions have significance in and of themselves. The actions must not encourage speculative decoding by isolated individuals. Rather, they must be robust enough to crowd out all that speculation and submerge people in what is happening.

Extravagance, like jumping into a pool with your clothes on, can be great fun. But when we are thinking about baptism there is much more at stake. If we want baptismal liturgy to transcend the realm of text and take on its true role as symbol; if we want it to create the unity of which it speaks; if we want it to embody the radical newness which comes with life in Christ: we have no choice but to be extravagant. Our actions must be excessive. They must overpower us so that they can make us into the community we are called to be.

A Survey of Current Anglican Initiation Rites
Kevin Flynn

> When we mean to build,
> we first survey the plot, then draw the model;
> and when we see the figure of the house,
> then we must rate the cost of the erection;
> which if we find outweighs ability,
> what do we do then but draw anew the model
> in fewer offices, or at last desist
> to build at all?
> *(Henry IV, Pt.2,* iii.41)

Many throughout the Anglican community have noted the abundant activity of liturgists, in recent years, who have attempted to produce a new model for the church through the reformation of its rites of initiation. This activity has arisen out of a sense that "the figure of the house" in which the faithful have been trying to live corresponds to blueprints more appropriate to the exigencies of another age. The following is a brief survey of initiation rites currently in use throughout the Communion, either as alternatives to an established Prayer Book or as part of a new Prayer Book. As many of the rites pre-date the World Council of Churches' document *Baptism, Eucharist and Ministry* [*BEM*], it would be too much to expect those rites to reflect the conclusions of that document.

BEM has been celebrated as significant of a good deal of convergence on important matters. One might wonder if that is a convergence more apparent than real. It is not clear, for example, how the churches are to reconcile the discussion of baptism as a once-for-all act that "is in water and the Holy Spirit" with the recognition that "Christians differ in their understanding as to where the sign of the gift of the Spirit is to be found."[1] And again, "Some churches consider that Christian initiation is not complete without the sealing of the baptized with the gift of the Holy Spirit...,"[2] i.e., in another rite. As this survey of rites will show,

---

[1] Faith and Order Paper No.111 (Geneva: WCC, 1982), Baptism, 14.

[2] Baptism, 14.

Anglicans may congratulate themselves on being at least as ambiguous on this point as is *BEM!*

That ambiguity is not to provide an excuse for complacency, however. The issue of our rites is of no small importance. The rites of Christian initiation are, for the faithful, a primary experiential contact with our ecclesiology. Given that fact, no matter how difficult the way forward may at times seem, we cannot "desist to build at all."

The rites under review have all emerged since Peter Jagger collected both Anglican and non-Anglican formularies in his *Christian Initiation 1552-1969.*[3] They include the following:

Australia	*An Australian Prayer Book* (1978)
	Holy Baptism and the Laying on of Hands (1990)
Brazil	*Livro de Oração Comum* (1988)
Canada	*The Book of Alternative Services* (1985)
Chile	*Prayer Book* (1973)
England	*The Alternative Service Book* (1980)
Ireland	*Alternative Prayer Book* (1984)
	Confirmation (1987)
	The Baptism, Confirmation and First Communion of Those Able to Answer for Themselves (1988)
Japan	*Prayer Book* (1986)
Kenya	*Modern English Services* (1975, a rendering of 1662 into modern English)
	A Service of Baptism (1991)
Kuching	*Admission of Catechumens* (1954)
	The Baptism of Children (n.d.)
	Holy Baptism of Those Who Are Old Enough to Answer for Themselves (n.d.)
	Revised Order of Confirmation (n.d.)
Mauritius	*L'Ordre de la Confirmation* (n.d.)
New Zealand	*A New Zealand Prayer Book* (1989)
Nigeria	*An Order for the Ministration of Public Baptism of Infants* (n.d., follows England 1928)
Papua/New Guinea	*Form of Admission of Catechumens, Baptism and Confirmation of Those Who Are Old Enough to Answer for Themselves, Baptism of Babies and Young Children, Confirmation* (n.d.)

---

[3] Alcuin Club Collections No. 52 (London: SPCK, 1970).

Singapore	*Diocese of Singapore Service Book* (1986)
Southern Africa	*An Anglican Prayer Book* (1989)
Tanzania	*An Adult Baptismal Liturgy, An Infant Baptismal Liturgy* (n.d.)
United States	*The Book of Common Prayer* (1979)
Wales	*The Book of Common Prayer for use in the Church in Wales* (1984)
	An Alternative Order for the Public Baptism of Infants, and an Alternative Order for Baptism and Confirmation (1990)
West Malaysia	*The Initiation Services* (1986, follows English *ASB* although with some interesting differences).

(In several provinces and dioceses initiation rites are still in the process of revision and copies of such work as has been done are not yet available.[4] To the best of my knowledge, this list is complete to July, 1991.)

Though there are many differences between the rites, all follow a similar basic order. Different names may be given to the various features of the order, but for the purposes of this discussion a general outline of the baptismal rite is as follows:

Gathering
The Word
Examination of the candidate
Thanksgiving over water
The baptism
Concluding prayers *or* Celebration of the eucharist
Dismissal

If confirmation is included as part of the baptismal rite, it follows the baptism and consists of prayer, laying on of hands, concluding prayers, and dismissal, or the celebration of the eucharist. On its own, confirmation follows an order similar to that of baptism:

---

[4]In a conversation with the Rev.Matthew Chung (May 1991), it was indicated that Korea uses a translation of the American *BCP*, though evidently with "adaptations." Dioceses such as El Salvador and Puerto Rico, being part of American provinces, use Spanish translations of the American book. The Scottish rites were not available at the time of writing.

Gathering
The Word
Examination of the candidate
Prayer
Laying on of hands
Concluding prayers *or* Celebration of the eucharist
Dismissal

Catechumenal rites, rare though they are, exhibit much the same order as well. After agreeing on the order, however, the initiation rites of the Anglican Communion ride off in all directions at once!

Gathering

Obviously, any liturgy must begin with the gathering together of the people of God. The rites of initiation are no exception. It is not apparent from an examination of the various rites, however, that we agree on who is being gathered, when we are gathering, or why.

Most of the rites are explicit that the preferred time for the celebration of Christian initiation is at an occasion of public worship. In Australia, the reasons given are those of the historic Prayer Books: so that "the whole congregation may witness the admission of the newly-baptized into Christ's Church and welcome them," and so that "Christians may be reminded of the profession of faith and obedience to God which they made in their own baptism" (p.500). In New Zealand, the congregation is expected to be more active, not simply to witness and be reminded, but to "renew their faith in Jesus as Lord and in the Creed profess the faith of their baptism" (p.380).

Though there is general agreement that initiation should be celebrated at public worship, there is considerable difference of opinion as to whether that should be the eucharist, morning or evening prayer, or a separate office. The majority of rites offer considerable latitude as to which public liturgy is appropriate. Canada and the US are unequivocal that the service should be one of baptism and holy communion. The only exception would be in a situation where a deacon was, through necessity, the presiding minister. Papua/New Guinea (adult baptism and confirmation) suggests that the normative pattern is baptism, confirmation, and eucharist. (Infant baptism, however, may take place at an office.)

On the whole, it is the rites developed most recently that reflect the *BEM* insistence on the connection between baptism and the eucharist. Thus Australia (1990), Brazil, New Zealand, Southern Africa, and Wales

(1990) all state, in one way or another, that it is *preferable* that baptism take place in the context of the eucharist. In some cases, such as Australia (1978, 1st and 2nd orders, adults and children), Chile, England, Ireland, Japan, Kenya, Kuching, Nigeria, Singapore, Tanzania,[5] Wales, and West Malaysia, baptism may take place as a separate office, though it is generally indicated that members of the congregation should attend. Kenya (1991) stipulates that when adults are baptized, "the context should be Holy Communion"; with infants, either the office or the eucharist are possible.

The direction of movement seems to be clear, i.e., towards a rite uniting baptism and the eucharist. Unless and until there is simply no option that baptism may take place at the divine office or as an office on its own, however, the essential unity of the two sacraments will continue to be obscured. The possibility that baptism may be celebrated apart from the principal Sunday liturgy continues to support those who understand the sacrament as an essentially private, family matter with no particular connection to ecclesial life.

In passing, it should be noted that virtually all formularies include some provision for emergency baptism, which obviously takes place in a more or less private setting. Southern Africa graciously notes that "parents and others requesting emergency baptism should be assured that questions of ultimate salvation or of the provision of a Christian funeral do not depend upon whether or not the person has been baptized" (p.396). This is undoubtedly true, and one wonders for what reasons we continue to provide a form for emergency baptism at all. Its existence can only continue to support the notion that "limbo" or "damnation" is the fate of those dying unbaptized. It can only undercut attempts to promote an understanding of baptism as initiation into the covenant community.

A final note about the occasion of baptism, whether or not its celebration is connected in any way with the liturgical year. Australia (1990), Brazil, Canada, and the US promote the understanding that baptism should be celebrated on particular festivals: Easter (especially at the Vigil), Pentecost, All Saints', Baptism of the Lord, and the occasion of a visit by the bishop. Canada offers, in addition (for those who are inundated

---

[5]This is a somewhat special case as the rite was developed for ecumenical use. It is not apparent from the text what Anglican practice actually is.

by requests for baptism), the Transfiguration of the Lord, and Holy Cross Day. The dates in these books do not appear to have the force of law, however.

The word

Not a few of the initiation rites come close to fulfilling Sydney Smith's rueful description of being "preached to death by wild curates." Unable to believe that the reading and homiletic exposition of scripture might be sufficient, the framers of many of the rites continue to display a tiresome didacticism. Usually this takes the form of a set piece outlining material that would probably better belong to prebaptismal catechesis. It is unclear whether the framers of the liturgies distrust the clergy's ability to fulfil their pastoral ministry or the people's ability to receive instruction. Chile has a form of instruction which precedes even the reading of scripture itself. Southern Africa has a brief introduction at the outset of the rite, and still more instruction after the sermon (in case the preacher forgets the occasion for which the sermon was prepared?).

The greatest anxieties seem to cluster around the baptism of children. The assumption is that the godparents have had little contact with the church previous to the celebration and must, therefore, be instructed in their duties during the celebration. This last-ditch effort to get people to do their duty appears to reflect a culture still expecting routine or indiscriminate baptism. Australia (1st order, infants), England (baptism of children), Wales, Nigeria, Kenya (1975), Singapore, Kuching, and West Malaysia all have set pieces explaining what is happening, why, and what duties are expected of the sponsors.

Curiously, for all the interest in instruction, there are a number of rites in which there is no provision for a sermon at all. These include Australia (1st order, infants; a sermon is optional in the 2nd order), Brazil (at the baptism of children there is no formal liturgy of the word at all, the presider *may* chose to speak from the gospels), Ireland (optional), Kenya, Papua/New Guinea (baptism of infants—unclear, probably not), Kuching (infants), Tanzania (infants, optional in the adult rite), Wales (infants, optional). Such rites make it difficult to see baptism as a response to the word read and proclaimed.

Kenya (1991) states unequivocally that a period of instruction (for adults, at least three months) is necessary before baptism can be celebrated. Candidates are presented by their instructor, who must vouch for the thoroughness of their preparation.

Which readings are to be used is another matter of contention. By and large, the division comes between the rites constructed before and after the publication of the *BEM* document. Australia (1990), Brazil (adults), Canada, Kenya (1991), New Zealand, Papua/New Guinea, Southern Africa, Wales (1990), and the United States support the use of the readings for the Sunday or Holy Day, although other suggested readings are also provided. In those cases in which it appears that the celebration of baptism is expected to be at a separate service, a complete set of readings or list of choices is provided. Such rites include Australia (1st order, infants and adults), England (infants, actually short quotations from scripture embedded in an exhortation), Ireland, Kenya, Nigeria, Kuching (infants), Wales (infants and adults), and West Malaysia. Even though baptism is expected to take place within the context of the eucharist or the divine office, the Japanese rite requires that a choice be made from a set of readings. Tanzania, on the other hand, features a *catena* of texts, read together.

Examination of the candidates

In most of the rites the examination of the candidates (and/or sponsors) takes place after the proclamation of the word. In a few instances certain questions are put before the word. Ireland, in this regard, asks the parents and sponsors whether they will see the infant Christianly brought up. So, also, Brazil and Wales (1990). In a sense, the questions asked before the word resemble a form of admission to the catechumenate, as the emphasis tends to be upon the sponsors' willingness to share formation and instruction in the Christian life with the child. Wales (1990) is the most unusual in this regard. Unique among all the rites, in the Welsh liturgy the signing of the (infant) candidate takes place before the word, even as happens in catechumenal rites.[6] (England allows for either a pre- or postbaptismal signing.)

Forms of admission to the catechumenate can be found in Japan, Papua/New Guinea, Southern Africa, and the American *Book of Occasional Services*. They include a signing of those admitted to the

---

[6] As was pointed out to me by the Rev. Dr. Keith M. Denison (August, 1991), the intention of this arrangement seems to have been to provide the Welsh church with a catechumenal rite.

catechumenate, which precedes the liturgy of the word. Kuching, though providing a form of admission to the catechumenate, does not prescribe a signing. In the case of Wales, curiously, the signing of an adult baptizand takes place after the word and after the candidate has renounced evil and turned to Christ.

The questions put to the candidates or sponsors all share in asking whether they turn from evil and turn to Christ. This may be done briefly as, for example, England:

P: Do you turn to Christ? R: I turn to Christ.
P: Do you repent of your sins? R: I repent of my sins.
P: Do you renounce evil? R: I renounce evil.

Or in a more extended fashion, such as in Canada and the US:

P: Do you renounce Satan and all the spiritual forces of wickedness that rebel against God?
R: I renounce them.
P: Do you renounce the evil powers of this world which corrupt and destroy the creatures of God?
R: I renounce them.
P: Do you renounce all sinful desires that draw you from the love of God?
R: I renounce them.
P: Do you turn to Jesus Christ and accept him as your Saviour?
R: I do.
P: Do you put your whole trust in his grace and love?
R: I do.
P: Do you promise to follow and obey him as your Lord?
R: I do.

Southern Africa has a similar set of renunciations but the affirmations take the form rather of a statement of belief and trust in the Father, Son, and Holy Spirit. In this rite, the renunciations and affirmations are divided from each other by the thanksgiving over water.

New Zealand has what is probably the most unusual arrangement of questions asked of the candidate. Following the New Testament lesson, gospel, or sermon (why present the possibility of dividing up the liturgy of the word?), the candidate is asked if he/she responds to God's promise of forgiveness of sins and the gift of the Holy Spirit. The candidate then renounces evil and, in faith, turns to Christ. Only *after* the baptism does the baptizand express a trinitarian faith (the Apostles' Creed is *not* used), and only *after* the baptism do parents and godparents indicate that they will share their faith with the infant baptizand. This is perhaps the first time that a part of the catholic church has not really asked anything of a candidate before baptism. As a further anomaly, if a person is baptized but not at the same time confirmed, there is no commitment made to any kind of Christian service.[7] This stands in stark contrast to such rites as Australia (1990), Canada, and the US, where the ethical implications of baptism are clearly part of the baptismal covenant.

Japan is unique in having the Apostles' Creed chanted after the baptism has taken place, but there is a trinitarian statement of faith before the baptism and other vows are made as well.

The participation of the congregation in this part of the rite also varies considerably. Australia (1990), Japan, Tanzania (infants and adults), Brazil, Canada, and the US ask the congregation a question such as:

> P: You have heard *these our brothers and sisters* respond to Christ's call. Will you support *them* in this high calling?
> R: We will do so.
>   (Australia, 1990)

There is also variety in how the Apostles' Creed is used. In certain cases the presider puts the articles of the creed in question form and the candidate or sponsor answers: "I believe": so Australia (1st order infants, adults) and Ireland. In others, the sponsors and candidates recite the Apostles' Creed: so Brazil (the congregation may join in) and Papua/New Guinea (infants and adults). It is not altogether clear who says the Apostles' Creed in the Welsh rite. In other instances the entire congregation joins in reciting the creed: so Australia (2nd order, infants and adults), Brazil (optional), Canada, Japan, Kenya, New Zealand, Chile, and the US.

The rest of the rites have briefer forms of credal statements. England is typical:

> P: Do you believe and trust in God the Father, who made the world?
> R: I believe and trust in him.
> P: Do you believe and trust in his Son Jesus Christ, who redeemed mankind?
> R: I believe and trust in him.
> P: Do you believe and trust in his Holy Spirit, who gives life to the people of God?
> R: I believe and trust in him.

---

[7]See "Additional Directions," *Arrangement of services* B., The Liturgy of Baptism only, p. 396).

The congregation then joins in as the presider says:

P: This is the faith of the Church.
R: This is our faith. We believe and trust in one God, Father, Son, and Holy Spirit.

In these rites this is the point at which the support of the congregation for the candidate becomes as explicit as it will ever be.

Thanksgiving over the water

The next element in the baptismal rite is variously named the "Blessing of the Water" or "Thanksgiving over the Water." Whatever the name, the rites differ on whether or not it is euchological (the emphasis being on blessing God), or an actual blessing of the water. If the prayer begins with a mutual salutation and call to give thanks, I have included it among the euchological forms. Others do not have such an introduction but demonstrate the euchological form in that which follows. This may include thanksgiving for any or all of: water at the beginning of creation; water as source of life and nourishment for all creatures; the delivery of Israel through the waters of the Red Sea; the crossing of the Jordan; the baptism of Christ; blood and water from the pierced side of Christ; Jesus himself passing through the "waters of death." There may also be thanksgiving for the work of the Spirit.

There is some division, however, over whether the Spirit is invoked upon the water or upon the candidate or both. In some cases, in true Anglican fashion, the text might be read in any of these ways. A detailed analysis of the structure and theology of these prayers is beyond the scope of this paper; it would, however, be a rewarding and valuable study. Among those rites which have euchological forms, I would include Australia (2nd order), Brazil, Canada (with a bold epiclesis over the water in the second of its two prayers), England, Japan, Kenya (1991), Kuching, Singapore, Southern Africa, Wales, Wales (1990), West Malaysia, and the United States. The emphasis in rites such as Australia (1st order), Ireland, Kenya, Nigeria, Papua/New Guinea, Chile, and Tanzania is on the candidate and his/her rebirth, followed by a petition that God bless the water.

The baptism

All the rites agree, of course, on the centrality of the water rite. It is on the question as to whether or not any other symbolic actions are to be used that the rites differ. Before the water rite, England (as noted above) provides the option of a prebaptismal signing, as does Wales. Malaysia, which follows England almost entirely, omits the prebaptismal anointing, however, believing that it would "create unnecessary confusion."[8]

Many of the rites provide for a postbaptismal signing, and the accompanying words, with one notable exception, are entirely christic. Whether the words are said entirely by the presider or whether they are shared with the congregation, the form is usually a variation of the familiar:

> I sign you with the cross, the sign of Christ. Do not be ashamed to confess the faith of Christ crucified. Fight valiantly under the banner of Christ against sin, the world and the devil, and continue his faithful *soldiers* and *servants* to the end of your *lives*.
>
> (Southern Africa, p.385)

The exception is the more pneumatic text of the American book:

> N., you are sealed by the Holy Spirit in Baptism and marked as Christ's own for ever. *Amen.*

This may appear at first to be only of passing interest. The American formula, however, may be a more helpful solution to the controverted nature of confirmation.

In all actions that follow the water rite, the word "may" appears with a great deal of frequency in the rubrics. Those rites which call for water alone are Australia (1st order, infants and adults), Ireland, Ireland (1988), Japan, Kenya (1975), Nigeria, and Chile. The giving of light, usually with some verbal formula, is an option in Australia (2nd order, infants and adults), Australia (1990), Brazil, Canada, England, New Zealand, Papua/New Guinea, Singapore, Kuching, Southern Africa, Tanzania, Wales, Wales (1990), West Malaysia, and the US (but with no words accompanying the giving of the candle).

The chrism is an option in South Africa where it is administered before

---

[8]As indicated in a letter from Bishop Tan Sri J.G. Savarimuthu (Feb.10, 1989).

the signing. In Tanzania, Wales, and Wales (1990) the chrism may be administered after the signing.

Oil may be used in Australia (1990), Brazil, Canada, Kenya (1991), Wales (1990), and the US. It is not always clear as to what significance the framers of the various rites attach to the oil, though it generally must be blessed by the bishop (though this is not explicit in Wales 1990). In England, oil is reserved for (optional) use at confirmation. The same applies in Papua / New Guinea and Southern Africa. In Wales, oil would be used at the confirmation. What, however, would be the significance of anointing a just-baptized adult who is not also being confirmed?

Laying on of hands

In the introduction to this paper, reference was made to the *BEM* document's somewhat ambiguous position regarding the necessity of a second rite signifying the gift of the Spirit. The majority of the rites surveyed here, however, are far from ambiguous on the matter. Most Anglican initiation rites require a second rite, that of confirmation. Just what this second rite consists of, however, is not so clear.

The form of the words attached to the moment in which the bishop lays on hands appears in basically three ways, as follows:

Defend, O Lord, your servant N. with your heavenly grace, that he/she may continue yours for ever, and daily increase in your Holy Spirit more and more, until he/she comes to your everlasting kingdom. Amen.

Strengthen, O Lord, your servant N. with your Holy Spirit; empower him/her for your service; and sustain him/her all the days of his/her life. Amen.

Confirm, O Lord, your servant N. with your Holy Spirit. Amen.

These do not seem to differ significantly from the words attached to "reaffirmation" in the American and Canadian books:

N., may the Holy Spirit, who has begun a good work in you, direct and uphold you in the service of Christ and his kingdom. Amen.

But, at this point, things begin to get more complicated. In England, the bishop has the option of using oil at the confirmation. This is also the case in Papua / New Guinea, Southern Africa, Wales (1990), and West Malaysia. How is this use of oil related to the use of oil (again, also optional) at baptism in the rites of other parts of the Anglican

Communion? To further complicate the matter, the Welsh form differs from the others in that the words accompanying the use of oil at confirmation are Christic rather than pneumatic.

The rite which seems most to suggest that the Spirit is given in confirmation is that of West Malaysia. The wording is: "Grant, O Lord, our Heavenly Father, Your Holy Spirit to your servant N. and confirm and strengthen him/her to live for your glory and honour. Amen." This is far stronger language than anything said concerning the gift of the Spirit to those being baptized.

Many of the rites attempt to unite baptism and confirmation, at least in the case of adults. It is held to be desirable (or at least possible) that adult baptizands be confirmed at the same service in Australia (2nd order, confirmation), Australia (1990), Brazil, England, New Zealand, Papua/New Guinea, Chile, Southern Africa, Wales, Wales (1990), and Ireland (1988). The American rubrics state that adults baptized by the bishop need not be confirmed, though others should be confirmed. Canada sees no requirement for those who have been baptized as adults to be confirmed. (It is far from certain that all Canadian bishops have noticed this feature of the text, however.)

In some rites, there is a hint of a theology of confirmation as the ordination of the laity. The *Veni Creator* or similar hymn is enjoined by Mauritius and Southern Africa, thereby making the service somewhat like an ordination. Chile's confirmation rite certainly suggests that the candidate has moved from a junior to a senior membership in the church: at baptism the candidate is received as a brother or sister in the church of Christ; at confirmation the candidate is received as a brother or sister who is now, with the congregation, a participant in the work of Christ and in the fellowship of the church. Further, the rubrics direct that the candidate may be received with an embrace by the community and the candidate's name is entered in the book of the church.

Summary

Clearly there are significant differences among initiation rites in the Anglican Communion. There has not been space here to analyze adequately the relationship of the catechumenate to the other rites, nor to delineate the various theologies incorporated in the prayers over the water or the other prayers of the rite. A general uniformity of order has been noted, however, though serious differences remain as to the relationship of baptism to the eucharist. Not only is this due to the requirement in many provinces that confirmation is still a prerequisite for communion, but also because the celebration of baptism at the divine office or as a separate office obscures the fact that participation in the Lord's supper is the logical expression of membership in his covenant community. Differing emphases may also be seen in the promotion of certain baptismal festivals, as opposed to (at the extreme) the celebration of the sacrament whenever convenient.

The promotion of certain festivals for baptism allows for a variety of scriptural texts to be heard, illuminating different facets of the baptismal mystery. This is in contrast to those rites which provide set texts which either defend infant baptism (Mark 10:13ff. being a favourite) or the divine origin of baptism (Matthew 28 and John 3). The Anglican penchant for didactic liturgy lives on in exhortations and instructions.

Some rites place more importance than others on the participation of the congregation, whether in the prayers, in declaring support for the candidates, or in the congregation's renewing of their own vows and recitation of the baptismal covenant in concert with the candidates. Might not such rites encourage the congregation also to see itself as the minister of the rite and become more engaged in prebaptismal catechesis?

There is evidently little agreement on the use of symbols or actions which amplify or interpret the water rite. In particular, there is confusion over the difference between the use of chrism at baptism and at confirmation.

Despite the ambiguity, the thrust of the *BEM* document is in the direction of water baptism being full initiation into the eucharistic fellowship of the church. Anglican rites display our reluctance to give up confirmation, even if it is tied more closely to the water rite than it may ever have been before. We do not yet appear to have heard what the Spirit is saying through the other churches.

Finally, a brief note about the different way in which the rites are set out in the various books. England probably stands as the book offering the most options: the baptism and confirmation of adults; the baptism of families and confirmation of adults; the baptism of adults; the baptism of families; the baptism of children; the confirmation of those already baptized. Other books provide a smaller menu. But does not even the existence of two forms, one for infants and one for adults, continue to suggest that there are, somehow, two species of baptism? This distinction becomes acute in the Southern Africa book where ambiguity remains about the status of adults who are ''not able to answer responsibly for themselves'' (p.378). As with children, they are baptized but not confirmed at the same service. While children will presumably grow to become happy confirmands, however, what happens to these adults "not able to answer responsibly"? Do they languish in a perpetual catechumenate, forever barred from receiving communion?

The Fourth International Anglican Liturgical Consultation achieved a high degree of accord on the form, content, and significance of baptism. Far from being idiosyncratic, the Toronto Statement reflects also the convergence of thought represented by *BEM*. Can we thus dare to hope that our formularies and practices might soon begin to reflect such broad agreement? We are speaking of rites which are foundational to our Christian identity. The churches of our Communion have much work yet to do before Anglicans everywhere will understand and recognize the baptized, of any age, as full members of the church, sharing in the eucharistic mystery and committed to a life of witness and service.

V Patterns of Initiation: An Anglican Mosaic

Child Communion:
How It Happened in New Zealand
Brian Davis and Tom Brown

History

The practice of admitting baptized children to communion before confirmation began "experimentally" in New Zealand in 1970 in the diocese of Waiapu. The 1968 Lambeth Conference had recommended to the provinces "experimentation" in the area of Christian initiation (Recommendation 25). In 1970 the General Synod endorsed this approach to reform and in 1972 recommended the following pattern:

  i. Baptism from infancy
 ii. Provision for Admission to Communion prior to Confirmation
iii. Confirmation as an event of adult life.

The Synod further resolved that "those admitted to Holy Communion prior to confirmation must be accepted as communicants throughout the Province." Initially Waiapu and only one or two other dioceses took advantage of the possible new approach to initiation.

In 1976 the General Synod recognized the 1972 pattern as "an alternative practice" and pastoral guidelines were provided to ensure orderly progress. Children could be admitted to communion "at not less than eight years of age and after at least one year's regular participation in the worshipping and/or educational life of the church." Appropriate instruction prior to a special service of admission was required. Names of those admitted to communion had to be entered in a diocesan register.

General Synod in 1978 re-affirmed the "alternative practice" by resolution, but the legality of the decision was challenged in an appeal to the Supreme Court. The applicants claimed that the "alternative practice" was in conflict with the confirmation rubric in *The Book of Common Prayer* (i.e., "there shall none be admitted to Holy Communion until such time as he be confirmed, or be ready and desirous to be confirmed"). Thus it became necessary for the General Synod to make canonical provision for the change, which it did in 1979. The new canon stated:

Not withstanding the provisions of the rubrics relating to Admission to Holy Communion, it shall be permitted as an alternative practice in the Church of the Province of New Zealand for baptized children to be admitted to Holy

Communion prior to Confirmation after instruction approved by the Bishop.

The canonical process was completed with the 1980 General Synod which also approved revised Guidelines. These incorporated both the traditional and the new practices. No lower age limit for admission to communion was stated. Admission could take place when:

> the family and parish priest judge appropriate, *or* after more formal instruction and at a special service, *or* after laying-on-of-hands by the Bishop following instruction.

The reference to ''instruction'' in the canon ruled out infant communion, though the dropping of any reference to the age of eight years encouraged a downward movement in the ages of those admitted. In fact, at this time (1980) some parents were beginning to communicate their very young children by sharing their own consecrated bread with them.

In 1972, fourteen parishes, all in the diocese of Waiapu, were admitting children to communion prior to confirmation. By 1984, 170 parishes (about half of all parishes in the province) were admitting children to communion. All dioceses were involved, and in one diocese all parishes were committed to the new approach. Today more than ninety per cent of New Zealand parishes practice child communion.

In the diocese of Wellington prior to 1986, the bishop was opposed to the practice and acted to discourage clergy from following the approved provincial Guidelines. In 1973, fourteen percent of all Wellington parishes were admitting children to communion prior to confirmation; in 1978 twenty-one percent, in 1983 eighteen percent, and in 1989 sixty-eight percent. These figures underline the significance of the bishop's role in encouraging or frustrating change. The 1983 figure reflects the negative move of the then bishop and the 1989 figure, the fact that his successor was a strong supporter of child communion.

The New Zealand approach of allowing both the traditional and the new practice to continue side by side has been pastorally helpful and avoided general hostility toward the change. Clergy and parishes more open to the new approach have tended to encourage those hesitant to change. Experience of the new way has been positive and, except under episcopal pressure, no parishes having begun to admit children to communion have returned to the traditional pattern or urged child confirmation as an alternative approach to the practice of child communion.

The present situation

A New Zealand Prayer Book, which came into use in 1989, offered the province new initiation rites. In 1990 further revised Guidelines for Christian Initiation were approved by General Synod to ensure pastoral consistency with the rubrics of the Prayer Book. In the introductory section to the baptismal liturgy, the Prayer Book states:

> When someone is baptized, that person is brought to Jesus Christ, and made a member of Christ's Church.
>
> When a baptism is of a baby or a child the baptized receives the love and shared faith of the family to grow up in Christ.
>
> Through prayer and fellowship within the Body of Christ, God strengthens and nourishes us (p.379).

Parents and godparents are exhorted to "encourage their child to take her/his place in the eucharistic community..." (p.382). The current provincial Guidelines, approved in 1990, state:

> The sacramental means of entry and incorporation into the body of Christ occurs through Baptism. The Eucharist is the sacramental means by which members of the Body are sustained and nurtured in that community and is the central act of worship in the Christian Church. Baptism confers full membership of the Church, and therefore provides the ground for admission to Holy Communion. All may therefore receive communion from the time of their Baptism regardless of age.
>
> Variations in pastoral practice in relation to admission to the communion may be found, but those once admitted (whether at Baptism, or when judged pastorally appropriate by priest and family, or at a special service after more formal instruction, or after receiving the Laying on of Hands for Confirmation), are welcome to receive communion in any parish in the Province.
>
> A process of education is essential in developing an awareness and understanding of the meaning of the Eucharist. Teaching on the Eucharist should be made widely available.

These new Guidelines were accepted by the General Synod even though the reference to "instruction approved by the bishop" as a prerequisite for admission remains as a canon. The repeal of this canon is now necessary to remove all legal obstacles to infant communion and give the Guidelines unquestionable force.

At this stage the practice of infant communion is exceptional and most children are being admitted to communion from about the age of seven years, after a period of preparation and special instruction. Teaching resources have been provided within the province, the best known being Graham Brady's *Going to the Supper of the Lord*. A handbook for teachers and a workbook designed for use by children in the 7-10 age group has been particularly popular. More educational resources are currently being prepared.

A constant factor in provincial guidelines has been the requirement of parental approval. Parents are expected to be present with their communicating children. Special adult sponsorship provision is made for baptized children who are admitted but don't have the support of their parents at worship.

Cultural factors

The New Zealand approach to reform in the area of Christian initiation, and in particular child communion, allows the main cultural groupings (Maori, Pakeha, and Polynesian), and also the individual dioceses and parishes, to move at their own pace, subject only to the provincial Guidelines. Though this has resulted in a diversity of pastoral practice, no serious pastoral confusion or difficulties have arisen. The process of change has been largely problem-free.

The rightness and value of child communion has won overwhelming acceptance among the seven dioceses of the province—what we are now calling "*Tikanga Pakeha.*" There has been a slower response to admission of children to communion in both the diocese of Polynesia and *Te Pihopatanga* among Maori Anglicans. *Tikanga Polynesia* and *Tikanga Maori* have been more resistant to ecclesiastical reform generally than has *Tikanga Pakeha*. Cultural rather than theological factors explain this best. No *Tikanga* is opposed to the alternative practice, however, and in time all are likely to follow more fully the lead given by the dominant *Tikanga*.

Some challenges

Currently the province is addressing some of the pastoral, educational, and liturgical implications of children at communion. These may be summarized by the following questions:

1. How does a eucharistic community recognize and provide for the presence of children?

2. How does the traditional Sunday school model of Christian nurture need to be modified once children are admitted to communion?

3. What parental or other adult sponsor support does a young child need if he/she is admitted to communion?

4. What teaching and liturgical resources do parishes need to improve the quality of their ministry to children who are participants in the eucharistic faith community?

Summary

The movement towards child and infant communion has been welcomed within the Church of the Province of New Zealand. It has required episcopal leadership and the leadership of parish clergy to win the support of the laity. In some places, however, it has been the lay people who have brought pressure to bear for change from the old pattern in the face of reluctant clergy. The province has allowed reform to take place at its own pace, and this has been well accepted. The unevenness of this process of acceptance has not been a pastoral problem.

The benefits of child communion could be identified as follows:

1. The practice recognizes the fullness of baptism as *the* sacrament of membership.

2. The participation of children in eucharistic worship nurtures them in their spiritual growth as members of the body of Christ.

3. The presence of children at the eucharist reminds the local church of the value and importance of children, and of the gifts they bring to the faith community as a whole.

4. The practice of child communion has the effect of transforming aging congregations into family gatherings with all age groups being represented.

5. The practice of child communion has an evangelistic dimension. Children can and do invite their friends to worship and this can lead to their baptism and/or admission to communion.

The Bishop in Initiation
J.C. Fricker

The longer I am a bishop the more I am persuaded that a major role in my relationship with the congregations within my pastoral care is to encourage them in their vocation as baptizing communities. As I publish the date of my annual visit to each parish about a year in advance, parishes are able to follow the guidelines in the Canadian *Book of Alternative Services* and plan that the visit of the bishop be one of the five occasions during the year when baptism is celebrated. Consequently, I preside at the baptismal liturgy (and therefore at the renewal of the baptismal covenant) most Sundays of the year, except during the lenten season. What once were confirmation visits have become baptismal celebrations in which all members of the community renew their baptismal faith and some present themselves for the laying on of hands for affirmation/confirmation.

On other Sundays, I make it a point to visit a parish for its regular celebration of the eucharist, at which I preside and preach. A theme that has taken on an increasing prominence in my preaching is reminding parish communities that they are the baptized and that, because they are the baptized, each person within the community has a baptismal ministry. The local community is, in its response to the call to mission, above all a baptizing community.

In preparation for my visit

Having set the date of my visit, I request the clergy to arrange with me a time prior to the designated Sunday when I can spend an evening or Saturday morning with the candidates for baptism, those seeking the laying-on of hands, and the parents and godparents of infants to be baptized. This visit serves several purposes. The first is to build a relationship with the candidates so that we are not total strangers when we meet for the liturgy itself. The second is to rehearse the liturgy, in much the same way as a wedding ceremony is rehearsed. Third, the rehearsal provides an opportunity to discuss with the candidates what the baptized life is all about. Fourth, since I preach each Sunday on the appointed lections, this prebaptismal meeting enables us to discuss together, bishop *and* candidates, how the lections might apply to specific aspects of baptized living.

A further advantage to the pre-liturgy visit is the opportunity to review with the clergy what will take place at the liturgy itself. In this way I manage to avoid most of the inappropriate liturgical additions that seem to creep into local practice.

The place of confirmation

I have presided at far fewer confirmations in my six years as bishop than did my predecessor. It is not that the number of confirmations is decreasing, but that there has been a dramatic change in their nature. Though there are still adolescents being presented for the laying-on of hands, there are certainly fewer of them. When I meet with these young people, there is inevitably the odd one who admits to going through with the confirmation in order to satisfy parents or even, occasionally, the parish priest. In all situations involving young people, I attempt to impress upon them the desirability of reaffirming their baptismal vows again sometime in the future. The repeatability of this liturgical reaffirmation is received with considerable interest, and the name is gradually changing from "confirmation" to "reaffirmation." I recently visited one of my parishes and met a young man, nineteen years of age, whom I had "confirmed" when he was 14. He was now seeking to reaffirm his baptismal vows once again and receive the episcopal laying-on of hands.

Perhaps the most exciting development within my episcopal area is in one of my parishes where there is a year-long parish program of preparation for baptism and reaffirmation, mostly involving new members. A date is set for my visit during the Easter season. During the liturgy, the baptismal and reaffirmation candidates briefly tell their story of journeying in the faith.

The seasons of Lent and Easter

There are four deaneries in my episcopal area, each of which has from ten to twelve parishes. I have led a "Journey of Faith" lenten program in three of the four deaneries. The program involves the gathering, one evening a week throughout Lent, of the adult baptismal and reaffirmation candidates from all the parishes in the deanery. Each gathering begins with a celebration of the eucharist. A coffee break follows, and then there is a presentation on some aspect of the Christian faith. Between fifty and one hundred people have attended each of these programs. The climax is a deanery-wide Great Vigil of Easter when the baptisms and reaffirmations take place. In the other deaneries, I have encouraged my clergy to arrange for "cluster" (i.e., two or more neighbouring parishes) confirmations during the great fifty days of Easter. These are usually held on Sunday afternoons or evenings.

Parish missions

Because I believe that a major accomplishment during this Decade of Evangelism can be the reclaiming of the baptismal ministry of the whole people of God, I have led several parish missions on this theme. The Friday evening and two or three Saturday sessions, focusing on the ministry of the baptized and of the parish as a baptizing community, have concluded with a renewal of the baptismal covenant, with the community gathered around the font.

Renewal of baptismal signs

One of the signs of reclaiming the church's baptismal vocation has been changing the time of baptism from a private ceremony attended only by family and friends to celebrating baptism within the principal parish eucharist on Sunday morning. In my experience, that is now universal. This makes clear the relationship between baptism and eucharist, and that all the baptized are entitled to be communicants by virtue of their baptism.

A more recent sign of the reclaiming of the church's baptismal vocation is the increase in the amount of water used in baptism and the repositioning of the font. Most parishes have refurbished their liturgical space, not only to reposition the holy table but also the baptismal font to places of obvious symbolic centrality. I have one parish where the tiny font has been replaced by a tank so that all baptisms are by immersion. In other parishes the place of baptism has been so reordered that it is now possible for a generous amount of water to be poured over the head of the candidate.

From "confirmer" to "baptizer"

Not very long ago bishops' liturgical schedules were almost completely occupied with parish visits for the purposes of confirmation. The change now to a schedule in which the celebration of baptism takes precedence has clearly altered the perception of the episcopal office. Bishops, therefore, have a critical role in restoring the vocation of the church as a baptizing community.

Baptizing the Nation:
The Problems of Baptism in an Established Church
Donald Gray

The problems surrounding infant baptism have an additional dimension for those of us in an established church. And some would say that they are of our own making. Within the Church of England we have talked (and taught) about the fact that every part of England is in some parish or other, that every dwelling is someone's pastoral responsibility. At induction services, this point is commonly made in the bishop's or archdeacon's address. Again, at these services, it is taken for granted that the Church of England has a particular relationship with the local community structures, so that it is very common for the mayor and the head of the neighbourhood state school to afford a welcome to the new vicar by virtue of the fact that they have responsibilities for the same "patch." This is not simply a matter concerning the church-state relationship; it has to do with geographical boundaries. These parochial boundaries are precisely drawn and can be changed only by legal process.

Legal exactitude

This same concept is further enshrined in other aspects of the law of the land. Not only are there specific provisions for parishioners (i.e., literally and precisely those who live within these strictly defined parish boundaries) concerning, for instance, marriage, but also there are other rights and obligations. Garth Moore and Timothy Briden have set them out in their introduction to the Canon Law of the Church of England:

> Everyone living in the parish is a parishioner regardless of his religious persuasion. So also is anyone who, though not living in the parish, occupies land therein and pays rates. So also is anyone on the electoral roll of the parish. Every baptized parishioner who is sixteen years old or over is entitled to have his name put on the electoral roll, if he declares that he is a member of the Church of England and that he does not belong to any religious body not in communion with the Church of England.

> A parishioner, whether or not on the electoral roll, and whether or not a member of the Church of England, has certain obligations and rights.

In strict law he is under an obligation to attend the parish church on all Sundays and holy days unless he has a reasonable excuse for his absence (Act of Uniformity, 1551 [5 & 6 Edw. VI. c.1]) or unless he dissents from the doctrine and worship of the Church and usually attends some place of worship other than that of the Established Church (Religious Disabilities Act, 1846 [9 & 10 Vict. c.59]). Attendance at another place of worship of the Church of England is good excuse (Britton v. Standish [1704], Holt K.B. 141), and in any event no pecuniary penalty can be incurred, but only ecclesiastical censure (Britton v. Standish, and since the passing of the Ecclesiastical Jurisdiction Measure, 1963 [No.1], it would seem that even censure has application only to a clergyman). The Book of Common Prayer (rubric at the end of the service for Holy Communion) further directs that none shall be admitted to the Holy Communion until such time as he be confirmed or be ready and desirous to be confirmed (rubric at the end of the Order of Confirmation).

As a corollary to his obligation to attend divine worship, a parishioner has a right of entry to the parish church at the time of public worship, so long as there is room for him, standing or sitting, and he has a right to a seat if there is one available, but not a right to any particular seat (unless one has been given him by faculty), and he must sit where directed by the church-wardens. He has a right (if it be so termed) to the burial of his body in the burial ground of the parish, regardless of his religion. He has a right to be married in the parish church, at any rate if one of the parties to the marriage has been baptized. In general, it is apprehended that, whatever his religion, as a parishioner he has a right to the ministrations of the church, so far as they are appropriate to his condition. It is further apprehended that a temporary visitor to the parish is entitled to the ministrations of the church so far as they are appropriate to his condition; he certainly has the satisfaction of knowing that, if he dies there, he may also be buried there (Halsbury, vol.10, para.1118).[1]

Against such a background as this it is perhaps not surprising that there should be a strong conviction among some parents in England that baptism should be available "on demand," being, as it were, part of the birthright of any English child. Indeed, a recent BBC television documentary made play on this phrase, claiming to be examining whether or not baptism as a birth *rite* was indeed each child's *birthright*. In the television program there were interviews with both clergy and lay folk who

---

[1]E.Garth Moore and Timothy Briden, *Moore's Introduction to English Canon Law* (London: Mowbray, 2nd ed., 1985), 39-40.

claimed that such a right certainly did exist, and that the Church of England would become nothing more than one sect among many if it adopted a rigorist line concerning baptism.

An established "duty"

The question is, then: Does an established church such as the Church of England best serve the nation by an open policy, or does it serve the nation better by preserving the integrity of Christian initiation and clearly delineating the boundaries of the Christian Church? The latter option would not necessarily be a desertion from principles. It would still allow the Church of England to exercise an effective "Apostolate of the undevout," as the recently deceased Alec Vidler described the role of the Anglican religious establishment in England.

However, this would not be the popular man (or woman)-in-the-street's concept of the Church of England. The Church of England is seen by many, who would not otherwise wish to identify themselves with its life, as a purveyor of certain functions which are traditional to English life. Like the Post Office or any other public utility, it ought always to be there, ready for whenever it is needed. And this seemingly simplistic attitude is fiercely defended by those who see the Church of England moving away from its duty to be the church of the nation, to be the Church *of* England rather than merely the Church *in* England.

Those who hold a traditional point of view regarding the "duty" of the church to baptize all who are presented for the sacrament would find themselves joining forces with those who find it irritating when the church "goes all religious on them." As the teenager said of the nativity scene in a High Street shop window: "They're even bringing religion into Christmas now!" The establishment traditionalists would defend their attitude against those who mutter about "cheap grace," believing that the Church of England has a right, a duty, and a responsibility to "baptize the nation."[2]

---

[2]The most recent scholarly examination of the establishment of the Church of England is Adrian Hastings, *Church and State: The English Experience*, The Prideaux Lectures for 1990 (University of Exeter Press, 1991).

Pastoral Care and Baptismal Practice on the Fringes of Society:
The Diocese of Cuba
Juan Quevedo-Bosch

Profile

To put it simply (though incompletely), Cuban culture is a fusion of the Spanish heritage brought by the colonialists, the African magical world of the slaves, and the influence of the French Enlightenment on the cultural elite. To this must be added, since 1959, the influence of orthodox Marxism-Leninism, mellowed somewhat under the heat of the tropical sun!

The present religious situation could be simplified as follows: There exists in Cuba a small minority of practising Christians, of both the Roman Catholic and Evangelical (i.e., Protestant) traditions. In addition there is a larger minority of "Catholics-of-their-own-style," as they call themselves (basically non-practicing Catholics). A third group consists of followers of the African syncretic cults which, though legal,[1] are non-institutional (i.e., without a regular place of meeting, regulated priesthood or membership procedures, or any national organization). A fourth group, the Spiritualists, is divided into three sub-groups: the first influenced by the French Kardecianism called Scientific-Spiritualism and two being dissident offshoots.

Among *la religiosidad popular*, membership in a particular group is not clearly defined and is marked by considerable mobility and overlapping. Due to the syncretistic mingling of Catholic saints with African deities, the people of *la religiosidad popular* attend the Roman Catholic Church when their rites require it of them. The Episcopal Church of Cuba, however, is the only Protestant church with followers of the syncretic cults included within a stable membership. They are one of the few Christian churches that do not consider the syncretistic faith of the cults to be either

---

[1]The Oni of Ife, Nigeria's High Priest-King of the Yoruba, visited Cuba some time ago and met a representation of the *babalaos* and other religious dignitaries. Yoruba religion is the most numerous and influential of the religious complex called by the generic name "African syncretic cults."

utter foolishness (as do evangelicals of the liberal left) or the work of satanic forces (as do those of a more fundamentalist persuasion).

The final group within the population are the Marxist-Leninists. By its own standards, communism requires that its adherents have nothing to do with religion. In popular understanding, however, it is recognized that various levels of private religious involvement are possible. There are Marxists who occasionally (on the basis of need) practise some form of religion—Roman Catholicism and the African cults being the favoured groups. There is also a large group of young people who basically have no feelings about religion one way or the other, and know very little about it.

People from any of these various segments of the population may, at some point, request baptism for their children. For those of Marxist-Leninist persuasion, or for those not wanting to jeopardize their upward mobility, the request will be made vicariously, that is, through a friend or relative.

The Cuban Episcopal Church

In 1966 the last Episcopal bishop appointed for Cuba by the American Church died in a hospital in the United States, after a long battle with cancer. His death occasioned a period of stressful change for the Episcopal community in Cuba. Autonomy was granted by the American Church, although this was more for political than ecclesiastical reasons and was not the result of a natural process of maturation and increasing self-government. In 1967 the Anglican Church of Canada was "persuaded" by the American Church to "nurse" the Cuban Church along. Shortly thereafter the Metropolitan Council for the Episcopal diocese of Cuba was set up, presided over by the Canadian primate. At the present time a new ecclesiastical province is in the process of being formed, to consist of the dioceses of Cuba (extra-provincial), Haiti (Province IV, USA), the Dominican Republic (Province IX, USA) and Puerto Rico (extra-provincial).

Today *La Iglesia Episcopal de Cuba, Diócesis Extraprovincial*, has forty organized missions and preaching points covering almost every area of the country. The church is served by one bishop, thirteen priests (one retired), seven deacons, and four seminarians. There are approximately three thousand Anglicans in Cuba, about seventy-five per cent being women in their middle years or older with a primary to secondary level of education, the majority being either homemakers or retired. Recently there have been some discreet signs of new life in certain communities, generally paralleling the improved situation for Christians within the Cuban socialist state. Though Christian roots lie deep in Cuba, the fringe character of contemporary Cuban Christian experience can hardly be denied. Within the very small, active Christian minority, Anglicans are a tiny group indeed.

Pastoral praxis

Baptism for their infants is one of the "services" that the general population in Cuba considers they are entitled to seek from the church. This is true for both the Roman Catholic Church and the Episcopal Church (many Cubans having a hard time distinguishing between the two). The Evangelical churches either practice adult baptism or are perceived by the general populace as being tied too closely to the "outsiders."

This continuing desire for people to have their children baptized may be explained by the extraordinary persistence of the medieval economy of salvation in the minds of the people. In the popular understanding, if a child is not baptized it is much more likely to fall ill. This view persists despite the availability of free public health care and an infant mortality rate of only 13.6 per thousand. This can only be explained by the obvious "success" of five centuries of Christian preaching which has made it possible for this understanding to become deeply embedded in the national consciousness.

The changes brought about by Vatican II have corrected, somewhat, the practice of indiscriminate baptism within the Roman Catholic Church. Popular understanding does not change overnight, however, and the reforms of Vatican II have resulted in increased pressure on the Episcopal Church to continue the practice of baptizing virtually any infant on demand.

To date the diocese has never actually dealt with the question of Christian initiation. Other problems, such as the survival of the church itself, seemed much more pressing. During the early years of socialism, most of the laity and clergy left the church, some going into exile in the United States, others remaining in Cuba. Pastoral care was left in the hands of the few remaining priests who were always overworked and often burned out. One of the results has been considerable laxity in the area of Christian initiation. From my own experience, I can say that very often it was considered sufficient to give the sponsors a homily on the meaning of Christian initiation and some stern injunctions against the popular "magical" understanding of baptism. To all of this they would simply smile, as if it was merely one of the things that must be endured in order to have the child "done."

The situation in Cuba is changing, however. Along with a considerable deterioration in the economy, the restrictions under which the Christian mission has been carried out are being eased. In October of this year (1991), the Communist Party will consider the possibility of allowing Christians to become members. With this changing position of the church or, as a fellow priest put it, with the "releasing of the social brakes," we may expect some of the lapsed to return, while, at the same time, new opportunities to reach out to the unchurched gradually open. The question of Christian initiation is rapidly becoming a priority.

How is the church to deal with the lapsed and the unchurched? While I do not expect that we will be swamped by the masses (Cubans have never been known to be overly religious), the present infrastructure of the church is operating on a significantly reduced basis. Even a moderate addition of people to the church could result in a dilution of the small but committed Christian community.

This is perhaps the church's best opportunity to deal with the question of Christian initiation as a whole. One of the most frequent rationales for the present practice is that, since the church is legally limited to action within "the temples," baptism is a service the church can provide to the people, and is the only significant bridge between the church and society. Others hold to the "autonomy of operation" of the sacraments, based on an interpretation of certain sections of the Articles of Religion. Some see baptism, then, as an opportunity for missionary work, a way of relating to new households within the community. Today, however, as new possibilities are being opened, it certainly can be argued that instead of holding on to a very frail and fleeting connection with society through the practice of indiscriminate baptism, new and more solid ways of relating to the larger community must be found.

The restoration of Christian initiation in Cuba

The Episcopal Church in Cuba must reclaim Christian initiation as a sacrament that basically pertains to the faith community. It is through the local faith community that the unchurched relate to the larger category church. It is through the local faith community that the signs of the church are present. Baptismal vows must be made in a context where it is possible for them to be fulfilled.

Only through the restoration of the catechumenate can candidates for baptism be tested and prove, over a period of time, their real commitment to entering into covenant with God. The length of time required in this candidacy should be governed by the Christian maturing of each person involved, and the local faith community should have a say in the admission of candidates. Comprehensive Christian instruction should be provided and the community of believers should be involved with the catechumens, supporting them and sharing with them their experiences of the Christian life. In this way the catechumens will learn from their sisters and brothers in the faith community and not simply from the priest or teacher alone.

Infant baptism should not be discontinued but should be limited to families which are already a part of the Christian community. Parents from outside the faith community, seeking baptism for their children, should be invited to renew their own baptismal vows (or be baptized themselves as the case may be), and only then would their children be eligible for baptism.

La Iglesia en la Provincia Anglicana/Episcopal del Caribe (The Church in the Anglican/Episcopal Province of the Caribbean) will soon be a reality. A new Prayer Book is in the making. It will incorporate elements from the American *Book of Common Prayer* (1979), still the *lex orandi* of most of the dioceses, and of "The Cuban Liturgy for the Eucharist." It is hoped that the new province will examine the question of Christian initiation in a comprehensive way, making its own unique contribution to liturgical development within the Anglican Communion. This will also be an opportunity to deal with some of the contextual and pastoral issues that will undoubtedly emerge from the proposed restoration of the integrity of the Christian initiation rite.

For the Cuban Episcopal Church, as a minority church within a religious milieu highly influenced by Roman Catholicism and in a society influenced by Marxism, the bishop is seen as the point of contact with the rest of the diocese and with the worldwide Anglican Communion. The bishop, therefore, must be a major source of pastoral stimulus to the local congregations. The recovery of the integrity of the Christian initiation rite and the consequent removal of the practice of confirmation will create a void in present liturgical piety. A number of possibilities could be explored as replacements for confirmation, including the renewal of baptismal vows accompanied by an appropriate liturgical gesture. This may be a solution, also, to the question of what to do with lapsed Christians returning to the fold.

Requests for indiscriminate baptism will not cease simply because the church has decided to change its practice. Often, however, members of the church are the ones who sponsor a child of parents who have nothing to do with the faith community (e.g., their own married sons and daughters). An adamant refusal by the priest will create any number of pastoral problems at the local level. A blessing of the infants (possible styled after the *BCP*'s the "Churching of Women") could possibly bridge the gap.

Regarding the inculturation of the liturgy, the Episcopal Church cannot afford to ignore the African component in the culture of the islands. In the 1930s a School of Afrocuban Studies was established. This institution could provide material that might well be helpful in the attempt to provide an expression of the catholic faith within the cultural "vernacular."

The church in Cuba is going through troubled but promising times. We have the opportunity, today, of recovering a place within the very heart of Cuban society. May God provide us with the wisdom to discern the right path to follow.

Adult Baptism:
A Pacific Perspective
Winston Halapua

The diocese of Polynesia, the largest in geographic area in the Anglican Communion, covers a vast area which is mostly ocean and fish. The diocese includes the Kingdom of Tonga, the Independent State of Western Samoa, the Republics of Nauru, Fiji, and Kiribati, the Government of Tuvalu, the Self-Governing Countries of Cook Islands, Niue, and American Samoa, French Polynesia-Tahiti, and the Marqueses. Our diversities include numerous languages and cultures.

I write particularly in the context of Fiji, which is at the heart of the South Pacific and the administrative centre of the diocese. Fiji itself includes many ethnic groups and religions. The two major ethnic groups are the Fijians and the descendants of those who came in the last century from India to work on the plantations. These Indo-Fijians are predominantly Hindu.

Our approach to adult baptism arises, first of all, out of our commitment to renewal within the church and our call to share our faith with others, and, secondly, out of our desire to respond to the varying needs of those who do not have a Christian background. In the complexity of our situation, we find that the inherited approach of teaching with words and reading materials falls short.

The need of our people in the Pacific is for quality of life, and a vital issue which our diocese continues to address is how to communicate the gospel. We need an approach which is not so much in terms of words but, rather, of allowing the good news to become incarnate in our lives. When we prepare adults for baptism in Polynesia, there needs to be a balance between the faith we impart and a vital experience of that faith within the worshipping community. Both the teaching of the gospel and the experience of the gospel are essential.

If we are to continue in this great task of preparing and nurturing adults for baptism certain steps will be important. The participation of all baptized Christians in the process of welcoming and enabling newcomers is vital. For years, in Polynesia, we have maintained a model of ministry in which the mission of the church has been entrusted to only a few—the ordained and the "semi-official," such as lay-readers—who are mostly male. It has been a model in which the few dominate and the majority are spectators.

Small groups scattered throughout the parishes have a vital role to play in enabling baptized Christians to participate in the mission of the church. Through such groups newcomers are welcomed and nurtured by the worshipping community: relationships are established, the gospel is seen to apply to everyday life, and community is formed. It is the very life of these small units that constitutes the celebration of the liturgy of the wider community in the Sunday eucharist.

Small groups for bible study, prayer, and fellowship provide fertile soil for the growth of people from differing ethnic and cultural backgrounds. They enable respect of persons rather than the labelling and caricaturizing which results from ignorance. In our experience (where the development of urban centres is a relatively new phenomenon), the role of small groups in the provision of acceptance, growth of understanding, and fellowship is imperative. The large gathering on Sunday, without the operation of the small units, may be daunting to newcomers and cause feelings of alienation.

Small groups provide continuity to the process of adult baptism. In our diocese, priests make space for teaching and preparing adults for baptism. The priest then encourages the newcomers to take an active part in the life of a small unit within the parish. In this way, Christian nurture is not limited to the period prior to initiation but is ongoing. The ministry of enabling newcomers is thus a matter of teamwork between clergy and laity, i.e., between all baptized Christians.

Polynesia is departing from its inherited pattern of preparing adults for baptism. Now small groups are instrumental in allowing the lay people to participate in the process of adult baptism. The joy of welcoming newcomers is the celebration of the whole church. This is a truly Pacific way. We in the Pacific work, struggle, and celebrate as a community.

Traditional Initiation Rites among the Ngunis and Their Relationship to Christian Initiation
Themba Jerome Vundla

Introduction

The Ngunis are the African people who occupy the eastern and south-eastern side of the present Republic of South Africa. They are of three tribes: the Xhosas, Zulus, and Swazis. The practices I discuss in this paper, however, are not purely Nguni. They are found also among the Sotho nations further to the west and north.

Initiation is a very broad term in African understanding, covering birth initiation rites, puberty initiation rites, and marriage initiation rites. Undergirding all of these rites is the strong bond between the living and the dead who, according to the Africans, are truly more alive than dead.

Birth rites

Every baby is born into a family. According to Nguni tradition, each child is a gift from God who sometimes can be seen as synonymous with a great ancestor. A family on earth is, as it were, holding the child in trust for the family in the other world. This means, therefore, that the earthly family must adhere to the family traditions and perform the required rites meticulously.

Among the Nguni, birth rites vary among the three language groups or tribes. Indeed, they may vary within a tribe according to which clan the family belongs. And when it comes to minute details, these may, in fact, vary from family to family. I will examine briefly the birth rites of three groups within the Nguni: the Mpondos (presently classified as a Xhosa clan, although I believe them to be a separate tribe joined to the Xhosas only by language); the Zondis and Zumas (both Zulu clans); and the Mbovus or Ngubanes (also a Zulu clan).

a) Amampondo (Pondos):
This people, who occupy the northern part of the present Transkei, have at least one outstanding feature: that of face marks. A child, while still very young, is ceremoniously admitted into a family by being scratched on the face with an instrument that leaves vertical scars. These usually

include a "blade mark" which cuts down from the centre of the fore-head on to the nose and chin. These marks are the same as those found among the Huasas of Northern Nigeria.

b) Zondi and Zuma clans:

Among these people there is a similar practice of cutting the face. The difference is that here the marks are short and on the cheek (four or five on each side) rather than over the entire face. I have worked in an area where these clans are prevalent and have discovered that these birth-rite marks may extend also to relatives of Zondi or Zuma clan members. For instance, if your maternal grandmother was a Zondi, you could end up being marked. The expression used is *"umntwana ukhalela uphawu lukaninakhulu"* (the baby is crying out for his grandmother's traditional marks).

This cutting is accompanied by other initiation rites which normally include slaughtering a goat and reporting the baby to the "living dead" members of the family. These facial marks are an outward sign which distinguishes any particular child from the children of other families.

c) Abasemabomvini, the Mbovus:

This clan is in the Kranskop area of Natal, on the Tugela River which forms the boundry between Natal and Zululand. I refer to them because their "outward sign" is more peculiar. Here the tip of the little finger on the right hand is cut off. When the baby's finger-tip is cut off, another member of the family receives a few drops of the baby's blood into a cut made for that purpose. Thus there is an "exchange of blood" between the two. This means that the baby literally becomes of "one blood" with the rest of the Mbovu family, both the living and the departed.

After the birth of a child, friends and relatives also welcome him or her with gifts. When a person sees a baby for the first time, it is assumed that he or she will give a present or some money. This is a sign of welcoming and of giving thanks to God for the baby's safe arrival.

Another rite associated with birth, formerly quite common among the Zulu though not very regularly observed these days, is the *imbeleko* or "baby-carrier" ceremony. When walking a long distance a woman uses an *imbeleko* for carrying her baby on her back. But as the name of an initiation rite, *imbeleko* has a more technical meaning.

In order to appreciate the *imbeleko* ceremony, it must be understood that the happiness of a Nguni bride lies mainly in her ability to bear children. A newly married woman who does not become pregnant within a year is looked on with serious disapproval. Because of the patriarchal nature of the African family, people do not normally stop to consider that it may be the man who is sterile. The prayer for God's blessing on the couple during the marriage service, that they may bear children, is taken very seriously among Nguni Christians.

In the *imbeleko* rite, shortly after the birth of her first child the bride returns to her parents' home with the baby. This is called *"ukuphindumkhondo"* (retracing the route back home). The family shower their daughter and her baby with presents. After a few days they accompany her back to her new home. Upon arrival, the bridegroom's family slaughter an ox or young cow and a celebration follows. The bride's family are proud of their daughter who represented them well by bearing a child; the bridegroom's family are pleased because their family has grown. So the slaughtering is in gratitude to the bride's family for having produced a woman who is capable of motherhood.

At the centre of all of these rites is a strong belief in the role of the ancestors. Ngunis generally, and the Zulus in particular, tend to attribute the cause of any sickness to something that is other than biological. After the traditional birth rites, therefore, if something goes wrong with the child's health, it is important that the baby be baptized quickly. Baptism, in this case, is seen as a therapeutic measure; God, as it were, is allowed to take over. If, even after baptism, the baby does not get better, the parents normally turn to the diviners and medicine men. These usually point to what they consider to be the root cause of the problem, namely that the birth rites were not properly done.

By the time a Nguni child is presented for baptism, therefore, a number of initiation rites have already been performed. When the priest says "name this child," that is merely a formality as the child has already received a name and much more from his or her "earthly family." So the new formula used in the Southern Africa *An Anglican Prayer Book* (1989) makes a lot of sense. The priest does not ask that the child be named. Rather, the godparent simply says "I present to you *N* to be baptized," acknowledging that baptism is not a naming ceremony.

Inculturation in the African context means appropriating some of the traditional rites into Christian practice and at least taking serious account of others. Proper handling of this inculturation can help the people see their traditional ceremonies through Christian eyes. Preaching and teaching must play a major role. But this inculturation can also be dangerous in that syncretism of any kind risks turning people back to traditional African worship and therefore away from Christianity.

Puberty rites

Traditional to Nguni life is the practice that every boy spends a consider-able amount of time out in the veld tending the family goats or, when he is older, herding the family cattle. Girls, on the other hand, spend most of their time at domestic chores such as cooking and tidying the house. So, as children grow, they are being prepared for adulthood.

When a boy has reached puberty, the other boys come to know of it in one way or another. Normally the cattle are led out to pasture early in the morning and returned sometime shortly before noon for milking and so that the calves may suck. One day, however, when the village awakens, it is discovered that all the kraals (the place where cattle are kept) are empty, except where the calves are kept. The boys do not return for the late morning milking, so the calves are noisy and want to be fed. There is general confusion in the village; the news leaks out as to which boy had reached puberty.

The girls are upset because they can't do their housework well. So, when the boys eventually decide to return to the village, the girls meet them on the way and hit them with sticks. The particular boy who has reached puberty must defend himself from his "sisters'" onslaught.

While the boys have been in the veld that day, the one who has reached puberty is given very serious instruction about the meaning of the stage he has reached, emphasizing responsibility both in terms of being able to defend himself and of taking responsibility if he makes a girl preg-nant. (This instruction is actually the culmination of a long period of teaching administered by a young man under the watchful eyes of the men in the community.)

There are puberty rites also for the girls which follow more or less the same pattern. A girl who has reached puberty wakes up quite early, tidies the house, and then leaves for the veld accompanied by other girls who have reached puberty. They go under the pretext of fetching wood or water, although the actual purpose is for instruction. When the boys return in the late morning, not only are the cows to be milked but also the boys expect to be fed. None of the older girls are available to feed them, how-ever. When the girls eventually return, there is "war" between the girls and the hungry boys.

After reaching puberty, the behaviour of boys and girls changes con-siderably. They begin behaving as adults. There are also certain ceremo-nies involved, including feasting. Although these traditions are no longer so prevalent as they once were, it is not difficult to see possible parallels between the traditional puberty rites and Christian confirmation.

During puberty instruction, the teaching and learning is extremely rigorous. It makes sense, therefore, that Africans tend to resist the idea of accepting baptism as the sole sacrament necessary for a person to receive holy communion. In the Zululand of King Shaka's time, after puberty a boy would go to the camp and therefore be eligible for battle. Because King Shaka Zulu took war very seriously, he did away with another puberty rite, that of circumcision—a practice which is still very important among the Xhosas. For a Xhosa male, unless you have been circumcised you cannot consider yourself a man, and are not regarded as one by the community.

Conclusions

In the foregoing description of Nguni initiation rites, two things in particular become clear:

1. For the African, baptism does not take the place of birth rites. The trend, at the moment, is to see these as two separate sets of rites in tandem. This can, in a way, be seen as playing it safe so that the ancestors do not turn against those family members who do not observe the traditional practices.

2. There are very clear stages in the growth and development of a Nguni child. Each stage has its own rites associated with it. A person cannot go on to a new stage without the appropriate rites and ceremonies being observed. Parallel Christian rites, therefore, must take serious account of this belief.

An Asian Inculturation of the Baptismal Liturgy

Francis Wickremesinghe

The basis

Even though insisting that the Jewish Law was not mandatory for Christians, St. Paul had Timothy circumcised "because of the Jews who were in those places, for they all knew that his father was a Greek" (Acts 16:3). So St.Paul writes: "Let us adopt any custom that leads to peace and to our mutual improvement." It is on this premise that the Christian Workers' Fellowship (CWF) of Sri Lanka experimented with the use of local birth customs in their baptismal liturgy. Some of these practices have been taken up by the CWF's parent churches in the *Proposed Ecumenical Baptismal Liturgy* for Sri Lanka (*PEBL*).

The CWF experiment was particularly far-reaching in that it involved worship patterns (and indeed even the clergy) of other faiths. The service begins, for instance, with a Moslem mullah chanting "God is great." Before the thanksgiving over the water, a Buddhist monk chants a religious stanza and passes a blessed thread dipped in the water for everyone present to hold as a sign of fellowship with the baptized. The basis for such involvement of other people is that, in the Jordan event, there is an identification of Jesus with the majority of the common people, even though baptism was not necessary for the Christ himself. In Sri Lanka, the common people are the majority communities of Buddhists, Hindus, and Moslems.

It would be too much to expect the Christian churches, with their roots in western civilization, to adopt customs from other religions in Asia, however good. But in the Asian context, religious and national traditions are inextricably intertwined. The *PEBL* attempts to inculturate by optionally permitting national (rather than religious) birth customs as part of the baptismal liturgy. The text of *PEBL* is also strongly ecumenical, being based on the World Council of Churches' document *Baptism, Eucharist and Ministry* and patterned largely on Fr. Max Thurian's baptismal text in *Baptism and Eucharist—Ecumenical Convergence in Celebration.* The pattern of any liturgy is necessarily traditional, and inculturation in Asian and African countries must come, then, in the incorporation of national ceremonies into the liturgy. This is what *PEBL* has attempted to do.

Pre-baptismal ceremonial

In *PEBL* baptism takes place after the liturgy of the word during the eucharist on a Sunday or festival day, when a large number of the congregation can be expected to be present. The particular days suggested are the Sunday in Epiphany week, Easter (the Vigil), Pentecost, and the Sunday after All Saints' Day. After the invitation, the president says a formal or extempore prayer during which he strikes each candidate with an *ekel* (cane) and breathes on their faces (a custom akin to exorcism). Several alternative prayers from various Christian sources are suggested. One, however, is clearly indigenous, using images familiar to Hindus and Buddhists as well as Christians:

> ...all blessings from the Ultimate Reality who said "I am who I am" be with you. May Jesus Christ, the Anointed One who liberates us, protect you from every kind of evil, keep you free from every blind fantasy of mind and will, and bring you from darkness into light. And may the Holy Spirit who sanctifies us dwell in your body and give you good health and the power to avoid all sin, that you may be well and happy. Just as the rivers swollen with rain flow into the sea and fill it, may you be filled with the plentiful grace of the Holy Trinity.

Following the prayer and attendant rites, the sponsors claim each candidate for Christ by signing them with the sign of the cross on the forehead, with the possible use of a paste of sandalwood and salt. The rubrics give a Christian meaning to this custom: It is "symbolic of God's protection and the spreading fragrance of a Christian example." Infants also may be given a ginger (palm) oil bath at this initial stage in the ceremony. This is a North Sri Lankan bathing practice which parallels similar patterns in the Old Testament and has associations with the Spirit. It is also reminiscent of the prebaptismal anointing in early Christian liturgies, including those of fourth-century Jerusalem.

(In an attempt to avoid a term closely associated with political favour and nepotism in this part of the world, *PEBL* refers to the sponsors as "spiritual parents." The biological parents are also asked to make the baptismal promises.)

After a hymn to the Holy Spirit, the thanksgiving over the water is offered in the form of a litany, the response being "Blessed be God." The prayer consists of a series of scriptural allusions to water and new life culminating in an epiclesis on both the candidates and the water. The "water-cutting" ceremony, enacted at national festivals in both North and South Sri Lanka, has been absorbed into the Christian blessing of water, the rubrics giving its significance as "the water cutting for cleansing and rain."

The exhortation and renunciation follow, and adult candidates may then make public acts of repentance. The renunciation is said by the entire congregation as a reaffirmation of their baptismal covenant. The question itself has both a trinitarian and a social dimension which are strongly contextual:

> So as to live in the liberty of the sons and daughters of God, to be a faithful follower of Jesus Christ, and to produce the fruits of the Holy Spirit, do you renounce being ruled by the desires of this world, the flesh and Satan, particularly the snare of pride, the love and worship of money, and the power of violence?

Immediately thereafter everyone makes a declaration of faith using the words of the (ICET) Apostles' Creed. Adult candidates may give testimony as to why they are seeking baptism/confirmation and the entire congregation prays. Before the baptism itself, a call for commitment by the congregation is made. (This involvement of the local congregation in the Christian nurture of those being baptized/confirmed is emphasized also in the rubrics.)

The baptism

The baptism consists of a threefold immersion or else the pouring of water three times, employing the trinitarian formula and naming each candidate. This eastern formula and concurrent ceremonial is derived from the historic association of the Malabar (Indian) Orthodox Church with Sri Lanka. A lock of hair is then cut from the crown of the head-a traditional custom at the first visit of an infant to a religious place. The president then lays his right hand on the head of the newly baptized saying, "Receive the seal of the gift of the Spirit." This laying on of hands is optional and does not in any way imply a two-stage rite of initiation. Rather, it emphasizes two separate symbols within the single sacrament of initiation through water and the Holy Spirit. Even in emergency baptism (outlined in the appendix to *PEBL*), both symbolic actions are recommended. (According to the rubrics, however, where confirmation follows baptism, the laying on of hands becomes a part of confirmation rather than of baptism.)

Following a period of silence, the candidates for confirmation and other members of the congregation may come to the font, place their hands in the water, and sign their foreheads in remembrance of their own baptism. The newly baptized then process around the font three times singing Psalm 32 or else the *Refuges* (an indigenous chant, christianized from Buddhism, concerning taking refuge in the Trinity). The Sri Lankan interpretation of this Orthodox circumambulation is that of dying to the old self and being born again into the new life of the Trinity. (This same rite takes place at Sri Lankan funerals.)

The welcome

The procession concludes with the newly baptized persons facing the congregation where they say together Wesley's covenant prayer and are then blessed by all the clergy and welcomed by the president. A white garment and a lighted earthenware lamp (a national symbol christianized to signify the fire of the Spirit) are given to each, and the newly baptized are signed with oil to show they are members of a royal priesthood. They are then presented to the congregation by their own "spiritual parents," and are welcomed with hallelujahs and shouts of "hurrah!"

The eucharist

During the baptismal eucharist which follows, the rubrics suggest certain symbolic actions. One is a demonstrable exchange of greeting with the newly initiated during the kiss of peace. Another is the placing of the clay lamps in the sanctuary during the offertory (as an act of commitment), as well as the offering of milk-rice, yoghurt, and honey, national symbols of new life and celebration. These will be consumed by the congregation after the service. (Here there is an intentional link with second-third- century practice, where drinking milk and honey at the baptismal eucharist signified entrance into the promised land.)

Conclusion

The rubrics state that "Confirmation, Reception, and Renewal are various modes of response to baptism, each directly related to the one covenant made in baptism, and should consequently take place primarily in the context of the Liturgy of Baptism." These rites are given in the appendix to *PEBL* and take place immediately after the water baptism ceremony. The *PEBL* lacks the rigid definitions of western European Christianity, not making an issue over a one- or two-stage rite, the moment of baptism, or the exact difference between confirmation, renewal, or reception to communion, leaving these as part of the mystery of eastern religion. This, in itself, is Asian inculturation.

The *PEBL* is still in draft form. If the churches of Sri Lanka (Anglican, Baptist, Methodist, Presbyterian, and Church of South India) give their authorization to this draft, however, it will be a landmark in the inculturation of the baptismal liturgy and in the ecumenical pilgrimage of the Sri Lankan churches.

Initiation in Anglicanism:
Where the Women Are
———————— Elizabeth J. Smith ————————

Introduction

There are some things in theology, as in life, that bear repeating: God is good; Christ is risen; we are forgiven; baptism is a great place to start almost any discussion of Christian life and the role of the Spirit in the church. Undoubtedly many of us can and do weave into our sermons, week by week, allusions to the importance of baptism. Slowly, almost subliminally, we aim to keep our people in a constant, joyful confrontation with the significance of their baptismal identity. And, from time to time, when baptism actually takes place in our assembly, we repeat our message with added urgency, with the impetus of the sacrament unfolding in our midst.

We do not apologise for rehearsing the same theme and variations so often. We know we are far from having exhausted the potential of the sacrament to teach and shape us. Baptism will continue to be among the most important of the lenses through which we view the church's life.

For many Anglican women, however, even as we rehearse our theology of baptism as the sacrament that includes and saves, we are also rehearsing our history of exclusion and oppression, inside and outside the church. Even as women explore the implications of the gifts of the Holy Spirit given to us through our membership in Christ, we are struggling to imagine a church and a world in which those gifts are truly welcome. Certainly, some of what follows has been said before. But it is too early yet for Anglican women to settle into silence, or for Anglican men to consider that enough has been said and done. For these reasons a discussion of initiation in Anglicanism cannot be complete without an examination of "where the women are." Women's experience is, at this time, a powerful and indispensable lens through which to view church and sacraments.

This paper offers one perspective on where the women are. I write as a deacon of the Australian Anglican church which does not yet ordain women as priests or bishops. I write as a scholar exploring the intersection of Christian feminism and mainstream liturgical theology. I write with Anglican women in mind: women who, though they, too, are born again by water and the Spirit, do not always have full access to the processes by which our church shapes our liturgies, names our God, and builds our future together.

There are four headings under which I want to review some of the issues for women about initiation in Anglicanism. The first concerns women's role as recipients and as ministers of initiation; the second involves the naming of God in our current liturgies of initiation; the third questions women's engagement (or lack of it) in the quest for Anglican identity that harks back so regularly to the haggling over ritual that characterized the English Reformation; the fourth looks forward to women's contribution to the kind of Anglican church that renewed baptismal liturgies might constitute.

"If you won't ordain us, don't baptize us": The theological credibility gap

This is perhaps the most oft-repeated call of women in the Anglican church. Yet it is also very slow to be acted upon in very many parts of the Communion. Some provinces have no women clergy at all, and women are not ordained to the priesthood in the majority of provinces. In only two dioceses in the entire Anglican world are women consecrated as bishops. As long as women may receive but not minister baptism and the laying on of hands, the theological credibility gap threatens to engulf every discussion of the significance of sacramental initiation.

So our first answer to the question of where the women are in Anglican initiation must be a literal, geographical one. Women are in the world as apostles, proclaiming the good news of God's love and forgiveness, but not in the church, absolving and blessing those who respond to the gospel. Women are standing around the font but not presiding at it. Women are passing through the water but not praying over it. Women are in classrooms preparing candidates for baptism and confirmation, but not in sanctuaries confirming them in the maturity of faith to which they have led them.

Celebrations of baptism thus become a painful time of contradiction for many Anglican women. The theology being proclaimed in word is of the radical equality of all people—male and female—before God; the rhetoric is of liberation and mission and of astonishing giftedness. Yet the theology being proclaimed in action, and in the visual impact of the robed ministers whose role is so significant in our tradition,[1] is that even baptism does not make a woman of equal worth to a man in our church. The church is not telling the truth. And this is not only a matter of distress and disorientation to women, it is also a scandal which ought to have all of us who use the rhetoric of baptism to motivate our people to ministry and mission jumping up and down to bring about change in the practices that contradict our high theology. Perhaps we need to call a moratorium on preaching about baptismal gifts and responsibilities until all who are baptized can do *in fact* what we say they can do *in theory*. Preachers would certainly feel the restrictions this moratorium would impose on their proclamation, and this loss might help them identify with the restrictions women experience on their ministry. Merely rehearsing the rhetoric without acting to eliminate the credibility gap does not put pressure on the church to end the lie.

In the Anglican Communion, although we have still so far to go towards an equal partnership for women in the community of the baptized, we have the advantage of including some local churches which *do* know what it feels like, sounds like, and looks like to have women ministering baptism and the laying on of hands. The Communion has much to learn from these churches, although structures which might help us to share information and reflections flowing from these experiences are not very firmly in place. Informal networks of Anglican women in various countries tend to be the channels by which insights and questions and explorations are exchanged.

The "official" liturgical bodies of all our churches need to be challenged to cast their nets more widely as they evaluate recent progress and look for new resources. Those churches which do ordain some of the women they baptize need to be asked to reflect intentionally on what they have learned from the experience: how it has changed their proclamation, their self-image, the credibility with which they enter into conversation with the world; and how far they still have to go before baptismal reality truly connects with baptismal rhetoric. In this evaluation, the responses of Anglican women especially must be sought.

---

[1]See the sections on visual and physical emancipatory language in Marjorie Procter-Smith, *In Her Own Rite: Constructing Feminist Liturgical Tradition* (Nashville: Abingdon, 1990), 71-84. Language is not limited to the texts of our rites but consists of "the word spoken and heard and touched, the word sung and danced and prayed; the word embodied and gestured and seen in vision and art, even the word which exists in silence" (p.60).

"God is not a boy's name":
Who IS God in Anglican initiation?

A major concern of feminist theology is the naming of God.[2] Again, the gap is immense between the rhetoric of humankind's having been created in God's image—male and female—and the reality of God's being consistently named in our tradition with male language, to the exclusion of female language.[3]

The bible has been a primary source for feminist Christians seeking to rediscover lost traditions and hidden fragments of female language for the divine. There is now pressure to include more prominently in the lectionary those passages which point to a biblical God who is not merely "Father" and "King." But the impact of this movement back to the scriptural sources has not yet been much felt in the way we name God in our mainstream liturgies. The "inclusive language" supplemental texts approved for trial use by the Episcopal Church USA probably represent the boldest attempt to move in this direction, yet those texts are hardly a radical departure from the mainstream. Feminist liturgies generated outside official church circles, on the other hand, have a characteristic commitment to experimentation and toleration of diversity, and "have not waited for theological consensus on the proper form of address for God."[4]

The task of renaming God is urgent for Anglican women because the words of our prayer books are so deeply formative for Anglican spirituality and identity. Even when, as Anglicans, we do not study our bibles with great diligence, we do perform a major part of our relationship with God as we rehearse the texts of our prayer books.

---

[2]"A feminist Christian spirituality...rejects the idolatrous worship of maleness and articulates the divine image in female human existence and language" (Elizabeth Schussler Fiorenza, *In Memory of Her: A Feminist Theological Reconstruction of Christian Origins* [New York: Crossroad, 1983] 346).

[3]For an elegant, witty and persuasive discussion of the shortcomings of actual Christian "God-talk" in the light of official trinitarian theology, see Brian Wren, *What Language Shall I Borrow? God-Talk in Worship: A Male Response to Feminist Theology* (New York: Crossroad, 1989), especially pp.115-22.

[4]Procter-Smith, *In Her Own Rite*, 89.

It may be helpful to consider the progress made in the area of 'God-talk' with some examples from the 1990 Australian rite for *Holy Baptism and the Laying on of Hands*, approved for experimental use.[5] In the presider's opening address to the people (the longest speech *about* God in the rite), there are no male pronouns used for God except for one reference to receiving Christ's continuing gift of "himself" at the Lord's table. Also eliminated are the italicized "he" and "him" used to speak about the candidate for baptism in the 1978 *An Australian Prayer Book (AAPB)*. This section addresses the candidates directly, and in the plural, as "you." Italicized plurals ("they," "them," "these our brothers and sisters") remain the rule throughout the rite, except for "he/she" in the prayer over each candidate at the laying on of hands.

While *AAPB* relies heavily on "Heavenly Father" and "Almighty God" throughout the initiation services, the 1990 rite shows a little more diversity. "Lord God" is still much in evidence, as is the perennial "almighty and everliving God"; the newly baptized still inherit God's "kingdom" and there is no attempt to shift the "Father" and "Son" from the creed or the trinitarian formula at the baptism and at the laying on of hands. But we do now have prayers which address a "merciful God," a "gracious God," and a "God of wisdom and love." These, together with the much more sparing use of male pronouns for God, constitute a reasonable effort to produce non-sexist or gender-neutral God-language.[6] The responsive character of the prayer of thanksgiving over the water (the congregation responds with "Blessed be God" after each of eight short paragraphs) also constitutes a more inclusive style of prayer in this rite than in *AAPB*.

There is, then, some evidence that Anglican liturgists are challenging the idolatry of a male God which has thus far been uncritically upheld. This progress represents more of a serious clean-up job on the old God-language than an attempt to build a new language, but it *is* progress and needs to be acknowledged and evaluated. But when we ask our governing question about where the women are, our answer is once again mainly negative.

---

[5]Prepared by the Liturgical Commission of the Anglican Church of Australia for use under section 4 of the Constitution (Sydney: Anglican Information Office, 1990).

[6]Procter-Smith has a helpful analysis of the potential and the limitations of non-sexist, inclusive, and emancipatory liturgical language. See *In Her Own Rite*, 63-66.

Women are at a distance from a God who is only ever "he," even if this God is "Father" with slightly less monotonous regularity than "he" used to be. Women and their bodies seem not to touch God's image in a sacrament which has birth as one of its key metaphors and our bodies as its indispensable subject. Women are not empowered for ministry in solidarity with other women by liturgies of initiation that do not show God in solidarity with the struggles of women, and that do not name sexism among the sins for which God offers forgiveness.

The problem for Anglican initiation is not that women are not coming to faith, repenting of their sins, learning to love themselves and their neighbours. The problem is not that women are not ritualizing their discoveries and contributing to the pool of resources from which the churches can enrich their rituals of initiation. The problem is that those who construct official liturgies (and most of these people are men) are not dipping deeply enough into that pool of resources. When it comes to naming God in terms of female images and women's experience, courage fails most liturgists and they beat a hasty retreat to the safe and familiar territory of Cranmer and the bible. Yes, liturgists are hearing and believing part of what women (and increasingly, men) are saying, namely that all-male God language is idolatrous. But for the sake of beauty, truth, and goodness the task must eventually be to add female language to our God-talk, not merely to delete the more obvious male language. In the God-talk we use in Anglican initiation, this task has barely begun.

Church"'man"'ship and the Anglican time-warp: What do we choose to remember?

In Anglican liturgical and theological circles, regretfully, it must be acknowledged that Cranmer is often safer and more familiar than the bible. The period between 1549 and 1552 has been the happy hunting ground of rival troupes of evangelicals and catholics seeking to snare the "Spirit of Anglicanism" and lead it home to matins or mass respectively. This is a caricature, of course. But one of my perennial frustrations, as a woman trying to do liturgical theology as an Anglican, is the fancy footwork required to keep the peace between the puritans and papists in our midst. To anoint or not to anoint? To bless or to consecrate people or things? To talk about sacrifice in the eucharist or to regard such terminology as anathema? One's credibility in the field of Anglican liturgy seems to depend on the correctness of one's party line on these issues. In the Australian church these questions are not incidental: our twentieth-century prayer books still bear the scars of sixteenth-century battles. "Churchmanship" they call it; and for increasing numbers of Anglican women it is one of those phenomena which deserves to keep its gender-specific language. These questions are not the ones which engage most Anglican women; and these answers are not the ones which will give Anglican women our sense of identity, our self-image as church.

Yes, identity is about history and memory: baptismal theology itself teaches us that. But women's history did not begin with the Reformation and contemporary women do not want to focus narrowly on the controversies of that period. And women's memories of struggle and liberation in Anglicanism tend to be either much more recent (looking to nineteenth- and twentieth-century developments), or much older (looking to the stories of women in the Old and New Testaments and in the early church). Our preferred points of entry into discussions of Anglican identity are not those of traditional churchmanship.

To take an example from the area of initiation: We may be glad of the introduction of chrism as an option in the 1990 Australian baptismal rite, but we will welcome it because it echoes for us the action of the woman who anointed Jesus, not because its inclusion represents a victory over the puritans. We will bring to its use not medieval symbolism but contemporary women's experience of oil used for healing and skin-protection, for fragrance and beauty.

Therefore, if Anglican liturgists want to engage Anglican women in creative liturgical remembering, there will need to be changes in the unwritten rules about where Anglican liturgical theology is anchored. Where the women are is in pouring through the scriptures, avidly exploring stories with baptismal motifs and resurrection commissionings, claiming empowerment for ministry not through a sixteenth-century pattern of church order but in a lived experience of the Holy Spirit.

Where the women are is in the midst of today's world, confronting personal sin and structural evil, seeking to be sustained in that confrontation by the knowledge that women before us have struggled, and women alongside of us are struggling in the power of the Holy Spirit given in our baptism. When we do not express a great interest in rearranging the crumbs under Cranmer's table, consider that perhaps the time has come for Anglican liturgists to try baking something new, using women's history and women's contemporary experience as the main ingredients.

Renovating the haunted house:
Changing the prayer, changing the church

Baptism and eucharist, we know, help to construct the church. Baptism and eucharist must also be enlisted in the struggle to reconstruct the church so that it becomes a home for women who are powerful and free. The sacraments support the old structure: women know this to our cost. As Marjorie Procter-Smith explains, our rites "initiate both women and men into a patriarchal ecclesial structure and...maintain their identity with that structure even when it is oppressive."[7] Clearly, a renovated household of God will need restructured sacraments to build and maintain it. What kind of church should we be dreaming of? What kind of church is seen in the visions of Anglican liturgists? What are the ways of approaching baptism, the laying on of hands, and the eucharist which will help to draw the church closer to this vision?

Where the women are, as we consider the future of the church, is *in* the church: living in it, praying in it, conceiving and creating new components for building it up. Women are in the church well aware of the ghosts of prayer books past—the ghosts of Cranmer and Arthur Couratin, of Massey Shepherd and Gilbert Sinden; but we are not too intimidated by those friendly shades. We know that the house is also haunted by the ghosts of the women who have never been named in the church's litanies nor acknowledged in the church's liturgical histories. Our loyalty is to those women and their struggles, and to the women of today's world who do not yet find in the Anglican church a safe home and a welcoming conversation space with God.

When the women of the church trust some people (and most of those people are still men) to shape and reshape the liturgy—to renovate the haunted house—those liturgists must trust, in turn, the women in the church. Trusting the women means believing the baptismal rhetoric that says that these women have gifts for building up the church: gifts of spirituality and administration, gifts of creativity and imagination. Trusting the women means acting on the baptismal rhetoric that says that the image of God can be found in women and named in women's language in the church's public prayer. Trusting the women means asking the women to bring treasures old and new out of our long-undervalued store-

---

[7] *In Her Own Rite*, 138.

houses, to be built into the new liturgies that constitute the renewed church.

Trusting the women means more than just accepting the resources women bring; it also means including the women in the task of planning, building, and evaluating the prayers that shape the living space we share. It means being willing to live—more, being glad to live—in the same house as women who are powerful and free.

Walk in Newness of Life
The Findings of the
International Anglican Liturgical Consultation
Toronto 1991

Sixty-four Anglican liturgical leaders met at Trinity College, Toronto, in August 1991 for five days of lively discussion of Christian initiation. Members of the Consultation came from many parts of the Anglican Communion, including Africa, Sri Lanka, the Philippines, India, Australia, New Zealand, and Polynesia, as well as North and South America and the British Isles.

The Consultation divided into four sections to consider its subject from different points of view. One section addressed the theology of Christian initiation, another the relationship of baptism, mission, and ministry. A third group considered the increasingly controversial subject of confirmation, and the fourth group provided suggestions for the appropriate celebration of baptism and for future revision of baptismal rites.

Each of the four groups produced a written statement. The statements were presented to the full meeting of all members of the Consultation in draft form and revisions in direction and content were made at that time. The Consultation had a further opportunity to propose amendments on its last working day, before the statements were adopted.

The four statements form the bulk of what follows. They are not uniform in style and method. They reflect different nuances and, in some cases, overlap each other in detail. They do, however, reflect a remarkable degree of agreement in a representative group of Anglican liturgical leaders, working at the same subject from different but interlocking points of view.

The statements have been edited for publication and approved by the Steering Committee of the Consultation.

In addition, and perhaps more important, the Consultation produced seven recommendations which are offered to the Anglican Communion as basic principles for Christian initiation. These recommendations were considered in detail by the whole Consultation and were formally adopted by vote. The small number of dissenting votes was recorded. The recommendations are printed before the statements.

Members of the Consultation noted that these recommendations on matters of principle build on the work of the first International Anglican Liturgical Consultation in Boston (1985), where the close relationship of baptism and the eucharist was emphasized and the communion of young (and unconfirmed) children was encouraged. The Toronto Consultation reaffirmed and endorsed the statements of its predecessor (with one dissenting vote, and one abstention). The Boston Statement appears in an appendix.

The convener of the Consultation was the Rev'd Prof. David Holeton of Trinity College, Toronto.

Introduction

It is now just ten years since the idea of holding the Anglican Liturgical Consultations was born. The Fourth IALC, held in Toronto, was the largest and most widely representative to date. Members of the Consultation were asked to come prepared to work on a document on the renewal of Christian Initiation in Anglicanism and it was to that end that most of our efforts were expended. As the Consultation worked towards that end there was considerable surprise and encouragement at the high degree of consensus that emerged both within and between the working groups.

It is almost twenty-five years since Lambeth 1968 set the renewal of patterns of Christian Initiation as a common task for the whole Anglican Communion. The document *Walk in Newness of Life* and its recommendations constitute a significant response to that ongoing task and represent the high degree of consensus which has emerged among Anglican liturgical leaders on the directions the renewal of baptismal practice should take within the Anglican Communion over the coming years. The reaffirmation and endorsement of the Boston Statement and its Recommendations from the first IALC represents a strong sense of continuity in the ongoing life of the IALC. Each and every province, diocese, and parish should feel challenged by *Walk in Newness of Life*. During this Decade of Evangelism it presents one ground-plan for the renewal of the church in mission and ministry and places the baptismal life of the church at the heart of its vocation to service in the world.

The fifth Consultation, to be held in Dublin in August 1995, will have as its principal topic the eucharist.

David R. Holeton
Chair, IALC

Recommendations of the Fourth International Anglican Liturgical Consultation at Toronto 1991 on

Principles of Christian Initiation

a   The renewal of baptismal practice is an integral part of mission and evangelism. Liturgical texts must point beyond the life of the church to God's mission in the world.

b   Baptism is for people of all ages, both adults and infants. Baptism is administered after preparation and instruction of the candidates, or where they are unable to answer for themselves, of their parent(s) or guardian(s).

c   Baptism is complete sacramental initiation and leads to participation in the eucharist. Confirmation and other rites of affirmation have a continuing pastoral role in the renewal of faith among the baptized but are in no way to be seen as a completion of baptism or as necessary for admission to communion.

d   The catechumenate is a model for preparation and formation for baptism. We recognize that its constituent liturgical rites may vary in different cultural contexts.

e   Whatever language is used in the rest of the baptismal rite, both the profession of faith and the baptismal formula should continue to name God as Father, Son, and Holy Spirit.

f   Baptism once received is unrepeatable and any rites of renewal must avoid being misconstrued as rebaptism.

g   The pastoral rite of confirmation may be delegated by the bishop to a presbyter.

Section One:
Renewal of the Theology of Initiation

Introduction

1 Through baptism with water in the name of the Father, and of the Son, and of the Holy Spirit, Christ unites us with himself in his death and resurrection, seals us with the Holy Spirit, and incorporates us into his body the church. Baptism does not happen in a vacuum, and its administration inevitably reflects the culture of particular faith communities. Baptism is the sacrament of once-for-all admission into membership in the catholic church, a particular expression of which is the local eucharistic community. Baptism, therefore, admits to communion.

Grace, faith, and sacramental efficacy in relation to baptism

2 All that is involved in becoming Christian is signified in baptism. This has both individual and corporate implications. Baptism springs from God's covenant of love and is thus the sacrament of justification through faith; baptism may be invoked interchangeably with faith in the New Testament (e.g., Gal 3.26f).

3 The inward part of baptism, including the promise of forgiveness of sins, rebirth to new life in Christ, and the gift of the Holy Spirit, is not only signified by the rite, but is also promised to all who receive it ''rightly'' (Art. XXVII). Where baptism accompanies or even conveys a personal experience of conversion to Christ, then that promised gift of God is received along with the outward sign. Yet clearly baptism is sometimes ministered where there is no active faith on the part of the recipient (just as faith can exist where baptism has not yet been given). Even in such a case baptism is still true baptism with an objective validity. If one baptized in this way later comes to active faith, any liturgical celebration of that faith must be based upon the original baptism, once given and still valid. The supposed ''baptism'' of one already baptized contravenes this basic principle and is deplorable.

4 Children of believers are baptized into God's people in the same manner as their parents and upon the same understanding of baptism. They thus participate in the one baptism common to all members of Christ.

5 The candidate's response of faith to the grace of God is not always simultaneous with the administration of the sacrament. In the case of infants the response will be gradual, related to the stages of the child's growth. There may be no apparent response in some cases, but even if the baptized person shows no signs of faith, yet she or he does belong by baptism to the community of the church — a God-given privilege which is to be respected.

6 There is need for the Anglican churches to relate the administration of baptism to the reality of the reception of the gospel. The sacrament must portray God's grace as both given and received, so that a realistic visible boundary to the church on earth is established. Thus baptism, in its frontier role, should both convey good news to the world and model with it conversion and commitment to Christ.

Baptism of infants

7 The context of the baptism of infants is the faith of the church as mediated by believing parents, other sponsors, and other Christians. This faith is extended in love and responsibility to the child and in this way the child is nurtured in the faith into which he or she has been baptized. Hence, it is appropriate to baptize infants when there is a reasonable expectation that the child will in fact be nurtured within the community of faith. Ordinarily, therefore, the baptism of infants requires the support of a believing parent.

8 This principle stands over against the practice of apparently indiscriminate baptism of all infants soon after birth. We regret that in the past the church has contributed to various popular misunderstandings of baptism, e.g., as a form of ''insurance'' for infants in case they die. This has resulted in the baptism of many who otherwise have no association with the church.

9 The current renewal of baptismal theology and consequent efforts to end indiscriminate baptism have significant implications for pastoral practice. Parents who have not participated actively in the eucharistic fellowship should be integrated into the worshipping community prior to the baptism of their children. Efforts to encourage a family's active participation in the community after the child's baptism are predictably unsuccessful where a parent has not already been integrated. Without prejudice to exceptional pastoral cases, it may be best for these families to defer the baptism of their children until

the children can make their own profession of faith, or until parent(s) and other members of the Christian community are prepared to nurture them actively in the Christian faith.

Baptism and Eucharist

10 Baptism is the sacramental sign of full incorporation into the body of Christ. Thus all who are baptized should be welcomed into the eucharistic fellowship of the church. We affirm the statement, ''Children and Communion,'' of the 1985 Anglican Liturgical Consultation in Boston.[1]

11 Communion of all the baptized represents a radical shift in Anglican practice and theology. Over the past two decades there has been an increasing acceptance of this practice in the Anglican Communion, although some provinces continue to require confirmation for admission to communion. We encourage provinces to reflect upon baptismal theology and eucharistic discipline and to implement the recommendations of the Boston Statement.

12 There is a general tendency to require instruction prior to admission to communion. We must recognize that none of us ever fully comprehends the eucharist and that each of us is welcomed to the Lord's table by the grace of God and not by our own merit.

13 Some provinces have considered it helpful to set a minimum age for admission to communion, but this should be only an interim step in transition to the norm of communion of all the baptized.

14 Unbaptized persons who through faith in Christ desire participation in the eucharistic fellowship should be encouraged to make their commitment to Christ in baptism, and so be incorporated within the one body which breaks the one bread.

Baptism and Confirmation

15 As part of the Prayer Book tradition, Anglican churches have inherited the post-baptismal rite of confirmation. Until the last two decades

---

[1]See paragraph 6 in Statement 3 on Confirmation. *Children and Communion* is appended to this collection of texts.

the rite combined ratification of baptismal vows, the bishop's laying on of hands in prayer and blessing, and admission to communion. Preparation of candidates has taken various forms.

16 Whatever its pastoral strengths, this discipline has lent itself to theological overvaluation and misinterpretation. There is little warrant in Scripture, the Reformers, or in the Prayer Book tradition itself, to support the notion that the imposition of hands somehow completes baptism and concludes the process of Christian initiation. This widespread notion has resulted in the exclusion of baptized children from full participation in the eucharist, with the further effect of forcing the age of confirmation downward, thus diminishing the possibility of a mature response on the part of the candidate.

17 In recent years various provinces of our Communion have recognized that baptism, of itself, admits to communion, as surely as it admits to the body of Christ. With this renewed understanding of baptism, the pressure for early confirmation is relieved so that the rite may actually express a *mature* ratification of baptismal faith.

18 Confirmation affords those baptized as infants an opportunity to affirm, as adults, the faith of the Christian community into which they have been baptized. Given this understanding of the rite, the administration of confirmation at or following adult baptism is unnecessary and misleading, and should be discontinued. This does not, however, preclude the bishop from administering baptism.

19 Confirmation therefore stands as a pastoral office in its own right, and not as a part of the initiatory process. If the title "confirmation" is retained, the status of the rite as a pastoral office must nevertheless be understood clearly.

Section Two:
Baptism, Mission, and Ministry

God's Mission

1 Mission is first and foremost God's mission to God's world. "As the Father has sent me, even so I send you."(Jn 20.21.) This mission is made visible in the person and work of Jesus and is entrusted by him to the church.

2   "When the Advocate comes, whom I will send to you from the Father, the Spirit of truth, who comes from the Father, he will testify on my behalf." (Jn 15.26) The primary agent of mission is God the Holy Spirit, who brings into existence a community of faith to embody this mission and to make God's new order manifest in a broken world. "You will receive power when the Holy Spirit has come upon you; and you will be my witnesses." (Acts 1.8; cf. Jn 15.27) The church needs the empowering of the Spirit to play its part in God's mission; it is called to proclaim the gospel, nurture people in the faith, care for the needy, and seek to transform the unjust structures of society.[1]

3   All that the church does is expressive of this mission, when it is true to its nature. This expressiveness must be so of its worship. As the church remembers its calling and waits on God in prayer, it is empowered for mission. Baptism in particular declares the gospel of God's saving love in Christ, establishes the church as Christ's body, and marks the individual believers as those called to participate in the work of the kingdom.

Baptism and evangelism
4   We welcome the developing awareness of the dignity and significance of baptism in the church, and believe that it needs to be consolidated by emphasizing the integral relation of evangelism and baptism. The journey into faith involves a process that includes awareness of God, recognition of God's work in Christ, entering into the Christian story through the scriptures, turning to Christ as Lord, incorporation into the body of Christ, nurture within the worshipping community, and being equipped and commissioned for ministry and mission within God's world. An adequate practice of baptism will recognize all these dimensions and will enable the church to play its full part in accompanying people on this journey. We therefore welcome the rediscovery of a pastoral and liturgical pattern which marks and celebrates these stages.

---

[1]*Bonds of Affection, Proceedings of ACC-6*, Anglican Consultative Council, London 1985, 48f.

Come and see: a bridge to the life of faith

5   Evangelism in our Communion often involves groups for enquirers and new believers which also include mature believers who accompany and nurture them. Many provinces recognize the status of *catechumen* in preparation for baptism, have a rite for admission to the catechumenate, and have rich community-based patterns of Christian formation. Patterns of formation vary greatly, taking different forms in isolated, rural communities, societies where natural community is important, and atomized, urban society. The strength and vitality of a culture's commitment to Christianity also affects patterns of personal formation. We recognize a debt to the Roman Catholic Church in making liturgical provision for marking the catechumen's journey into faith, through the Rite of Christian Initiation of Adults (RCIA). We welcome also the initiative in the Episcopal Church (U.S.A.) in making available in its *Book of Occasional Services* (second edition, 1988) rites for the catechumenate for the unbaptized and similar rites for baptized persons who seek a renewal of faith.

6   The catechumenal process begins with the welcome of individuals, the valuing of their story, the recognition of the work of God in their lives, the provision of sponsors to accompany their journey, and the engagement of the whole Christian community in both supporting them and learning from them. It seeks to promote personal formation of the new believer in four areas: formation in the Christian tradition as made available in the scriptures, development in personal prayer, incorporation into the worship of the church, and ministry in society, particularly to the powerless, the sick, and all in need. The catechumenal process commonly includes four distinct stages, with the transition between them liturgically marked within the assembly:

— enquiry,
— formation, properly called the catechumenate,
— immediate preparation, sometimes known as candidacy,
— post-baptismal reflection, or mystagogy.

7   We see this revival of the catechumenate as strengthening the ministry and mission of the church in a number of ways: it offers those seeking faith a way of exploring Christian discipleship and taking their place in the life and mission of the church; it respects the

integrity and humanity of those seeking faith and avoids the danger of squeezing them into a pre-arranged and scheduled program; it challenges all the baptized to take evangelism seriously, and to become more effective in it. The catechumenate provides a model for other processes of personal formation. It restores to the community of faith its essential role as the minister of baptism. It challenges the church through the questioning and enthusiasm of new believers. It subverts the dominance of the clergy by recognizing the responsibility and ministry of all the baptized.

The Baptizing Community

8   "One Lord, one faith, one baptism." (Eph 4.5) We see the catechumenal process affirming and celebrating the baptismal identity of the whole community. As people participate in the process, whether as enquirers, catechumens, candidates, and initiates, or as sponsors, catechists, and clergy, the *one baptism* by which all are incorporated into the one body of Christ will be apprehended. In this way the whole church is formed as a participatory community, one whose members share life with one another, while at the same time being conjoined to the missionary purpose of God for which baptism calls the community into existence. Through the lens of baptism the people of God begin to see that lay ministry is important not simply because it allows an interested few to exercise their individual ministries, but also because the ministry and mission of God in the church is the responsibility of all the baptized community.

Baptism: fount of justice and ministry

9   "For as the body is one and has many members, and all the members of the body, though many, are one body, so it is with Christ. For in the one Spirit we were all baptized into one body—Jews or Greeks, slaves or free—and we were all made to drink of one Spirit." (1 Cor 12.12-13) Baptism affirms the royal dignity of every Christian and their call and empowering for active ministry within the mission of the church. The renewal of baptismal practice, with a consequent awareness of the standing of the baptized in the sight of God, therefore has an important part to play in renewing the church's respect for all the people of God. A true understanding of baptism will bring with it a new expectancy about the ministry of each Christian. It will also provide an important foundation for allowing different Christians their true and just place within the

life of the church. This is of particular significance for categories of Christians who are marginalized by church or society. Baptism gives Christians a vision of God's just order; it makes the church a sign and instrument of the new world that God is establishing; it empowers Christians to strive for justice and peace within society.

The Gospel for the Baptized

10 ''Do you not know that all of us who have been baptized into Christ Jesus were baptized into his death?'' (Rm 6.3) There are many reasons why the gospel should be preached to those who have been baptized. They may have fallen away from Christian fellowship and discipleship. They may never have had the will or the opportunity to respond to God's gracious gift offered to them in baptism. They may have continued within the life of the church without a deep personal grasp of the reality signified in baptism. It is important for the integrity of the church's sacramental practice that such people are not treated as if they have not been baptized. For this reason the baptized are not to be called catechumens. An opportunity for them to renew their baptismal commitment may be provided through a rite of confirmation or reaffirmation of faith; such a rite should reinforce rather than undermine their awareness of baptism. In many situations it may be helpful to provide personal formation similar to the catechumenate, including the involvement of sponsors as companions on the way. The Episcopal Church (U.S.A.) has made a valuable contribution in creating a series of rites to mark such a journey of renewal. As in the ancient practice of the order of penitents, Ash Wednesday and Maundy Thursday frame the final stage of reaffirmation. In other cultures and contexts other appropriate forms could be created to support people in their return to the dignity and ministry of baptism.

Baptism of infants: patterns of preparation

Parents and sponsors

11 When infants are to be baptized, parents and sponsors are the main focus of preparation and formation, since parents have an important part to play in the spiritual formation of children. In the past, parents and sponsors have undergone meagre (or no) preparation. Christian formation and the renewal of the baptismal process demand that this change. A few classes which simply instruct in a small amount of theology do not provide the necessary renewal

of faith. What is required is a holistic approach in which the goal is formation, not simply the provision of information. The catechumenal model for the renewal of faith is helpful. A program on catechumenal lines, with the involvement of lay persons, will help build bridges between the local community and parents and sponsors as well as encourage and help them to renew their own faith commitment. (See, for example, the *Book of Occasional Services*, second edition, 1988.)

The catechumenate for infants or children?

12 The formation of a catechumenate for young children has been discussed in a number of places. It might be useful to admit to the catechumenate those young children whose parents/sponsors are going through a renewal process as described above. Until the parents are ready to accept the faith responsibilities in presenting their children for baptism, the children may continue as catechumens. It might also be useful to admit to the catechumenate those children whose parents choose to delay their baptism (for whatever reason). Proposals for adapting and using some of the liturgical rites of the catechumenate merit further investigation and experimentation. Limited experience has shown some initial benefit in doing this. A warning, however, should be sounded in this discussion: some clergy and parishes may be tempted to use the admission of young children to the catechumenate as a roundabout and non-confrontational way of refusing baptism. Therefore, infants should not be admitted as catechumens without an expectation of continuing nurture and formation. The whole area of a catechumenate for children needs to be explored further.

Clarifications on the Catechumenate

13 It may be helpful to identify three areas of possible confusion or difficulty:

14.1 Terminology: The word *catechumenate* is often used as a shorthand term for the whole journey of faith leading to baptism and the emerging ministry of the baptized. In contemporary rites, *catechumenate* describes only one of four periods in the journey into faith.

14.2 The term is often used as a synonym for a similar process provided for those already baptized. We would urge that the term *catechumen* and *catechumenate* should only be used for the unbaptized, while the term *catechumenal process* may be used for any pattern of Christian formation.

14.3 The term *catechumen* is regarded by some as antiquarian. However, there are advantages to using a word that resonates with the historic practice of the church. At the same time, simple terms may need to be found for liturgical rites that mark the stages of the journey in faith. *Baptism*, *baptismal process*, and *reaffirmation of baptism* may be better general terms than catechumenate. *Initiation* also has wide currency although it may give rise to difficulties in cultures with developed rituals to mark birth or puberty.

15 Some believe that the catechumenal approach to baptism is in conflict with the New Testament practice of baptism on profession of faith. They think it may undermine the priority of grace made explicit by placing baptism firmly at the start of a person's public discipleship. Three points diminish this difficulty:

15.1 The period between welcoming enquirers as catechumens and the acknowledgement of their call as candidates for baptism must not be seen as a period of probation to see whether their discipleship matches up to certain criteria. All practices that appear to apply this sort of probation must be carefully avoided. This period should rather be seen as a period of growth and discernment in which both individual and church are involved.

15.2 The practice of baptism in the New Testament cannot be separated from the process of entry into the gospel, nor from the Christian community's welcome and reception of the candidate. Baptism was not simply a formal, official act devoid of profound personal encounter and communication. If baptism is properly to effect what it represents, the church as well as the candidate must be fully and meaningfully present for the sacramental act. In most social contexts this will imply something like the sort of extended process to be found in the ancient and modern phased rites of initiation. *Catechumenate* and *candidacy* should not be seen as stages of preparation for an eventual baptism, but as part of the extended process of baptism: conversion and baptism unfolding together.

15.3 It may be helpful to make a clear distinction between the stages of *enquirer* and *catechumen* on the one hand, in which the decision for Christ and baptism is being made, and the stages of *candidate* and *neophyte*, in which candidate and church are involved together in an extended and full celebration of the baptismal reality.

16 Another concern raised by the catechumenal approach to baptism is a fear that it will raise barriers between the church and the surrounding culture. Some are anxious not to alienate those who are associated with the church as God-fearers. Where the church is a culturally distinct community in the context of a plurality of religious faiths, some are concerned that baptism may wrongly be seen as involving the denial of one's cultural heritage. Properly practised, the catechumenal approach to baptism can lower the barriers between church and society in two ways: first, it creates a bridge to enable people outside the church to find their way in; second, it encourages the church to value and respect the cultural heritage of those coming to faith.

Section Three:
Renewal of Baptismal Faith

1 Many Anglicans assume that their current confirmation practice (or something like it) is of great antiquity, going back perhaps even to New Testament times. History will not support this point of view.

2 There is no proved link between (i) the event described in Acts 8 and (ii) the imposition of the bishop's hand and the second anointing after baptism which we find in baptism as described in the *Apostolic Tradition* attributed to Hippolytus of Rome (third century). There is very good reason to believe that the second anointing by the bishop was a local Roman practice which was extended to the rest of the Western church only as the influence of Rome expanded. There is no good reason to conclude that chrismation in the east is the oriental counterpart of Western confirmation; it is more likely to be the counterpart of the first, not the second, anointing. Some believe that confirmation has never existed in the Eastern churches.

3 Nor is the medieval picture less clouded. Confirmation (in those days, of infants) was included among the sacraments only in the twelfth century and was required in England by Archbishop Peckham as a prelude to communion only in the thirteenth century by a regulation whose very existence implies that another practice was

normal. It was a regulation much disobeyed where the vast size of dioceses, the non-residency of many bishops, and the difficulties of travel prevented the access of many Christians to the rite.

4   The Reformation emphasis on conscious and intelligent faith[1] raised the age of candidates. However, practical problems continued in post-Reformation England, and were magnified in those colonies where bishops were not provided. Confirmation was unknown in the American colonies and during the early years of the new republic because there were no bishops. American clergy were regularly confirmed just prior to their ordination in England. In Australia the problem was solved by a more imaginative exercise of economy: archdeacons presided at confirmations prior to the availability of episcopal ministry, even after the first bishop had arrived.

5   None of this history obviates the value that the laying on of hands with prayer has had in the lives of many people, whether it occurred before or at puberty or at some later turning point in their pilgrimage. What it does mean is that no single model may be claimed as absolute and inviolable, a completion of baptism, and a necessary rite of passage to the eucharist.

Affirmation of the relationship between baptism and eucharist

Relation of baptism and eucharist

6   Baptism is the public act which marks the beginning of the Christian life. Its meaning, however, stretches both backward and forward beyond the rite itself into a wide range of experience and events which create the larger context of Christian initiation. For many people, baptism is the natural consequence of having been born into a Christian family and indicates incorporation into the faith of the parents. For others, the path to Christian membership has been influenced by some person, perhaps a friend or even a stranger, whose own faith has been a witness to the presence and love

---

[1]Michael Ramsey, review of Gregory Dix, *The Theology of Confirmation in Relation to Baptism* (London: Dacre, 1946), in *Journal of Theological Studies* 47 (1946), 256.

of God. Whatever the particular factors, which can be infinitely varied, baptism is a sign of a person's entrance into the visible community of the church as a participant in the common life of the body of Christ. The fundamental expression of that life is found in the gathering of all the baptized around the word and table of the Lord. Eucharist is the ongoing sign of the identity which is established through baptism, and fulfils the intention of Christian membership by the nurture of all God's people in the eucharistic gifts as the instruments of grace and the expression of the common faith into which all have been baptized. Although this essential link between baptism and eucharist came to be obscured through the infrequency of the communion of the laity, recent decades have seen a recovery of the earlier tradition of the church that eucharist is in fact the fulfilment and sacramental completion of the initiatory process, and also the continuing expression in the Christian life of our shared baptismal identity.

Types of belonging

7   The church's fellowship is participation or communion in the life of the Holy Trinity, as revealed in the life, death, and living again of Jesus Christ. Those who are baptized with water in the Name of the Father, and of the Son, and of the Holy Spirit, are fully received into the church's fellowship as members of the body of Christ.

8   An active member of the church of Christ is one who has been baptized and who shares regularly in the life of the eucharistic community and in its service in the wider world.

9   Baptism admits to full membership of a eucharistic community which, because of its missionary character, is open and inclusive rather than closed and exclusive. Within its fellowship, those who have been baptized may find the freedom to come to faith and express their faith in their own way and at their own pace, and to feel always that they have access to all that the worshipping community is able to provide for them and to offer all that it is able to receive from them.

10   Baptism admits to full membership of the universal church of God, even though that church is divided. A person who has been baptized within another part of the church, and who wishes to be

received into the Anglican Communion, should be required only to produce evidence of baptism and to be welcomed and received through the laying on of hands. Rites of reception should respect the prior church allegiance of those received.

11   Full membership of the church is conferred through baptism. The right to hold particular offices in the church or to exercise a vote at church meetings may be governed by regulations specifically drawn up for the purpose.

12   Those who have been baptized in infancy are to be nurtured and formed in the faith as people who already are in full membership of the body of Christ, and who at some later stage may choose to make public profession of their faith.

Celebrations of significant moments / awakenings in the Christian life

Affirmation / commitment

Understandings of confirmation

15   Anglicans have assumed that confirmation includes the laying on of hands with prayer, at some time after baptism. A distinct Anglican custom is that the hands are those of a bishop (though there have been exceptions to this). Further, the rite has generally been used to admit baptized Christians to the holy communion. Among Anglicans, at least five notions of confirming (not necessarily exclusive of each other) have been identified.

15.1   Confirmation is a person's ''confirming'' the baptismal covenant[2], after preparation and reflection. This is the major understanding in the 1662 *BCP*. It assumes that the candidates were baptized as infants, and must respond in a life of active faith to God's grace given them.

---

[2]The term ''baptismal covenant'' is used in this document as having scriptural and Anglican heritage. Other terms which are used in our tradition are ''baptismal vows'' and ''baptismal promises.''

15.2 Confirmation is the ratifying of a Christian's belonging to the church of God. Such an act takes place in the presence of the bishop, who represents the wider household of faith. Anglicans who hold this view look to the phrase "to be confirmed by the bishop" in the 1662 *BCP* as pointing to a wider view than the candidates "confirming" their covenant.

15.3 Confirmation is the last act in a sequence of rites of entry to the church. Those holding this view trace the separate laying on of hands back to third-century rites of initiation. While other actions came to be delegated by the bishop, hand-laying to complete initiation continued to be the bishop's role.

15.4 Confirmation is sealing by the Holy Spirit. This view gained popularity in the late nineteenth century, and was understood in various ways. Some saw the bishop as the only minister who could impart the Spirit in continuity with Christ's gift to the church. Some used confirmation as a means of relating "conversion" experiences to the church's rites. Some wanted to move beyond a "civil religion" view of baptism by stressing the Spirit's role in confirmation. Some used confirmation as a denominational marker, excluding any not episcopally "sealed" from holy communion, since they did not have the Spirit.

15.5 Confirmation is a form of "commissioning" by the bishop for the ministry of Christian life. This has mistakenly been called "ordination of the laity," a notion which diminishes baptism.

15.6 In addition, it has been argued in recent liturgical work that the laying on of hands as a dismissal blessing is the origin of what came to be known as confirmation.[3] Such a view may be helpful in endeavouring to renew the meaning of confirmation as commissioning.

16   The fourth view has been firmly set aside in the past two decades in New Testament and liturgical scholarship, where it has been made clear that sacramental initiation is complete in baptism. Therefore the role of confirmation as *necessary* for admission to communion is

---

[3] Aidan Kavanagh, *Confirmation: Origins and Reform* (New York: Pueblo, 1988).

is undermined. An increasing number of Anglican provinces have moved to admit children to communion before confirmation, and to receive communicant members of other churches at the Lord's table and also as regular communicants.

17 Many agree on the first view of confirmation but whether this rite should be required of candidates for baptism making the baptismal promises for themselves is a moot point. Many Anglicans consider a separate act of commitment to be necessary for those baptized as infants, but not as an essential prerequisite to participation in the eucharist. Some prefer a single rite of baptism in water, with provision that illustrative ceremonies such as anointing and imposition of hands may be separated from it in point of time to mark stages in the Christian's growing life. Any or all of these stages could be delegated by the bishop to a presbyter.

18 The laying on of hands, with prayer for further strengthening by the Spirit, is open to many uses. Such a "stretched" rite, perhaps termed *commissioning* or *affirmation*, able to be repeated as different pastoral needs arise, and creatively adapted to various times and places, may bring new life to this distinctive Anglican heritage. To such a broadening view we now turn.

Renewal of faith

19 Baptism is the unrepeatable sign of initiation into Christ and his church, the validity of which does not depend on the age of the candidate, the amount of water used, or the manner of baptizing. But the church long ago recognized that the journey of the baptized in their exploration of the life of faith is a process punctuated by failure and forgiveness, repentance and renewal. These experiences are sometimes marked by signs recalling baptism — sprinkling with water, making the sign of the cross with ashes on Ash Wednesday or with water on entering church, laying on of hands in reconciliation, and affirming of baptismal promises.

20 Many provinces in the Communion now make provision for the affirmation of baptismal promises, some of them including the explicit use of water. The assumption is that there is no limit to the number of times baptismal promises may be affirmed. This is an assumption with which we would agree. We would want to distinguish:

20.1 a simple remembering of baptism, for instance in the course of witnessing someone else's baptism;

20.2 a serious affirmation of the baptismal covenant by all or most of the congregation on a special occasion, such as at Easter or New Year. However, since the regular renewal of the life of the baptized is in the eucharist (with confession and absolution), the solemn affirmation of the baptismal covenant — a comparative innovation in Anglican liturgy in any case — should be infrequent and preceded by due notice and preparation;

20.3 a celebration of the renewed faith of an individual or group. When someone baptized as an infant — and sometimes never nurtured in the faith — has a "conversion experience" or finds new faith in Christ, there is often a need for a dramatic celebration of this experience in the local Christian community. The same is sometimes true when someone has an experience of the Spirit so overwhelming (and marked by an initial speaking in tongues) that some are tempted to call it a "baptism in the Spirit." For some, one of the corporate affirmations described above will be sufficient. But the requests of those looking both for immersion in water and for the laying on of hands to mark a significant experience of the Spirit must be taken seriously. For them, a lesser ceremony will not do, and a more specific rite, which may include both the laying on of hands and the use of water, as well as provision for public catechesis or testimony, should be provided. We believe that care should be taken not to deny the baptism that has already taken place in the person's life or the mode of that baptism by affusion.[4] No province should adopt a form of this kind until it is satisfied that neither those involved nor others who are aware of it will confuse it with baptism.

21 To avoid confusion with baptism we urge that the following be noted in the preparation of any rite for local use:

21.1 words which define what is happening should be said by the whole congregation;

---

[4]Methods of baptism vary from submersion (the water completely covering the candidate), through immersion (the candidate kneels or stands in water which is also poured over the head), to affusion (water poured over the head).

21.2 words should be used to affirm clearly the baptism which has already taken place in the person's life;

21.3 water may be used by a minister in a manner which is not suggestive of baptism, e.g., sprinkling a number of people at once, but not individually;

21.4 the sign of the cross in water or oil may be made by the persons themselves or by sponsors.

Reception from other churches or Communions

22   Reception of a baptized Christian from another Communion is a significant moment in that person's life which calls for public affirmation. At least since the nineteenth century Anglicanism has distinguished between those already confirmed or sealed in a Christian tradition which has retained the historic episcopate, and members of other Communions. If confirmation is not regarded as an essential part of full initiation, this distinction is no longer appropriate. Nevertheless reception should be made available as a public act at which the bishop usually presides. A rite for this should include:

22.1 affirmation of Christian faith;

22.2 expression of a willingness to live within Anglican life and order;

22.3 laying on of hands with prayer for perseverance in the faith;

22.4 welcome into fellowship both by the bishop (or bishop's delegate) and congregation.

Reconciliation of the lapsed

23   Reconciliation of the lapsed concerns those who after baptism ceased for a period to take any active part in church life. This should be an optional rite for use when a public affirmation is needed, but an unobtrusive return will often be the appropriate way back.

24   If present the bishop should preside. The elements in any public rite should be:

24.1 affirmation of Christian faith;

24.2 prayer for perseverance in the resolve to return to practice of the faith;

24.3 the welcome, appropriately expressed in the context of the Peace.

Restoration of the penitent

25   Restoration of a penitent concerns restoration of those who have repented of sin, even when there has been no lapse of participation in church life.

26   This rite will usually be celebrated by minister and penitent alone, but its corporate dimension should always be clear.

27   There will be contexts where a public celebration is appropriate after grave and notorious sin. In such circumstances the rite should take place in conjunction with the act of penitence in a public liturgy.

28   The elements should include:

28.1 expression of penitence (including appropriate confession of sin);

28.2 absolution and prayer for perseverance;

28.3 restoration to fellowship. In a public context this would appropriately be expressed in the Peace, leading to shared communion.

Cultural celebrations

29   The 1988 Lambeth Conference affirmed that the gospel judges every culture on its own criteria of truth, challenging some aspects of the culture while endorsing others for the benefit of the church and society. The Conference urged the church everywhere to work at expressing the unchanging gospel of Christ in words, actions, names, customs, liturgies which communicate relevantly in each society.

30   It should be noted that the historic liturgies we have inherited were influenced by the cultures in which those liturgies developed. The Anglican provinces should therefore be encouraged to develop liturgies which are culturally relevant while remaining faithful to the Christian faith.

31   In the African context, for instance the issue of Christian initiation can find great enrichment when the traditional initiation ceremonies are understood, and the same is true elsewhere. In most African cultures initiation into the life of a community begins with a celebration of the naming of a child. For those who are believers in Christ, the ceremony of naming of a child can now be associated with the initiation of the child into the family of God's people in baptism. Some of the traditional rites of naming may be included

in the baptismal process. Just as women helping the mother burst into allulations of joy at the birth of a child, so allulations may mark the climax of baptism when the child is baptized in the name of the Father, the Son, and the Holy Spirit. In every culture death is marked by significant rites. For Christians, funeral rites mark the completion of the earthly journey in Christ begun in baptism. Customs marking the end of life should therefore be associated with baptismal symbols. In this way the transition of Christians into the full presence of Christ recalls their initiation into Christ in baptism.

32 The next important ceremony in some societies is the initiation of boys and girls into manhood and womanhood at the time of puberty. The ceremony is preceded by a period of intense instruction in what it means to be a man or a woman. When the rite is performed, those initiated are regarded as no longer children but adults. The service of confirmation by a bishop has been regarded as equivalent to this initiation into manhood or womanhood. In cultures in which initiation into adulthood is a significant event, we encourage churches to develop rites to observe this passage, whether these be services of confirmation, commissioning to Christian witness and service, commitment to Christian life, or other appropriate rites.

The role of the bishop

33 Any contemporary discussion of the theology of Christian initiation in the Anglican Communion must inevitably lead to a discussion of the ministry of the bishop. As admission to communion becomes less dependent upon confirmation and the age and numbers of candidates presenting themselves for confirmation change, questions are being raised as to how bishops will continue to exercise a visible ministry among the members of the local congregation and what shape that ministry might take.

34 There are some who fear that changes in confirmation practice and renewed emphasis on baptism might deprive episcopal ministry of its primary pastoral contact with the faithful. However, it must be stated that the Anglican tradition has a consistent liturgical tradition which has a broader vision of the scope of episcopal ministry.

35 This vision, contained in the traditional and contemporary ordinals of the Anglican Communion, calls the bishop to be first and

foremost a pastor.[5] The bishop is "to know (the) people and to be known by them."[6] This pastoral ministry extends to the ordained and to the laity, since by the bishop's personal care and provision of ministers to share in this ministry of pastoral care, the church is built up in love. It has also been a consistent element of the Anglican vision of the episcopate that bishops are to care for the poor and needy, speak for the voiceless, defend the helpless, and exercise a prophetic role in their society.[7]

36   One expression of this episcopal ministry of pastoral care is found in the bishop as teacher of the faith. This ministry takes place in two arenas. First, within the local church, the bishop is called to preach the word of God, "enlightening the minds and stirring up the conscience of (the) people."[8] By this and other means, bishops encourage and support the baptized in their gifts and ministries.[9]

37   Second, bishops are responsible for seeing that the good news of God in Jesus Christ is proclaimed to the world. Their life and teaching, as well as the life and teaching of their people, are to be a public witness to God's saving love. As leaders of a community of faith, bishops are to enable the church to fulfill its mission.[10]

38   Bishops also exercise pastoral care in their role as guardians of the church's unity. They are the personal signs that the local congregations form a larger and diverse diocesan community that is itself part of a national and international community of dioceses.

39   The bishop expresses the unity of the church by presiding at its liturgical rites.[11] Whenever possible, the bishop presides at baptism,

---

[5]See the collect for the consecration of a bishop, *BCP* 1662, 373.

[6]*ASB* 1980, 388.

[7]*BCP* (U.S.A.) 1979, 518. See also the examination of the 1662 and parallel liturgical units of contemporary Anglican ordinals.

[8]*BCP* (U.S.A.) 1979, 518.

[9]518.

[10]*ASB* 1980, 390.

[11]See Scotland 1984, 3. See also *BCP* (U.S.A.) 1979, 517, 518, and *ASB* 1980, 388-389.

whether of adults or children, and eucharist, leading the people in offering the sacrifice of praise and thanksgiving. Bishops also exercise their authority through delegating or presiding, as we have indicated above, at the church's other rites of commitment, such as confirmation, affirmation, the reception of Christians from other communions, and celebrations of reconciliation.

40 These other rites of commitment are articulations of the ministry which all Christians enter at their baptism. The bishop's presidency at these rites derives from the bishop's role as the chief pastor of the baptizing community.[12]

Section Four: Rites of Initiation

1 Baptism is the rite of admission to the body of Christ; but other liturgical rites may be appropriate to mark different stages in a person's journey to faith. These should involve the local congregation and sponsors with the candidate. Such catechumenal rites have already been adopted and found to be valuable in some provinces of the Anglican Communion, and others may wish to learn from their experience. In some cultural contexts it may be fitting to include within these rites exorcism and the giving of a Christian name. In the case of those unable to answer for themselves, parallel rites for parents and sponsors may be devised as part of the process of preparation. Care should be taken to distinguish rites which properly belong to the process of becoming a Christian from those which celebrate different stages of human development, such as the birth of a baby and the onset of puberty.

2 Since baptism is the full and complete rite of initiation into the church, no further rite of admission to communion is essential. However, until this principle can be fully implemented in the Anglican Communion, pastoral need in some places may call for the provi-

---

[12]See the prefaces and related statements in *BCP* (U.S.A.) 1979, 510; New Zealand 1989, 887, 890, 918; South Africa 1989, 571-572, Wales 1984, 2:716-717, *ASB* 1980, 390,394.

sion of such a rite for those baptized in infancy. Liturgical opportunities may also be needed for individuals and groups to reaffirm the baptismal profession of faith from time to time. No pre- or post-baptismal rite should overshadow the centrality of the sacrament of baptism itself.

The occasion of baptism

3   Whenever possible, the rite of baptism should take place within the principal eucharistic celebration on a Sunday or holy day, immediately following the ministry of the word. Provinces may wish to designate appropriate seasons for baptisms, of which Easter is one. When the bishop is present, it is particularly appropriate that baptism be celebrated, so that the bishop may preside over the rite.

The structure of the baptismal rite

4   The same rite, with only a minimum of adaptation, should be used for both those able and those unable to answer for themselves. The following order is desirable:

4.1 Presentation of the candidate(s). Sponsors should present each candidate by name to the presiding minister and to the congregation. They may also attest to the candidates' faith and manner of life. The congregation may respond by indicating their support.

4.2 Renunciation of evil. This expression of repentance may also include candidates' individual testimony to conversion.

4.3 Prayer over the water. This may take place before or after the renunciation of evil, or after the profession of faith. In giving thanks for the gift of water, the prayer should draw upon the wealth of appropriate scriptural imagery, and especially the great themes of Exodus and Covenant. At the very least it must make reference to God's act of creation, to the redemptive work of Christ, and to the action of the Holy Spirit in baptism.

4.4 Profession of Christian faith. A question and answer form is most effective for the affirmation of trinitarian faith.

4.5 The administration of water. Whenever possible, candidates should be thoroughly immersed in water, or at least have it generously poured over them, as traditional Anglican rites direct. If appropriate provision for this method of administration cannot be made in the church building, the baptism may take place in another location. The construction or renovation of church buildings should allow for the abundant use of water in baptism. Whatever language may be used in the rest of the rite, both the profession of faith and the baptismal formula should continue to name God as Father, Son, and Holy Spirit, to ensure acceptance both within the Anglican Communion and in the wider church.

4.6 Post-baptismal ceremonies. Not only traditional ceremonies, such as anointing and consignation, but also symbolic acts drawn from local culture offer valuable means of explicating the significance of baptism. But, while it is important that these be vivid and expressive, they must not obscure the centrality of the baptismal act itself.

5 It is important to note that effective celebration requires much more than the provision of suitable texts. The setting, choice of music, catechesis of the local congregation, and the incorporation of symbols and customs which are appropriate to the candidates and the community also have important contributions to make.

Ministries in relation to baptism

6 The church is the baptismal community into which new members are incorporated. The congregation should therefore not only witness the rite but also play an active part in the whole process, from evangelism to nurture of the newly baptized in Christian faith and life. Some expression of this responsibility should find a place within the baptismal rite.

7 The sponsors, in addition to presenting the candidates, may also lead prayer for them during the rite, and, together with the newly baptized, perform appropriate ministries within the eucharist. In the case of those unable to answer for themselves, the sponsors make the renunciation and profession of faith. This may be understood as speaking on behalf of the candidate; as expressing future intentions for the candidate; as speaking on their own behalf; or as a combination of these. It is also appropriate for them to give public acknowledgement of their continuing responsibility for the Christian formation of those whom they have sponsored. Parent(s) should normally be among the sponsors of infants.

8 The minister presiding at the eucharist also presides over the baptismal rite, and should say the prayer over the water, receive the candidates' profession of faith, and take some part in the administration of the water. Deacons or other ministers may assist in the administration of the water; and other parts of the rite may be delegated to them.

Statement of the First International Anglican Liturgical Consultation
at Boston 1985 on

Children and Communion

i That since baptism is the sacramental sign of full incorporation into
the church, all baptized persons be admitted to communion.

ii That provincial baptismal rites be reviewed to the end that such texts
explicitly affirm the communion of the newly baptized and that only
one rite be authorized for the baptism whether of adults or infants
so that no essential distinction be made between persons on basis
of age.

iii That in the celebration of baptism the vivid use of liturgical signs,
e.g., the practice of immersion and the copious use of water be
encouraged.

iv That the celebration of baptism constitute a normal part of an episcopal visit.

v That anyone admitted to communion in any part of the Anglican
Communion be acknowledged as a communicant in every part of
the Anglican Communion and not be denied communion on the
basis of age or lack of confirmation.

vi That the Constitution and Canons of each province be revised in accordance with the above recommendations; and that the Constitution
and Canons be amended wherever they imply the necessity of confirmation for full church membership.

vii That each province clearly affirm that confirmation is not a rite of
admission to communion, a principle affirmed by the bishops at Lambeth in 1968.

viii That the general communion of all the baptized assume a significant place in all ecumenical dialogues in which Anglicans are engaged.

Members of the Fourth International Anglican Liturgical Consultation

Toronto 1991

Australia
The Rev'd Canon Albert Mcpherson
The Rev'd Ronald Dowling
The Rev'd R.W. Hartley
The Rev'd Dr. Charles Sherlock
The Rev'd Elizabeth Smith

Brazil
The Very Rev'd Santos de Oliveira

Canada
The Rev'd Dr. William R. Crockett
The Rev'd Kevin Flynn
The Rt. Rev'd J.C. Fricker
The Rev'd John Gibaut
The Rev'd Paul Gibson
The Rev'd John W.B. Hill
The Rev'd Prof. David Holeton
The Rev'd Matthew Johnson
The Rev'd Gregory Kerr-Wilson
The Rev'd Prof. Richard Leggett
The Rev'd Phillip May

Chile
Senor Frederic Smith Bravo

Cuba
The Rev'd Juan Quevedo-Bosch

England
The Rev'd Canon Peter Ball
The Rt. Rev'd Colin Buchanan
The Ven. Dr. Mark Dalby
Miss M.D. Fraser
The Rev'd Canon Dr. Donald Gray
Mr. David Hebblethwaite
Dr. Janet Hodgson
The Rt. Rev'd Colin James
The Rev'd David J. Kennedy
The Ven. Gordon W. Kuhrt
The Ven. Trevor Lloyd
The Rev'd Ian H. Robertson
The Rev'd Dr. Kenneth Stevenson
The Rev'd Michael Vasey

Ghana
The Rt. Rev'd G.A. Okine

Ireland
The Rev'd Harold C. Miller

Kenya
The Rt. Rev'd David M. Gitari

New Zealand
The Most Rev'd Brian Davis

Nigeria
The Rev'd Dr. Solomon Amusan
The Rt. Rev'd Gideon Olajide

North India
The Rt. Rev'd Pritam B. Santram

Philippines
The Rev'd Joseph Laus

Polynesia
The Very Rev'd Winston
Halapua

Scotland
The Very Rev'd B.A. Hardy
The Rev'd Canon Gianfranco
Tellini

South Africa
The Venerable Themba J.
Vundla

Sri Lanka
The Rev'd Sydney Knight

Tanzania
The Rev'd John Simalenga

U.S.A.
The Rev'd Dr. Paul F. Bradshaw
The Rev'd Canon Robert J.
Brooks
The Rev'd Sister Jean Campbell
OSH
The Rev'd Richard Fabian

The Rev'd Canon Chester A.
LaRue
The Rev'd Dr. Richard Cornish
Martin
The Rev'd Ruth Meyers
The Rev'd Dr. Leonel Mitchell
The Rev'd H. Boone Porter
The Rev'd Timothy P. Perkins
The Rev'd Dr. Thomas J. Talley
The Rev'd Dr. Louis Weil

Uganda
The Rt. Rev'd Joram Bamunoba

Wales
The Rev'd Dr. Keith M.
Denison
The Rev'd Canon Walter H.
Williams

West Indies
The Rev'd Eric Lynch

Ecumenical Partner
The Rev'd Dr. Eugene L. Brand